Travels With Susie

A Hilarious Account of One Couple's RV Journey Across America

Gordon Grindstaff

Bloomington, IN Milton Keynes, UK
authorHOUSE®

AuthorHouse™
1663 Liberty Drive, Suite 200
Bloomington, IN 47403
www.authorhouse.com
Phone: 1-800-839-8640

AuthorHouse™ UK Ltd.
500 Avebury Boulevard
Central Milton Keynes, MK9 2BE
www.authorhouse.co.uk
Phone: 08001974150

© 2007 Gordon Grindstaff. All rights reserved.

No part of this book may be reproduced, stored in a retrieval system, or transmitted by any means without the written permission of the author.

First published by AuthorHouse   1/8/2007

ISBN: 1-4259-5597-5 (sc)

Library of Congress Control Number: 2006908220

Printed in the United States of America
Bloomington, Indiana

This book is printed on acid-free paper.

For my wife, Carole, who because of my column's weekly visits to Newspaper opinion pages, is now known to complete strangers only as "Susie". When I first took pen to paper, she told me, in no uncertain terms, ever to use her name in any of my "corny" stuff or she'd break my arm. Needing both appendages to type, I had to find a new wife. That's how Susie came into existence and why Carole remained anonymous.

I couldn't exist without either one of them.

Acknowledgments

The Author wishes to acknowledge the help and encouragement of his children Joe, Jason, and Julie. Also, the support of the writing group, "In Broad Daylight", especially Carole Carlson, Sheila Sowder and Dick Stott, was invaluable.

No acknowledgment of this book would be complete without mentioning the one casualty of out travels, my dog, Murphy. He hated traveling so much that he went to live with the farmer down the road. I cannot begin to tell you how much I regret this.

This is probably also a good time to tell you that some of the stories in the book first saw daylight as newspaper columns or magazine articles.

Introduction

My back was killing me, my wife Susie was yelling at me, and my new retirement warm up suit was in ruins, thanks to the permeated soapsuds and the smell of wet dog. On top of that, I had suds in my eyes and my overly full kidneys were ready to explode. This wasn't what my idea of leisure was supposed to be. Here it was, my very first day of retirement and Susie had me in this predicament with a half crazed dog who hated getting wet.

What happened? Why was I even retired? I was still a young man. I might still be on the clock had the newest batch of MBA grads not arrived at the giant corporation when they did. I normally looked forward to the arrival of newly hired graduates because it meant training for these new people and more importantly, it meant free lunches during their training sessions.

This time around, though, something was different. As my manager brought the five of them around for introductions, I noticed all of them seemed to be life sized versions of Ken and Barbie dolls; not a misshapen body, not a hair out of place nor a rumpled suit in the bunch. My God! It appeared as if BMI scores had joined the ranks of GPA as qualifiers for entry into this company's work force.

The look of the new people irritated me some, what with my being a tad overweight and prone to being disheveled. That wasn't all that bothered me, though. Besides their apparent arrival from some cloning operation they weren't telling the older generation about, they also exhibited signs of wanting to manage the damn place. One of the things they brought with them from MBA School was the concept of Corporate Mission and Vision Statements.

I had been going to the office for 40 years without needing a department mission to guide me but suddenly, we could not do one more thing without one. One minute we were working away on a new computer system and two minutes after the MBA's arrival, we had dropped everything to gather together informally and stew over what we might come up with that best described our departmental Mission.

The management felt that these informal meetings to hammer out a Mission statement might get more results if food was served during the sessions. Probably another MBA idea, but one I appreciated. So between handfuls of potato chips, I contemplated the idea of Missions and Visions and found myself trying to figure out why we needed two.

"What's the difference?" I asked Ken #3 and Barbie #2, both of whom were laboring over a white board full of quotations that had been tried and rejected for our Mission statement.

"The difference in what?"

"In Mission and Vision statements."

"Well, one is the mission for our group and the other is what we see our group doing down the road. You know, the Vision."

"Right." I said, turning my attention to the ham sandwiches and potato salad that had just been delivered.

There was more to this than just eating. The new grads soon had me 'blocking off time' for something called 'one-offs'. I had never blocked off time nor attended a one-off. I didn't even know what they were and suddenly I was in the middle of so many one-offs, I couldn't get any work done. Nor could I get any food. One-offs were, by their nature, impromptu affairs so there was not time to schedule a food delivery.

We eventually gave birth to a magnanimous Mission statement that promised, among other things, full color, user-friendly computer systems that would strive to benefit the payroll department, if not possibly the whole of mankind. Our departmental Mission, printed in a Broadway BT font, joined all the other little bits of framed corporate wisdom hanging in a hundred cubicles around the I.T. area, including my own.

The new grads moved on to the departmental Vision and I, five pounds over my fighting weight, settled back into my routine of work, lunch, nap and a little more work.

That wasn't the end of it, though. I instinctively knew it was time for me to step aside when I went to the restroom one late spring morning and found Ken #3 brushing his teeth in preparation for a staff meeting. Now this was a good idea,

My first real job was in a furniture factory where ninety percent of the workers chewed tobacco to counteract the sawdust laden air. A fresh breath in that place was as hard to find as a free lunch so Ken practicing his oral hygiene at work was a welcome sight.

While Ken #3 was flossing, Ken's 1 and 2, not to be outdone, were lined up at the row of ceramic urinals, each with his red power tie slung over his dark blue-suit clad shoulder. Why would that be, I thought. I supposed it must help to keep the tie dry during this process but that maneuver also left the shirt exposed. I tried to recall the number of times I had stepped up to the urinal and wet myself in the vicinity of my chest and stomach but no recollections were forthcoming. They must teach this practice in MBA School, I decided and then wondered what you'd call a class like that. Was it for men only? Do lady MBA's have some similar problem? I'm sorry to say I never found out.

I guess if I would have stopped to remember my own entry into the workplace, I would have been a little more understanding of these guys with the clean ties. As a young man, I couldn't understand why my older coworkers weren't as excited about their jobs as I was about mine. Now I realize, it must be this way with every generational changeover as the old folks are shoved aside to let the next generation take charge.

I still wasn't thinking about retirement. I thought maybe a fresh start in another location would do the trick and put the magic back into my job. It wasn't to be. Several companies, including the giant firm where I labored away, decided the job that I performed could be done cheaper in India. In less time than it took to figure the corporation's ROI, the demand for people with my skills disappeared. I decided to quit.

We had a little money in the bank, a decent 401k and I was only six months away from early Social Security eligibility. We decided to go ahead and retire at the end of the year 2001. What we weren't prepared for was what we would do when we didn't have to get up and go to work every day. That is why I found myself trying to stand up straight after giving the dog a bath on New Year's day of 2002. We were about to learn that retirement was not as easy as just going off into the sunset and living happily ever after There was a lot to learn and a lot more to do. This book is one result of that quest.

Oh, about the wet dog. You can read more about it in the Chapter entitled 'Cujo wannabe' on page 25.

Contents

Part One
Okay, so we're going to retire. Then What?

A Trip to Amarillo 3
A hometown Visit. 7
Life aboard a Cruise Ship 13
9/11- A Dark day for America 16
Finally, a decision 22
Cujo Wannabe. 25

Part Two
The Southwestern United States

Off to Arizona 35
A quick trip to Santa Fe 38
Truck troubles – Just pull over, Damn it. 42
An apparent Immigration problem. 46
Quartzsite, Arizona 49
Just go behind that cactus! 52
Where do I find the U-bolts? 57
The Salton Sea. 60
Who you calling maggot shit? 65
San Diego 68
Area 51 or a reasonable facsimile 73

Part Three
The Birth of Riley Marie.

Chapter One 79
Chapter Two 83
Chapter Three 88
Chapter Four 91
Chapter Five 95
Chapter Six 97
Chapter Seven 100
Chapter Eight 105
Chapter Nine 109
Chapter Ten 112

Chapter Eleven...115
Chapter Twelve..118
Epilogue:...121
Punkin? What punkin you talkin' about?..................................122
She had me there. I couldn't insult the Pope. 126

Part Four
Winter in the sunshine state.

Bring 'er on back...131
I swear I'm not a pervert..134
I'm not going a penny more. 137
Who you calling an old geezer?..141
Don't look down, whatever you do...144
Anyone know if alligators eat Yankees?.....................................147
Boobs at nine O'clock 150
Que Pasa yourself..153
Say hello to Rodney...156
I'll have those Clearance Lights, Clarence.................................159

Part Five
Autumn in the east.

Oh God, Susie, please don't say anymore. 165
Your frigging what??..170
A solemn moment. 174
Belt buckle? That looks like a dinner plate. 176
I need that grandma gear. 179
My God Susie, Put some socks on..183
Walk or get the hell out of the way..186
Pass me the peanuts, please. 190
I didn't push nothing. 194

Part Six
The Lone Star State.

You ain't nothing but a hound dog. 199
Free popcorn?? Where do I sign up?..203
The horror of it all. 206
Oh God, just let me die..209
Randolph Scott was no scaredy cat. 215
I like my steaks medium rare. 218

Give my compliments to Mr. Tchaikovsky. 223
The answer is blowin' in the wind. 227
Ich Bein Luckenbach? Ya, Ya, Ya. 230
Really? I look that good? Honest? 233
It tastes like sweat? I'll have a bowl. 237
Pass me another crawdad, please. 240
Ten dollars? Not a problem. 243

Part Seven
The great Northwest

Imitating Daniel Boone never hurt anybody. 249
Air. I need air. 252
How much fat will ten inches of Spandex hold? 256
Sweet Jesus, Get me to the bottom. 261
I'm moving to Oregon. 265
Don't talk with your mouth full. 268
How does one identify an organic cow? 272
Move it, pilgrim. 275
Where's Babe, the blue ox? 278
The land of the free and the home of the arrogant. 282
How did Oysters get to the Rocky Mountains? 285
Idiot? Your mother thinks I'm an idiot? 291
I wish I would have thought of that. 294

Part Eight
The Florida Keys

Now that's a new use for a sock. 301
Eight thousand dollars? Sign me up. 305
Paddle for your life. 309
Tricky Dick Nixon does it again. 312

Epilogue
Slow down and smell the sweet corn. 319
Would we do it again? 323

PART ONE
*Okay, so we're going to retire.
Then What?*

A Trip to Amarillo

When I first considered what I would do to keep myself amused after I quit working, one of the things that kept popping into my head was the idea of becoming a gourmet chef. Many of my relatives, including my mom and my sister, had worked in the restaurant business and it seemed like a natural progression for me to do the same. I was already pretty good at hamburgers and fried chicken, so it didn't seem like much of a stretch to advance to the next gastronomic level. I bought a cart full of spices at the closeout store, a bottle of sherry at the gourmet deli, several kinds of cheese at the cheese shop and set out on my culinary journey.

Oddly enough, as I began producing beautifully garnished haute cuisine dishes, not one of my kids, my relatives or my friends were ever hungry when they came to our house. After my dog turned up his nose at my hollandaise sauce for the third time, it hit me over the head why they didn't want to eat. It wasn't good. Gourmet cooking was just not my bag.

Fortunately, I found a new direction for my hobby. My cousin, Randy, showed up at a family reunion bringing along a gigantic cut of meat and I found my kids standing in line to get some of this stuff. The 'stuff' turned out to be a smoked beef brisket that Randy had cooked at his home in Amarillo. I knew he was no gourmet genius so when I asked him how he cooked that brisket, he told me all it took was a good smoker and his marinade that contained several secret ingredients.

A smoker, eh? This was good news because I had a meat smoker, sort of. In a fit of asserting the macho side of my nature, I had purchased a combination deep fryer, barbeque grill and smoker. It was a cylindrical thing about eighteen inches in diameter with three thin aluminum legs. My only adventure with this baby had been deep-frying a turkey for the family Easter gathering and it had turned out pretty well despite the third degree burns. If you could disregard the fact that I also lost my eyebrows and severely damaged the finish on my brother-in law's deck, it would have been termed an unequivocal success no matter what Susie said. She told me there was to be no more deep frying and even though I was a little bit leery myself, like the just thrown horseback rider, I vowed to try again as soon as my eyebrows grew back.

The year before I was to retire, Randy called and invited me to Texas to attend the annual Amarillo meat smoking festival. He was a contestant in this cook-off and wanted me to join him on the cooking team. Obviously, he had heard from some of our relatives about my cooking know-how. I cleared the trip with Susie and took off for Amarillo. It was invigorating to be out on the road looking at some of the things our country has to offer. The drive through Missouri and Oklahoma was just what I needed. My job was becoming intolerable and the closer I got to quitting, the worse it seemed to get. I stopped in Oklahoma City to visit the bombing memorial and came away saddened at the loss of human life. That visit also made me realize that wasting any of the precious time we've been allotted for our lives is foolish. I mulled all that over and by the time I reached Amarillo, I was determined that I would not squander one more minute of mine.

I arrived at Randy's home and found within the first few minutes that smoking meat in Texas is not just some Sunday afternoon activity. It's a big deal. It's also mostly a manly sort of activity and the cook-off festival in Amarillo gives the guys a chance to compete for bragging rights. Randy took me outside to see his smoker. I had envisioned something like mine sitting in the corner of his garage. Instead, he shows me this huge steel box mounted on a fire engine red trailer custom built for the smoker and its accessories. The smoker resembled the hog roasters seen in the Midwestern part of the country, only it was larger. The smoking surface was about three feet by eight feet. A large firebox contained maybe a hundred pounds of charcoal and a couple of hickory logs. Mounted on the trailer were a two burner gas stove and a griddle big enough to cook two dozen pancakes at a time. Both of these appliances were on hinges so that they could swing out to the side of the smoker. Good Lord, the whole thing was beautiful.

"I want one of those." I said, using my best primal, caveman voice.

"I can get you one custom built for around three thousand."

The bean counter side of me overruled the caveman. "Maybe next trip."

We spent the next day buying the meat for the contest. We drove twenty or so miles south of Amarillo to an out of the way butcher shop Randy had found some years earlier. We bought six briskets, a dozen slabs of pork ribs and eight Rib eye steaks. Late in the afternoon, we pulled the smoker to downtown Amarillo and set it up in our assigned slot on the blocked off street.

When we were finished setting up, a gentleman who had been watching us work, invited us to 'sit a spell' and offered us a drink. He was wearing faded jeans, boots and a ten gallon hat so I assumed he must have been a cowboy. Having always had a deep seated desire to be a cowboy, I sat right down and took the beer he handed me.

I immediately tried to impress the guy by telling him about my smoker. I described it, embellishing the size a little.

"I've been thinking about smoking a turkey and maybe even a brisket." I told him, bragging a bit. I babbled along, not realizing I sounded like some awestruck cowboy wannabe. I also was about to learn that I should have kept my mouth shut when I bragged about my outfit.

"Shoot, son," he says to me even though I'm probably twenty years older than he is, "you ain't got no meat smoker. What you got is one of them weinie cookers."

Weinie cooker? Was he insulting my smoker? My God, was I going to have to call him out on that? I didn't even own a gun. Randy saw my distress and explained the remark. Cowboys in Texas like to refer to hot dogs as weinies and this guy was only being truthful telling me that what I had was a hot dog grill.

"Now that's a meat smoker." The cowboy said, smiling and pointing at his rig, It was parked next to ours and occupied about half a city block. It even dwarfed Randy's cooker. It was an immense black metal chamber mounted on a dual axle gooseneck trailer pulled by a one ton Ford Diesel truck. The lid was raised by a chain attached to an electric motor. It had it's own generator, hot water tank and a cord of hickory wood stacked on the back. It also had a built in sound system that endlessly played Willie Nelson CD's. A flag pole about twenty feet tall was attached to the side and the Lone Star of the Texas State flag flew over the whole outfit.

"I'm cooking up 84 slabs of ribs and a goat."

"A goat? A whole goat?" I said, instantly wanting to look inside that thing belching smoke into the afternoon Amarillo sky.

"Yep. A goat. It's good eating, especially with those pintos." He told me, gesturing toward a five gallon pot perched on a stove built into the front of the trailer.

"Pintos?" I asked, mistakenly picturing parts of an Indian pony crammed into a pot.

"Beans, son. You got to have pinto beans when you're eating smoked goat."

"Well, alrighty then." I said.

Having no more to say, I gathered up my wounded pride, excused myself and went to help Randy as Willie Nelson pleaded with me to get on back to Luckenbach.

The smoking went on all night and well into the next day before Randy pronounced them done.

"I wish we had a full moon. Meat tastes much better smoked under a full moon." He had told me sometime during the night. "holds the juices in somehow."

After the judging, the event was open to the public. Several thousand people attended and for fifteen dollars each, they could sample food and drink from any of the ninety teams as well as two beer distributors and a group from the quarter horse association who were giving away margaritas. The teams came from different organizations and businesses, including the state prison. I think the cooks on that team were guards and not inmates but I was afraid to ask.

Our team didn't win anything.

"I told you we needed a full moon." Randy said.

Even though the cooking team didn't win anything, I came away from there with a victory. I thought back on the goat smoker, the Oklahoma City memorial and all the things in between. I had done all that in just one trip. I realized there is a world full of experiences out there that are just waiting on us to partake of them. Travel was in my blood and it had taken a trip such as this to find it out.

A hometown Visit.

A few months before Susie and I retired, we made a trip to my hometown in Southern Indiana. Moving back to this little town was an option I wanted to explore even though I couldn't wait to move out of there when I was young. There was never anything to do back when I was twenty years old and the excitement of the big city beckoned.

I moved to that big city and after several years there, the hectic pace required to work long hours, raise kids, coach little league and make a daily fifty mile round trip commute made the memories of the slow pace of life back home grow fonder as the years went by. I promised myself I would eventually return and spend the rest of my years observing the frailties of the human condition as found in Southern Indiana.

The only fly in the ointment was Susie. She was not one to sit around and do nothing and she cared little about observing the human condition. She also enjoyed the cultural advantages of being around a real city therefore Loogootee, Indiana was not high on her list of places to spend her golden years.

Nonetheless, I still wanted to consider it. The town had about 2500 citizens when I lived there in the decades of the forties and fifties. Maybe half of the streets were paved and the rest were oil covered gravel or dirt. The best paying jobs in town were at the Post Office and at Carnahan's Planer mill, one of the three factories in town. It employed about fifty people making doors and windows. The other two employers of note were the Shirt factory and the Loogootee Clay Tile Company.

The Planer Mill steam whistle was an important part of the townspeople's daily lives because it could be heard in the farthest reaches of the town. It was blown in the morning at 6:45 and again fifteen minutes later when the workmen were expected to be at their machines. It blew again at 12:45 to signal the impending end of the lunch hour and then again at four o'clock to dismiss people for the day. The Catholic Church bells played the Angelus at Noon and at Six P.M. so between the two establishments, you always pretty much knew what time it was.

When I was a kid, there were endless summer days spent at Tater's Mobil station talking baseball. Mobil was a gasoline brand name that used a mythological character called Pegasus, a horse with wings, as their logo. The sign with that horse was the biggest thing on the property. There were two gas pumps out in front of a small building with one bay for oil changes and another bay in back for parking Tater's car. There was a tiny office where Tater and John, who was Tater's only full time employee, kept the radio tuned to a baseball game. You could always count on finding a kid or two in there listening to a game. In addition, a half dozen other local business men with colorful nicknames like Spindle, Popeye, Buzz, Skip Jack and Dupes would drop in and out during the day to discuss baseball. Any time of day could always be counted on to find a lively discussion about the nation's pastime. The question of whether Stan Musial or Ted Williams was the better hitter was a daily topic as was Jackie Robinson's entry into the Major leagues. This was a little disconcerting for some of these guys whose Grandfathers could have worn the Gray uniform in the Civil War. Most days, you could listen to Joe Nuxhall doing the Cincinnati play by play or catch Harry Caray broadcasting the St. Louis Cardinal games. This was the same Harry Caray who later became a Chicago Cubs legend. A lot of the games were played in the afternoon in those days and it was a good thing because Tater closed up at five o'clock and went home to his wife and his dinner.

If there was a night game to listen to, we had to find other accommodations. We had a Muntz console radio at our house that probably weighed seventy five pounds. Most night games meant we would drag it outside and onto the front porch where the reception was a little better, even though it required minor location adjustments as the signal bounced around any cloud cover. Being outside also meant being a little cooler and it also gave us a chance to stand under the streetlight and re-enact any exciting plays that came in over the airwaves. All it took for us to spring into action was to hear Harry Caray shout excitedly.

"There's the windup and the pitch. Swung on and THERE SHE GOES. It might be. It could be. IT IS. HOME RUN."

The next instant, two of us would be in the street with bat and ball, reliving the play.

There was another way the town kept track of Major League baseball. Nip's Pool Hall was a place my brother and I weren't allowed to go in because we were too young. Even had we not been underage, our mom wouldn't have let us go in there for fear of contacting some terrible character destroying addiction. We had no idea about addictions. All we cared about was the big blackboard on the wall just inside the front door. The blackboard had been divided into eight blank inning by inning box scores using white paint to draw the lines. Next to the blackboard was a ticker tape machine that sat quietly during the off-season but by noon of each day during the baseball season, it would spit out some mysterious hieroglyphics on the narrow tape on a regular basis. A rotund man with a permanent cigar stuck in the corner of his mouth worked for Nip. His name was Mike and it was his job to maintain the board and the tape machine. He would begin his day putting each of the sixteen teams in their assigned slot for that particular day's games. His printing, as he filled in the blank slots, was so meticulous that it looked like a machine did it. We could stop any time during the morning hours and look in the window to see who was playing. Not that we really needed to do that, we usually had the whole season schedule memorized by the middle of April. After lunch, the ticker tape would begin to rattle it's information and Tip would record the box scores. I would stand outside the window shading my eyes from the hot afternoon sun and watch him. Out at the end of the inning by inning boxes, he would inscribe any home runs. 'Musial, two on'. I would read and joy would fill my heart. Stan was my favorite player.

We didn't just listen to baseball, we also played it. There was always a baseball game going on at Bicycle John's empty lot. It wasn't an organized thing, not "Little League" and no parents were involved. It was just a bunch of boys choosing teams using the hand over hand on the bat method. Most of the time, I was the last one chosen and it probably would have damaged my self esteem had that term been invented then.

Gordon Grindstaff

There was no game on Wednesday afternoon because Wednesday afternoons were reserved for the twelve mile school bus ride to Washington, Indiana's swimming pool.

Tuesday nights meant the movie because the Ritz theatre had their Jackpot drawing that evening and we had to be present or registered as being present to win. The registered as being present meant that you had paid a quarter and signed a sheet saying that you wanted to be included in the drawing.

There was also a cowboy movie every Saturday afternoon at the theatre. The cowboys were my heroes and I vowed to grow up like Lash Larue, saving the day and riding off into the sunset. The Ritz took on a new role when we got to be twelve or thirteen. Then our Saturday afternoons were used for the first tentative interactions with the opposite sex. Holding hands with a girl while watching Lash or Roy or Gene take on the bad guys somehow wasn't the same. Girls didn't understand why you'd yell "Look out Lash, he's behind the rocks."

Every Sunday meant the ten o'clock High Mass. It also meant frequent visits to my Aunt and Uncle's farm where fried chicken and mashed potatoes with thick milk gravy awaited us. That milk gravy and my Uncle left me a memory that I'll take to my grave. He would take the last biscuit, always reserved for him, and with slow circuitous motions, wipe his plate clean with that fluffy morsel. It was mesmerizing to watch that biscuit moving around the plate, snagging bits of chicken and maybe a green bean that had been caught in the gravy. I picked up the habit and it remained with me through my adult life and is probably why I'm wider around the middle than I should be.

If we ever found ourselves with nothing to do, there was always the half dozen old men who sat on the town square watching the world go by. The square really wasn't a square because the street bordering the east side ran diagonally. This ended up making the square more trapezoid than anything else but town trapezoid sounded stupid so we called it the town square.

There was always some topic for discussion to be found here amongst the town's elders. It might only be the weather and the corn harvest but it also could be the prospects of that year's crop of high school basketball players. Politics was another favorite subject. Bringing up President Truman and later, President Eisenhower, always made for a lively debate. One of these old guys was a man who had something wrong with his left eye so he had a nickname that was insensitive but true. I don't even know if he had another name since everybody in town called him Popeye. The hardware store display window had one of those new television sets in it, one of a half dozen in the whole town and mention of that TV set always upset Popeye.

"That thing is gonna be the ruination of civilization." he would say. Now that I look back on it, several of these guys probably had no more than an eighth grade education and except for the war, had never left town, yet in my opinion, were right on the money with predictions like that.

When I became a young man, there were burgers at Jerry's drive-in restaurant. Not Drive-thru, mind you. It was a Drive-in where you parked under a tree and had a car hop bring you a cheeseburger and a root beer. As I grew into my early twenties, the root beer became just beer and there were nightly, unsettling discussions at either Frank's or Stormy's tavern about what we were all going to do with our lives.

When I look back on it now, it all seemed so idyllic and I guess it was but I don't want to paint you some untrue picture. The fifties weren't always some sort of Eden in my hometown. Three of our town's sons were lost to the Korean conflict. We had a town drunk and when he couldn't get to town, we had two or three stand-ins ready and waiting to take his place. There were men who beat their wives and children. Some kids didn't have shoes, at least in the summertime. Outdoor plumbing was the norm and central heat was a novelty. Polio was a constant threat. There was a photographer who set up shop and besides taking pictures, he also fondled some youngsters and was run out of town. Although only a few people in town even knew a black person, racism was still the order of the day.

The union eventually moved in on the mill and it ended up going out of business. No, it wasn't all Ozzie and Harriet. I just recall it that way.

Fast forward forty plus years and you find me returning to Southern Indiana to check on what few relatives I have left down there and maybe to find a place to settle down.

I spent the day visiting my old haunts. Not many survived. The site where Jerry's Drive-in stood is a dusty gravel parking lot filled with grain trucks. Tater's gas station corner now contains an abandoned quick mart and the Pegasus sign is God only knows where. All of the regulars as well as some of the kids who hung out there, have gone on to the big baseball game in the sky. I wondered where today's kids gather to talk baseball or if they even do that anymore.

Bicycle John's empty lot has been filled to the gills with six or seven mobile homes. An empty weed filled area between two buildings on the square is all that's left of a burned out Stormy's tavern. Frank's tavern, where I first legally drank a beer, had been torn down and a garish Chinese carryout place uses the space for parking. The gang at Tater's Mobil or the patrons at Frank's would never in a hundred years have dreamed that a Chinese restaurant would exist in the United States, much less in Loogootee, Indiana.

Larkin's Department Store where my mom bought my first communion outfit is gone and a dollar store occupies the front half of the building. The Hardware store now contains a video place and most of the other storefronts are either empty or occupied by insurance agents. The thriving downtown area of the fifties has the makings of a not to distant future ghost town. It has that look of many towns victimized by the gargantuan big box stores.

The Pool hall is still there but Nip and Mike are long gone, replaced by Murray, Nip's older son. The blackboard with the baseball scores is gone also. It wouldn't have been able to hold all the teams playing today, anyway. The Ritz is no longer there, either. Oh, the building is still standing but it appears empty now. The word 'Gospel' is painted in faded and chipped letters on the brick wall nearest the street. That seems to be the only reminder of the building's most recent past. I looked in the doors but the popcorn machine was gone. You can't tell there was ever a movie house filled with cheering kids in there.

The old men sitting on the town square are long dead and nobody has replaced them. The Cars and SUV's patrolling the streets with their deafening BOOM BOOM stuff rattling the car windows have made sure nothing like that happens again.

The mill and it's whistle is long gone, the site now occupied by a bank and a drug store. This leaves me to wonder how people in the town know what time it is.

What happened to the town? Maybe nothing. Most likely, it's me getting old and sentimental about my childhood days but it's not at all like I remembered it. I think Susie can relax because I'm going to pass on retiring there and I wonder if that's why she didn't object when I talked about it. She probably knew it all along and I should have learned because someone whose name escapes me said it best; You can't go home again.

Life aboard a Cruise Ship

The trip to Amarillo had served to whet my appetite for travel and then when Susie and I visited my hometown, we met a couple who was seeing the world by ship, taking cruises on a regular basis. They told us that this is what retirement is all about. To hear them tell it, this seemed to be a great way, albeit a bit expensive, to see the world.

I wasn't real comfortable with leaving dry land, not really seeing any need to do that. But Susie wanted to try it so a few weeks later, when a chance to go on a cruise popped up, I relented and agreed to go, figuring it would be nice to drop such an experience into casual conversation.

The thought of being out in the ocean where you can't see land did make me queasy but it turned out not to bother me at all and of course, it didn't bother Susie. She'll try anything once.

In addition to seeing new places, we found that the food was an added bonus of cruising. Those of you who have been down to the sea in ships know about the food. It's always very good and served with seemingly unlimited portions. How the kitchens turned out such beautiful food meal after meal is beyond me. After three or four days of six course meals, I went to sleep vowing to quit eating. However, the morning after taking my vow, I found myself surrounded by an omelet, hash, grits, a fruit plate and a bagel with fresh smoked salmon, cream cheese and a big slice of Bermuda onion. I was helpless. First of all, I am a tightwad so I hated to pass up the food that was already paid for and secondly.... Well, secondly, I had to face the fact that I had no willpower. This realization almost brought me to the point of tears. I knew I shouldn't eat all that stuff but I couldn't help myself. On top of this, Susie was sitting across from me with a piece of melon and a cup of blueberry yogurt. She was very nice and didn't say anything even as I sat there working on committing one of the seven capital sins.

When I wasn't eating, I was busy trying to educate Susie in the ways of the ship's sewage disposal system. The toilets on the ship were not your everyday water flushers. The flushing mechanism was driven by a powerful suction device. A little button on the wall next to the toiler paper activated it and when pushed, there was a loud "SWO-OOO-SH" and everything in the vicinity of the bowl was vacuumed out of sight, ending up somewhere in the ship's innards. Susie had confessed to me that she was terrified of this thing. She was certain that, were she to be seated on it when the button was pushed, her private parts as well as several other important organs would be sucked out of her by the roots, most likely to be propelled out of the ship and into the depths of the North Atlantic.

I told her that was nonsense and thought it might be educational for her if I could get that button pushed when she was perched on the apparatus. I had tried mightily to figure out someway to do it myself but she was wise to me. She kept the bathroom door locked allowing me no access to the button. I realized that my efforts were fruitless and the only way that button would get pushed was if she did it herself.

I first appealed to her sense of cooperation.

"Susie," I said through the closed bathroom door. "The room steward called and said there is a problem with the toilets on this deck. He needs you to flush it while keeping the bowl covered."

"He wants me to do what??"

"Flush the toilet while you're sitting on it."

"Right. In a pigs eye."

Seeing that cooperation was not in the offing, I thought perhaps a promise of self actualization might work.

"Susie, I think you should try it. It's really very refreshing, sort of like a fresh ocean breeze on your bare bottom.. "Don't give me that stuff. I've seen what happens and if that's an ocean breeze, I'm Sam Donaldson."

I tried another approach. Prurient interests normally didn't faze her but I thought I'd give it a try.

"Susie dear, I've heard that in the orient, these suction devices are used in combination with inhaled ivory dust to provide a sense of sexual pleas….."

"You're full of it, you pervert. Ivory dust, my butt. You can forget it because I am not pushing that damn button. "

I tried everything in my book of tricks but to no avail. I have to report that I couldn't outsmart her. Her gizzard arrived home intact.

9/11- A Dark day for America

The time for our retirement was fast approaching when my well heeled brother, Ron, called me and offered to spring for a trip to Europe. He and his wife, Julie, were going to tour several countries in a rented car and they wanted Susie and me to go along. Susie was ready to pack her bags but there were two things holding me back. I hated the idea of having someone else pay my way and even more, I hated the idea of flying. I did want to go though and not knowing any other way to get there, I convinced myself that even if the plane should crash, I had already had a good life and any other experiences were icing on the cake.

I also went to the doctor and got a prescription for four Valium tablets. Two to get me over there and two to get me back. I got around the dilemma of having my brother paying for the trip by telling myself that his gift was probably in gratitude for all the times I hauled him back to the University while he was a student. He made the trip from Purdue to home as often as possible and invariably missed his ride back. I made the two hundred and fifty mile round trip on many a Sunday evening in his four years of college.

I took a valium tablet with two cans of beer and slept through most of the flight to Ireland; a method of travel that I highly recommend. Susie told me that the flight went without incident. We planned to visit as many Western European countries as we could during five weeks of travel. The trip was going marvelously and was well worth the two or three years of my life probably lost by the initial fright of the plane trip. We spent a few days in Ireland and then flew to Paris to see the continent. There, we were met by a couple named Francois and Danielle, good friends of my Ron and Julie. Francois's escorting us around the city made the visit a once in a lifetime event.

We were about two weeks into our journey and left Paris headed for Switzerland. Along the way, we stopped to visit the King Louis XIV palace at Versailles. I marveled at the opulence of the place and while my only exposure to the history of this era was attending 3 performances of Les Miserables over a five year period, I could well understand why the French populace revolted.

We rode around the grounds in one of those open air buses used by tourist attractions all around the world. I was seated next to a man who lived in New York City with his family. Ten million or so people live in that city and this was the first person from there that I had ever actually met. He was by himself, combining a business trip with a short vacation. He was also a New York Knicks fan and we had an enjoyable conversation about Reggie Miller and Spike Lee. He completely changed my perception of New York basketball fans. They were human after all.

We left the palace in our rented car headed for the Burgundy region in the South of France. We stopped sometime during the afternoon at a service area and restaurant along the highway to get something to eat. While we were waiting on our food, I wandered over to a cluster of eight or ten people gathered around a television set. A cloud of smoke around a bunch of buildings was on the screen and a newscaster speaking in French was saying something about the United States.

"What's happening?" I said, once again forgetting that I was in a foreign country where no one understood me. Luckily, one man did. He looked up and said in a heavy French accent.

"Someone attacked New York City."

"Attacked? With what?" I said, not particularly alarmed.

"I don't know. Chemicals. I think."

Chemicals? Did some crazy fringe group gas the subways? I thought, not stopping to wonder what was causing all the smoke on the screen.

I went back to tell Susie and a man stopped me. "Are you from America?" he said, in perfect English.

"Yes, I am."

"I live in Copenhagen and I just talked to my wife at home. Someone is flying airplanes into buildings in New York. "

My brother walked up to see what was going on as more and more people gathered in front of the television. I told him about the attack.

He ran to a phone to call his son as the rest of us watched the TV screen.

He frantically came back to where we were standing. "I can't get through to anybody. I think Marcus might be in New York." Marcus, his son, traveled extensively and the terror in my brother's face was overwhelming.

The man from Copenhagen interpreted the news for us. "They think it might be Palestinian terrorists."

My brother shouted an expletive that made everyone turn around. Never one to mince words, he said "Those raghead SOB"S. We ought to take out that whole damned area with an A-bomb."

Fear had obviously made him irrational. His face was so red I was afraid he might have a stroke. I was also more than a little concerned about all the Middle Eastern garb being worn by people in the gathering crowd.

"Let's get to the car." Susie said, grabbing him by the arm as we left the place, forgetting all about our food. We turned on the car radio but got only snippets of words that we understood. We drove for hours twisting the radio dial while at the same time trying to find a hotel that had access to CNN. Along the way, a dozen or so fighter aircraft screamed over us at a very low altitude scaring the daylights out of all four of us. Was the whole world at war?

I thought of the man from Manhattan on the open air bus. Did he say his office was in the twin towers? I was pretty sure he did. We were panic stricken and I could only imagine what he was going through. He must have really been going crazy.

We finally located a hotel in Beaune near the Swiss Border. We tried calling our kids and couldn't get through. We stayed up all night watching CNN and the BBC and trying the phone every few minutes. More details came in. Collapse of the buildings. Thousands dead. The pentagon attacked. A crash in Pennsylvania. Palestinians dancing in the streets. All airplanes grounded and the U.S. borders closed. Probably more terrorists out there.

Someone at the hotel advised us not to wear any clothing that identified us as American. I packed my baseball cap with the American flag on the front of it and stuck my Indiana University sweatshirt in the bottom of the suitcase. A feeling of fright and hopelessness like none I'd had before or have had since came over me. The images of those planes flying into the towers had been played over and over on the television screen and were permanently lodged in my consciousness. I didn't know if I would ever be able to get on an airplane again nor did I think I would ever let Susie. None of us had any idea how or when we would get home. In the meantime, there was nothing for us to do but go on with our trip, so we loaded up our bags and headed for Zurich.

Two days after the 9/11 attacks, we finally reached our kids via e-mail and found everything okay with them. They had been as frantic about us as we had them. Marcus had not been in New York nor had he ever even considered going there. My brother had just panicked.

During the next few days, our fears took a back seat to the plight of dozens of people that we met who couldn't get back to the U.S. because of the border closing. We met dozens of stranded Americans and heard their stories. One young couple in particular had a harrowing tale to tell. They had flown over for a wedding and left their two children with a babysitter. They had driven to cities in three countries trying to find a flight home. The babysitter needed to move on and was threatening to take their children to a government agency for care. Their credit card was maxed out and they were sleeping in their rental car; a car that was supposed to have been returned on the eleventh. We let them take a shower in our hotel room in Zurich and they left for Innsbruck to try and find a flight. We weren't scheduled to leave for three weeks so we decided not to worry until then and just try to enjoy our trip.

It was good that we did. We were shown extraordinary kindness by the citizens of the European cities that we visited. We went to a Cathedral in Munich where maybe a thousand people had gathered for a mass. While we didn't understand much of it, we were able to figure out that they were praying for the United States. A makeshift memorial on the Marienplatz, the town square in front of the city hall, contained hundreds of candles, thousands of flowers and just as many notes from the citizens of Munich. We found these same kinds of memorials in a dozen cities; Caen, France, near the Normandy beaches, had a huge memorial as did Koblenz, Germany on the Rhine river. Everywhere we stopped, when people found out we were American, they went out of their way to express their sympathy.

A particularly poignant encounter happened during a breakfast Susie and I were having on the outskirts of Amsterdam. Two burly truck drivers introduced themselves to us. They lived in Belfast, Northern Ireland and were either transporting potatoes to or from their country, I've forgotten which. The smaller of the two, but still a very big man, introduced himself as Michael and took me by the hand.

"We wanted to reassure ourselves that you weren't British before we spoke." He said quietly. "I'm very sorry for what has happened in your country. Our prayers are with you."

His voice cracked and he said in his Irish brogue, "Nothing makes any sense. There are terrible, crazy things happening in my country as well so sure and I'm knowing how you feel."

Then the tears welled up in his eyes and in an instant, he was crying and I was too. Susie was way ahead of us. Her tears had started at his initial expression of sympathy.

Flights had resumed somewhat of a normal schedule by the time our traveling was over and we headed for terminal C at Charles DeGaulle airport in Paris. I was hanging on for dear life to my little vial of Valium tablets.

There were thousands of people of every conceivable description and nationality milling about the terminal like so many ants in a pile of sand and I was suspicious of every one of them. A giant of a man, perhaps six and a half feet tall and wearing an Arab headdress and bright blue flowing robes stared at me as he went by. I couldn't figure out what was wrong until I realized I had been staring at him.

We surrendered potential weaponry to the baggage inspection people before boarding the plane. A nail file, fingernail clippers, a pair of scissors and my newly purchased Swiss Army knife went into this huge crate filled with such paraphernalia. It had not dawned on me to pack it away.

Two middle eastern men sat together in the center row of seats on the Paris to Dublin part of the flight.

"This is the Irish National airline." I thought. "Why are two olive skinned Arabs on an Irish airliner?"

I resolved to keep an eye on them and it turned out that I wasn't by myself. My five foot one inch tall sister-in-law got in her purse and kept her eyebrow pencil ready to inflict a crippling injury on either of them had they shown any inclination toward mischief. My brother, artificial knee and all, clutched a bottle holding an airline sized serving of Cabernet Sauvignon. He had plans to break it off at the neck, like some motorcycle gang member in a bar fight and stab them if it became necessary. Susie had no weapons but had already decided if either of them charged the cockpit, she was going to jump them and not let go.

I'm certain that more than half the other passengers were prepared to do the same thing because the tension in the cabin hung heavy over all of us as the plane lifted off. There was very little small talk as most everyone was locked into their own private thoughts. The apprehension stayed on people's faces until we arrived in Dublin.

We switched planes in Dublin and the trip from there went much more smoothly since all the passengers looked more or less like us. I sincerely had to resist the urge to kiss the ground when we stepped off the plane in Chicago. I swore that I would never, ever let my feet leave North American ground again.

Finally, a decision

The horror over the 9/11 attacks eventually abated somewhat and I was back in my routine of work and found myself dreaming of the day when I didn't have to work anymore. It was a good thing I was close to retirement because the jobs were drying up fast. The East Indians were willing to work for a fraction of what I had been making; still, I could have muddled through for another few years but I had about had enough. It was time to try something else and set about achieving some sort of personal goal. But what it was to be, I didn't know.

I had not had the good sense to be an employee in one of those industries that promised to take care of me for the rest of my life so there was no pension in the offing. I had fortunately put some money away in a 401K and it did well. We looked at those savings that were growing by leaps and bounds with the stock market explosion of the nineties. All the financial experts said the market was sure to continue in that direction so it was pretty obvious I needed to retire and start spending some of that money before there got to be too much to manage.

Susie had her own goals. She wanted to paint and play with her grandchildren, if our children ever got busy and had any. In fact, unbeknownst to us at the time, we did have one on the way, thanks to our daughter and her Husband, Rick. Only later would that matter.

I sat down to list my long term goals and realized I didn't have any, other than not working. I did want to develop some proficiency with the only hobby I had, my writing pastime, but I didn't consider that a goal. I looked around and decided I should devote some time to efforts that had some lasting purpose; maybe a book. Yeah, that's it. I'd write a book as soon as I could think of something to write about.

We also looked a little more seriously at a backup idea we had. We had discovered during our forty years of marriage that we both liked traveling and seeing new places. The idea surfaced about the time our youngest child played her last soccer game. We realized that, God willing, there would be a time when we weren't tied down with raising kids and we would be free, within some financial constraints, to do what we wanted. There was nothing complicated about the idea. We would dispose of everything we owned, kiss the kids goodbye, hook up our newly bought camper, climb into our equally new truck and drive away into the sunset to see the world.

It sounded like a great idea but actually doing it took more courage than we could muster. The older couple we'd met on the cruise ship weighed on my mind and then one Sunday after church, we talked to another older couple that were acquaintances. The gentleman was in a wheelchair. They told us they had plans to travel when he retired but it never happened. For several years, at the end of the year, they would put off retirement in favor of working just one more year.

"Just one more year and then we'll do it."; they promised themselves but a debilitating illness wiped out their plans.

In the next few weeks, we ran into all kinds of people who felt the same way but family, sickness, financial difficulties or just being too cautious to give up their daily lives prevented them from striking out. There were so many encounters that it seemed like someone was telling us to go while we could. So we took a deep breath and decided to do it.

It would take some doing for us to work out this business of living together day and night in 240 square feet of camper. Susie and I are exact opposites when it comes to our outlook on life. Old habits die hard. Thirty years of being in the information technology business and analyzing everything to death, is not a habit that goes away easily. That kind of training left me poorly prepared for taking it easy. Susie, on the other hand, just goes with the flow. She doesn't care why things work and is not at all concerned when they don't. If we logged ten miles in a day, or five hundred, it would make no difference to her. I was worried that her positive attitude might drive me crazy.

Also, there was the problem of schedules. These meant nothing to her while attendance at a thousand business meetings had made me paranoid about being on time. If someone says, "We'll see you at 'four o'clock'", I hear 'three thirty' and Susie hears 'five'. She also delights in detouring off the road to see something she just read about in a tour guide even though it's not on the itinerary I'd planned for the day.

There were a lot of kinks to sort out but we had made the decision. I spent most of my life being wishy-washy about decisions but resolved that would not be the case this time.

We sold our home of thirty years and got rid of almost everything we owned. We gave some to our kids, had a garage sale to get rid of some more and donated what was left to a homeless shelter. We ended up with less stuff than we had the day we got married. It was starting all over but that was okay. From now on, every day would be a Saturday. There would be no more stress battling the morning traffic. No more washing storm windows. I cut up all my neckties and considered pitching my blood pressure medicine out the window but thought better of it. We found a truck and a fifth wheel camper on the Internet and bought it without ever even looking back. We were on our way.

Cujo Wannabe.

My first full day of retirement found us in an environment of freezing temperatures and seven inches of snow on the ground. I woke up that morning and panicked because I thought I was going to be late for work. Then I remembered that it was New Year's day and we were retired. No hurrying to get ready for work, no more stoking my heartburn with a quick breakfast. The most pressing thing I had to do at the moment was start thinking about getting our camper hooked up so that we could head for warmer weather in Arizona.

After selling our home, We had been bunking with our son, Jason, in Indianapolis. Besides providing us with a place to stay, he had also solved a problem with our dog, Murphy, a sixty pound Border Collie, who didn't care for the vagabond life. A weekend trip to a state park had convinced us that camping was not his forte. It was obvious that he could not accompany us on the trip and we weren't sure what we would do. Jason had come to the rescue and offered to watch Murphy until spring.

The coffee that Susie brought me took effect and the fog in my head began to lift. I could hear Murphy barking at something outside that he felt needed to be herded into the shed for shearing. No matter that it might be a garbage truck or an eight year old kid on a bicycle. If it moved, it needed herding.

Jason was spending the New Years' holiday with friends so we had the place to ourselves. Susie brought me a second cup of coffee and the fog brought on by our previous late night totally evaporated. This being New

Year's day, I considered writing down a list of resolutions we needed to make in our lives now that we no longer had to get up and go to work every day. Resolutions came easy to me. I had been making them for Susie and myself on New Years Day for thirty five years and for just as many years, she had been ignoring them.

Since she didn't pay attention anyway, I decided to forget about improving Susie's life and instead work on improving mine. I had decided a few days earlier that since my first day of retirement would be the first day of the rest of my life, it was also time to turn over a new leaf and get rid of all my bad habits. Getting into shape was to be the first of my new avocations. Susie and I were planning all these golden year activities and most of them required a moderate amount of fitness so our first day of retirement seemed like a good time to get started.

I propped myself up in bed and balanced the cup of coffee on my stomach. I wanted to start planning my exercise regimen for the day and I needed something to record all the things I would be doing. I yelled for Susie to bring me a pen and paper.

"Why do you need a pen and paper?" she asked.

"I need to make a list of the exercises that I'll be starting today." I said. "In a few weeks, you'll be married to a sixty year old man with the body of a thirty year old."

"Ha!" she said. "A thirty year old what?" Susie had been hearing me make these New Year 'getting into shape' resolutions for almost as long as we'd been married and she tended to treat them lightly but I was ready to show her. This New Year's day was different. I didn't have to get up tomorrow and go to work. I was free to exercise until I resembled the guy who kicked sand in the faces of ninety eight pound weaklings.

"Why don't you start this exercising by rolling out of bed and getting your own pencil?" Susie asked me as I handed her my empty coffee cup.

I sat up on the edge of the bed and scratched my ears. I was tempted to scratch my stomach but I'd already seen one too many underwear clad beer bellied characters doing that and knew that it was not a pleasant sight. There were plenty of other areas that needed a little tending to, though. Susie watched as I went through my morning scratching ritual. The first thing that needed my attention was my head, scratching hard to wake up my scalp, then my nose, my ears and finally my chin hair. The last thing to do was a bit of stretching.

"You know what?" she said.

"What?"

"You should've been an umpire."

"An umpire?."

"Yes. an umpire. If you'd scratch your crotch, you'd have all their signals down pat."

"That's not an umpire."

"Well, whatever it is."

"I think you mean third base coach."

"Okay then, a third base coach. Call it whatever you want. You still got all the signals." .

It looked like I wasn't going to get a pencil so I decided to incorporate only a few activities performed at a vigorous pace to restore my body to it's former state. I forgot about the pencil and paper. No need to write stuff down. I would just start out by running a mile or so and then knock off a few push-ups to start trimming the old spare tire.

I was also mulling over a plan to make up a vitamin laden concoction for my morning sustenance. The "Rocky" movies were the inspiration for this plan but I had only a vague idea of what went into that glass that Rocky gulped down in the pre-dawn light before setting off to run thirty five miles around Philadelphia. As I remembered, Raw eggs were the main ingredient in the drink and the thought of that made my stomach turn so I decided to forego the drink and substitute a bowl of chili instead.

With my plans for the day in place, I more or less jumped up and got dressed in the new warm up suit I had purchased for this occasion. I was removing my new cross trainer shoes from their box when Susie told me that we were going to give the dog a bath before we did anything else.

"Not so fast, Buster." She said. Anytime she called me "Buster" meant that she had plans for me. "The first thing you need to put on that list is giving Murphy a bath."

I let out a groan but to no avail. Susie was having none of that. Lord knows that dog needed a bath. He had a habit of rolling around in the woods and he picks up a lot of nasty-ass stuff back there. Have you ever smelled the doughballs that some guys make for catfish bait? The kind that makes your head snap back when the old olfactory nerves get a whiff of 'em? That was pretty close to what our dog smelled like. There were compost heaps that put out a better scent. That alone was reason enough to beg off that job. I wanted nothing to do with trying to clean up that dog. I had always used the work excuse but now I could only point out that I was busy preparing for my workout and that she would have to do it by herself.

In reality I knew I was barking (so to speak) up the wrong tree. She couldn't do it by herself. She always enlisted one of our kids to help when they came to visit but they were nowhere to be found on this day. I whined around a little while but in the end I resigned myself to helping out since it takes at least two people to give Murphy a bath. The little woman likes to think of him as a little fu-fu lap dog but in actuality he's anything but. He runs everywhere he goes and wouldn't dream of sitting still for even a minute. He would make a great candidate for a dog version of Ritalin.

Even with all his liveliness, he's a pretty gentle dog who goes about minding his own business unless he's faced with being dipped in a tub of warm water. A whole new personality emerges at that point and he drops any pretense of being civilized and tends to make the task as unpleasant as possible. That dog hated getting wet more than I hated Christmas shopping and he would let us know about it in any way that that his little dog brain could conjure up.

The bath thing was further complicated by a couple of problems. The first of these was that we no longer had a home or a garage to do this in. We would have to attempt this bath in the half-double where we were currently nesting. The other half of the double was occupied by a person who really and I mean REALLY, liked his peace and quiet. When he was disturbed by noises that we made, he banged on the walls or came flying out his front door to yell thru the screen door that we should be quiet. I harbored suspicions that he was a budding homicidal maniac because I had read somewhere that Ted Kazincski of letter bomb fame got his start in much the same manner.

The second problem involved the tub that we were going to have to put the dog in. It was an old-fashioned bathtub that had four legs holding it off the floor. The legs were not attached very well so the whole thing was kind of loosey goosey. When anyone got into the tub, they had to move very carefully so that the tub didn't tip over and rip the plumbing right out of the wall. This possibility alone was enough to argue that we should not put the dog into that wobbly-ass thing. Add to that the pathological neighbor who was just waiting for an excuse to reek mayhem on us and it seemed to me like there was no way to complete our task.

The first thing we had to do was capture the dog, no mean feat in normal circumstances. Because of previous adventures in bathing, Murphy avoided any water bearing container like the plague so we had to try to coax him into the room but we were wasting our breath because he wouldn't get near us. Giving the dog a bath always winds up with someone shedding a little blood. Sometimes it's the dog but more often than not, it's the person holding him. In this case, that was me.

I tried arguing these points with the little woman and when I had exhausted these and all of my other arguments, I again, so to speak, threw in the towel. Neither of us could lift the squirming Murphy by ourselves so our only choice was to each grab an end (front and back)) and dump him in the tub. He landed with a huge splash and commenced to thrashing around somewhat like I imagine the Tazmanian devil would do if put in the same circumstances. Susie assigned to me the job of grasping him firmly by the collar and the rear legs and holding him still while she scrubbed him down. It sounded simple enough but Murphy had not listened to her instructions. He wanted to get loose and he didn't care who got injured in the process.

Once we had him in the water, I grabbed him and pointed out to Susie that she should start scrubbing. She moved in slow motion, putting one handful of shampoo on his back and soaping down what appeared to me to be each individual hair. Another handful of shampoo went to a scrubbing action on each leg in a deliberate counter clockwise motion. I noticed a red stain growing in the churning water and realized it was blood. My blood. Murphy had scratched my hand and the blood was seeping from the cut much like I imagined my life itself was slowly seeping away.

I was bent over the tub, trying not to put any pressure on the tub legs. The dog was about three seconds away from getting loose, I had a terrible pain in the middle of my back and there were soap suds everywhere; on my glasses, in my nose..... Oh God, Susie, please hurry up.

I knew we would never get all the soap out of that fur and she just kept adding more. She got another handful of shampoo and started to work on his head. I could see the shampoo getting in his eyes and pushing him over the edge into an uncontrollable fury. A sopping wet, soap laden and madder than hell dog in a small enclosed area can do a serious amount of damage and I tried with what little strength I could muster to prevent this from happening.

"That's enough shampoo, Susie. Please don't get it in his eyes.". I said this in what I perceived to be a reasonable tone of voice because I didn't want to disturb Ted whats-his-name next door. All my plea got was a look that told me my quality of life was about to take a turn for the worse. All it got the dog was a soapy hand across his eyeballs. He actually handled it very well. He was fast approaching a demoralized state from his frantic attempts to get loose so he managed only a weak protest and a slight scratch, maybe three stitches worth, on my arm from a flying paw when the burning suds hit his eyes. She poured another gob of shampoo into her palm and proceeded to wash the dog's nether regions. Oh God, Susie. Don't touch his private parts, I prayed, not having any idea how he would react but pretty sure he wouldn't take it as a sign of affection.

I couldn't take it anymore. The fact that my back was killing me and my eyes were burning from the soap caused me to throw caution to the winds and to utter in a slightly louder and firm (but still self-controlled) tone, "Just wash the damn dog before one of us has a stroke.".

I said this at great danger to my person, knowing full well that the little woman possesses a hair trigger temper and my bout of cursing stretched that hair trigger past the breaking point. If you remember when Shrek's dragon shot one of those fire breathers at the donkey, then you have a general idea of the reaction my little outburst received. If you've not seen that movie, another movie comparison would be 'Carrie' where she locked the gym doors and let all hell break loose.

The end result of Susie's outburst was me in a pout, covered in unused shampoo and muttering to myself about learning to keep my mouth shut. On top of this, the neighbor was unhappy with our noise making and had started a steady rhythmic pounding on the wall. I knew It was only a matter of time until he showed up at the door with a machete.

The rinsing piece of the job, what with the glut of soap suds, was another sloppy operation that took an endless amount of time but I kept that observation to myself. I got a further soaking while we attempted to rid the dog of the sudsy mess and also clean the loose hair out of the tub and off of us. The pain in my back had reached critical mass but my mental state was getting better. While the task at hand was bad, it was also the light at the end of the tunnel. I knew we were in the home stretch.

I was beginning to think that a little toweling off, a hot cup of coffee, some iodine for my scratches and I would be none the worse for wear. This mood was quickly destroyed when I saw the little woman reach for another bottle. Another bottle? What the hell was going on now?

It was a bottle of hair conditioner! The dog's locks were about to get conditioned, for god's sake, and I was powerless to stop the person who was going to do it. I thought I should point out that dogs have no desire to be fluffy and I was certain that split ends are the last things on their mind; but I knew better than to say anything for I would then have not only an angry neighbor and a half crazed dog on my hands, but a mad woman as well.

To my astonishment, the little woman went about her business as though she were working on Goldilocks instead of a frothing at the mouth Cujo wannabe. I did not understand how she could be so calm at a time like this. The dog was shaking like he had just contracted a palsy germ and was shedding water like a garden hose that got too close to the mower. There was more water on the floor than there was in the tub. Hell, if you could have wrung me out, there was more water on me than in that tub.

The dog had had enough. He wriggled loose and with a hearty leap, he cleared the tub, flew out the open door and was gone down the hall to roll in the carpet. He disappeared before I could straighten up enough to grab him. But at that point, if that dog had been Whistler's mother, I believe he could have gotten away before I could straighten up. My back was killing me and I was bent over like a disheveled question mark. I would have made Quasimodo look like one of the Queen's guards.

I stood there picking wet fur off my shirt waiting for the man next door to burst into the bathroom with an axe and dismember all of us. I half preferred this to the prospect of Susie reaming me out like an enlarged prostate for letting the dog loose. But she didn't have it left in her to protest. All she could do was ask me to find the earring that had been knocked off when the dog cleared the side of the tub. Her earring, for lord's sake!

"Why in God's name would you wear earrings when you're giving the dog a bath?" I asked quietly, very quietly, in fact. She didn't answer right away, preferring to give me that incredulous stare that I always get when I question an activity for which the purpose is perfectly obvious to her.

Summoning up some line from the past, she said "You ARE the weakest link. Goodbye!"

Relieved that I had been dismissed, I was nonetheless too tired to go for that mile run and besides that, my brand new warm up suit with the wet dog hair all over it looked like an old department store Santa outfit on the day after Christmas.

Gordon Grindstaff

    I waited for a visit from the lunatic next door, axe in hand, but that failed to materialize. Maybe the whole episode hadn't been so bad after all. Perhaps if I would let the suit dry out, I could start my new regimen the next morning. No point in trying to do it all in one day, anyway. This exercise stuff needs to be eased into or else you're liable to get shin splints or something.

Part Two
The Southwestern United States

Off to Arizona

Getting the dog washed and dried left us with nothing to do but pack. It took us two days to get our camper ready to go because Susie wanted to take everything we owned. You would have thought we were going to China with all the stuff she packed instead of Quartzsite, Arizona where we were headed. We picked Quartzsite because it was a winter time Mecca for RV'ers and we had decided that should be our first stop on our full time RV adventure. Really get our feet wet, as it were. Actually, I was the one who decided to go there. Susie was ambivalent about the whole thing.

I figured I could make it in four days with a little hard driving. I had not yet learned we were retired and could take as long as we wanted. My original task list had us leaving early on Sunday morning but with all the re-arranging necessary to find a place to keep everything, it was late in the afternoon before we actually started the truck.

There was five inches of snow on the ground when we left. I was convinced that I wouldn't be able to get the trailer up the hill at the end of our six hundred foot driveway. I stationed Susie in the road to stop any traffic that might be coming and said a little prayer. I gunned the engine, rolled down the hill, crossed the creek and started up the hill on the other side. The tires were spinning as our four and a half tons of camper obeyed the laws of gravity and resisted the climb. I kept my foot on the fuel pedal, praying under my breath.

"Please, God. Please, God. Oh, please, please, please, God."

I gripped the wheel for all I was worth and hung on until I cleared the drive and was in the newly plowed road. Our first hurdle was cleared and we were on our way.

We eventually left the snow behind, driving eight hundred and fifty miles in the next day and a half. I figured I was good for another fifty miles before halting but Susie insisted we stop because I was getting a little bleary eyed. We found a small, Spartan campground in Elk City, Oklahoma and pulled in. We walked into the tiny combination office and living room of the campground owner. The smell of tobacco smoke was overwhelming. A Marlboro cigarette dangled from the lips of a thin man bent over the counter. The smoke was in his eyes and he waved it away as he checked us in. The stale, smoky air was too much for Susie and she backed out of the room murmuring something about food.

The man remained bent over as he moved from the counter to grab another cigarette from five open packs laying on the small coffee table behind him. He lit the new cigarette using the remnants of the now defunct one. Between wheezes and coughs, he pointed to a small hand made sign announcing that the business was for sale.

"You inter.., cough, cough, interested?

I waved the smoke away and shook my head no. There was a time when I had wanted to own a campground but I knew the work involved and the thought of what liability insurance would cost discouraged me from even thinking about this one. Still, the price on the small sign was attractive and most of the sites were filled with oil well workers. Okay, it had more of a trailer park atmosphere than it did campground but the wheels were rolling in my head.

"Elk City, eh??" I said to myself deciding to tell Susie about the opportunity a little later.

We got the camper set up and headed for the showers. The owner had promised us plenty of hot water and he was right. I wanted a long shower to get the kinks out of my back but the tobacco smell in the shower room forced me to cut it short. I looked around the room as I dried my lily white body and noticed all the cigarette burns in the area. Every conceivable flat spot; the floor, the sink and even the soap dish in the shower, contained multiple burns. This guy even smoked in the shower, for God's sake. How'd he do that without getting his cigarette wet? I decided to forget about buying the place.

Elk City wasn't just the home of that campground either. U.S. route 66 passed thru the middle of town and the city fathers had put together a route 66 museum. I was a fan of the old television show so we stopped for a quick visit even though it wasn't built into the schedule. That fact caused a problem when we were leaving the parking lot. Trying to hurry a little, I cut a corner too short and banged the side of the trailer into a light pole. It bent up some of the aluminum siding on the Camper slide out but didn't seem to do any other damage. I hoped the slide would still work like it's supposed to but I was afraid to try it until we got to Quartzsite for fear I couldn't get it back in.

About ten miles from the Texas border, we had another unscheduled stop; a blowout on one of the camper tires. It was on the opposite side of where I hit the pole so that didn't have anything to do with it. I was certain we had too much crap in the trailer because of Susie packing everything we owned and I pointed that out to her but she wasn't buying any of that. Neither of us knew what we were talking about.

When we got to Amarillo, I asked the guy at the discount tire place about the weight of the camper and he told me that I really should have heavier load range tires. The man who sold me the camper had put Automobile tires on it and that was the likely cause of the blowout. I wasn't even aware that tires had load ranges but took him at his word. I read the pamphlet he gave me and quickly became an expert on the subject.

"You got anything in a load range E?" I asked the guy.

"Nope. The biggest in your size tires are only eight ply."

"Ply?" Another term to toss around in conversations, I thought. Eight Ply also meant Load range D. Being a quick learner, I soon had this down pat.

The blowout had been a bad experience that I didn't want to repeat so we left Amarillo with four new tires, load range D, on the camper. I also left there with a new hobby. Six months ago I didn't even know tires had load ratings and now I wandered parking lots reading people's tires to see if their load range was adequate. I had no plans to tell people of their vehicular inadequacies; not having a clue as to how I could work it into any conversations.

North Texas west of Amarillo is flat and you can see for miles and miles from any little rise in the road. The adventure of traveling had me. We were in the west and I was hooked. Now if only Lonesome Dove lay ahead in our path, I could sit a spell and swap yarns with Augustus McRae. But I wouldn't be able to talk long because I wanted to reach Santa Fe before nightfall.

A quick trip to Santa Fe

Santa Fe was out of our way but it is one of the cultural icons of the west, if not the whole country. I didn't need a lot of exposure to culture, having grown up in Indiana. Still, Susie wanted to visit the place. There is a lot to see in Santa Fe and I already knew we wouldn't get it all in. I was looking to make up the time we lost with the flat tires so I considered bypassing the town altogether but Susie would hear none of that.

We found a small campground on the edge of the city, got the camper set up and jumped on a bus heading downtown. Figuring to get a jump on the sightseeing and save a little time in the bargain, I grabbed the Triple A tour book and turned to the Santa Fe section. There was no Santa Fe section.

"Susie, why is there no Santa Fe section in our guide book.?" I said to her as she looked out the window.

"I tore it out so we wouldn't have to carry the whole book but then you brought the book anyway." She answered without turning away from the window.

"The book really isn't that heavy, dear, but okay, thank you for thinking of that. Could I see the torn out piece?"

"I left it in the truck but it's your fault. You were hurrying me along to catch the bus and I forgot it."

"Alright. We'll do Santa Fe without a guide."

"We can probably find another one." She turned and finally looked at me.

"Susie dear, we have less than eight hours to visit this place. "I looked at my watch for emphasis. "There's no time to find a new tour book."

The central plaza in the downtown area is several hundred years old and none of the buildings, even the new ones, are more than three stories tall. There's some requirement about the height of buildings but without my guide book, I couldn't tell you what it is. These buildings are also very old but I'll have to leave it at that because of the missing Triple A pages.

The Palace of Governors is an Adobe building on one side of the Plaza. It has a porch roof about a block long covering the sidewalk and the Native American artisans displayed their wares along the sidewalk under this porch. Most of the things were jewelry with a lot of it being of the turquoise variety. There were some carvings and a few people had paintings. Two different stalls had blankets for sale. I asked Susie if she wanted to take a chance on an Indian blanket, but all that got me was an elbow in the ribs.

Another thing of note about the plaza. It's the beginning (or the end, depending on your direction) of the old Santa Fe trail where many of the legendary cattle drives took place. I'm almost positive I could hear the ghosts of cowboys hollerin "git along, little dogies" as I stepped onto the trail and walked, bowlegged, down the street.

There were two things that we didn't want to miss in Santa Fe. The first of these was the mysterious staircase built in a Catholic church located on the trail. The original architect forgot to put stairs up to the choir loft when the church was built a few hundred years ago. . I'm sure the architect had impeccable credentials but I was unable to say for sure, failing to see any empirical evidence of that.

The loft was too high for a regular stairwell because it would have taken up too much room and it appeared to the original congregation that the choir would just have to sing from the bottom floor.

An order of nuns settled at the church and prayed for a solution short of tearing down the church. A mysterious carpenter showed up one day and announced that he would build the sisters a stairway. This gentleman somehow acquired the necessary wood even though it was not native to the region and spent the next several years building the stairs. I don't know the exact number of years; The triple A thing, you know.

The finished product is beautiful. It is circular in shape and there is no central stabilizing pole. It just starts at the bottom and winds around three times up to the loft floor. When it was finished, the carpenter disappeared without accepting any payment. Susie is convinced that the carpenter was St. Joseph reincarnated. No one at the church is saying that it was but they're not saying it wasn't, either.

The other place we wanted to see was the San Miguel mission. This church was built in the early 1700's. It is still in use and is run by the Franciscan brothers. The really interesting thing about this church is the bell that is used in the mission. It's the oldest bell in the United States and was cast in Spain during the war with the Moors in 1348. The Moors were trying to take over this little Spanish village but the villagers successfully turned them away. In gratitude, everyone in the village donated all their gold, brass and other precious metals to be melted down and poured into the cast. As I read this, I wondered if everyone donated all their precious metals as it said. If it was me, I might have been tempted to hold back a little gold or silver, just in case. I mean, there might have been another battle or something and the villagers might have wanted to cast another bell. If all the gold was gone, then what would they have done?

Susie was allowed to ring the bell a few times because a couple of the Franciscan Brothers took a fancy to her. They didn't ask me. Incidentally, All this information about the bell came from a sign inside the door of the mission. Luckily I saw the sign because it just happened that I didn't have the Santa Fe section of my AAA guide book.

The Georgia O'Keefe Museum was another stop we planned to make and Susie, being an artist, was pointing us that way. I was hungry and still reveling from the walk with the cowboy ghosts on the Santa Fe Trail. I figured that was enough sightseeing for the day. I promised her we would do it first thing in the morning before we left.

We had an early dinner at a place called Tomastino's across the Santa Fe River from the plaza area. It was a local place built in the old railroad station. Their specialty was New Mexican cuisine which meant an introduction to red and green chile. This isn't chili like we have in Indiana or even Texas. It is a sauce and it is used in many New Mexico dishes. Chile peppers are a big crop in this state. The red Chile is composed primarily of fire and the green has chopped peppers and onions swimming in a thick chicken broth. Both are very hot and the restaurant had a warning on the door about understanding the meaning of "HOT". Every time I ordered something to eat in New Mexico, even eggs, the waiter would ask me: "Red or Green?"

We had samples of both with nachos and then ordered enchiladas and tacos with the green. In order to keep our lips from scabbing over and in the spirit of our south of the border meal, I drank two bottles of Corona and Susie had two huge Marguerites with our dinner. She should never have more than one.

The influence of the tequila had Susie deciding to christen our fifth wheel. She got tired of saying 'fifth wheel' so she decided to give the camper a feminine gender and call her Fionna. Neither of us knew anyone by that name so we figured there wouldn't be any danger of hurt feelings or confusion when we brought up the name in a social setting.

We stayed a little long in the restaurant and ended up walking hurriedly over the cobblestone streets in order to catch the bus. The rough surface of the street along with the two drinks could have resulted in Susie breaking an ankle or getting us arrested but we arrived at the bus stop without incident.

We woke up about 5:30 a.m. with my stomach loudly protesting the ingested chiles. I looked outside to see a light dusting of snow and the TV guy was talking about three to five inches before the day was over. My God. It was fifty degrees outside when we went to bed and now it was twenty five and snowing. We were at seven thousand feet and surrounded by mountains. We couldn't get stranded by snow. All I could think was "Get this rig south as fast as possible". Georgia O'Keefe would just have to wait until the next trip. We got up and I started preparing for us to go while Susie made a pot of coffee. We left without any goodbyes and headed south for Albuquerque.

According to the chart I had laid out before we left, I had less than thirty six hours to reach Quartzsite. We were still six hundred and fifty miles from our destination and if I was going to meet that schedule, we'd need to do a little hard driving.

Truck troubles – Just pull over, Damn it.

Our brief visit to Santa Fe had convinced me that traveling full time was our destiny. The jury was still out on Susie's feelings. The new tires had also eased my mind about the overloading of the camper and I was itching to put some more miles behind us.

The miles were clicking by when a problem with the passenger side rear view mirror developed. The wind was forcing it to droop and by the time we reached the outskirts of Albuquerque, all I could see in the mirror was the bottom of the trailer. I pulled over and fiddled it with it trying to find a nut or something to tighten but nothing was apparent. Of course, Master Mechanic is not one of my titles. I jammed a piece of one of the pages from the Santa Fe section of the Triple A tour book into a pivot point hoping to keep it steady until we reached our destination. It helped some, but it still tended to droop as we made our way west.

"Stop in Albuquerque and get it fixed." Susie told me.

"It's Sunday and nothing is going to be open. Besides that, We don't have time. I'll fix it when we get to Quartzsite."

"We're retired, remember?"

"I know that but we have this schedule…"

She grumbled somewhat but I convinced her to roll down her window every 20 minutes or so and adjust the mirror. That sounds simple enough but in fact, it turned out to be pretty exciting because Susie is not one to take orders, especially from me.

"Down a little." I told her, after she had rolled down her window and moved the mirror.

"What?"

"DOWN A LITTLE." I yelled over the roar of the wind.

She made an adjustment.

"Whoops, Way too much."

She tried again.

"That's much better but still a little too much".

She pushed again.

"Okay, good. Now out."

"Out, what do you mean, out?" she said, looking a little perturbed

"Push on the right side."

"You need to be more specific. How much do I push?"

"Just a little."

She wiggled it but not enough.

"Not bad, now, just a lit-"

"LOOK OUT FOR THAT TRUCK."

I looked up at the very big grill of a Peterbilt coming our way and jerked the wheel.

"Jeez, Susie, You scared the water out of me.".

"Oh, I guess you would rather have hit that truck."

"You didn't have to yell so loud."

"Do you want to come over here and do this?"

I made a mental note that my next truck will have electrically adjusted mirrors.

We had no more than gotten our mirror adjusting technique down pat when I noticed that neither of the turn signals were working. I pulled over on the shoulder and checked everything that I knew how to check but I couldn't get them working. All the lights worked but no turn signals. I know what you're thinking. Fuses. That must be it. A fuse. Nope, I tried that and it didn't help.

Well, that was just great. I did not have time to unhook the trailer and take the truck somewhere to get it fixed. As it was, I was going to have to drive all night to get back on schedule.

"I'll get it fixed when we get to Arizona." I told Susie.

"Are you crazy? How are we going to pull that thing behind us around without any turn signals.?

"Easy. I just won't change lanes."

"And if you have to turn?"

"I'll just make right hand turns. You don't need a signal if you're turning right."

It was a dumb argument but I was already way behind schedule and it didn't seem like it could be that much farther. After all, it was just one more state.

Not having turn signals made it a little hairy when we went through Albuquerque. My plan of staying in the same lane got a severe test because of construction that kept shifting the lanes back and forth. Naturally, about that time, the rear view mirror began to slide down. I put Susie to work keeping the loose mirror straight so that I didn't run over anybody.

A mile or so further we spied a barrier up ahead in our lane. We had to move right.

"Pull over." She yelled, the wind whipping her hair into her eyes. Off schedule or not, I knew I had to get off the road but I was in the middle lane and couldn't signal my intention to get off the road. I didn't see anything in my mirror but I was afraid there was someone I couldn't see who might whip around to my right. Susie's arm was blocking the mirror on her side.

"Is there anybody behind us? I asked loudly. She adjusted the mirror in order to look back and let me know if anyone was coming. This required an incredible amount of trust on my part. I've never been one to do spur of the moment things and you couldn't get any more spur of the moment than letting someone tell you when to change lanes. The conversation:

"Okay, Susie, I'm moving over. Is it clear?"

"Okay now. Go now."

"Are you sure?"

"Of course I'm sure. Why would I tell you to go if I wasn't sure?"

"Okay."

"WAIT! There's a car coming now. You have to go when I tell you. You just have to trust me."

"How about now?"

"Not yet."

"Susie, I'm running out of road."

"I guess I'm supposed to do some ... NOW. GO NOW, DAMN IT ."

Trusting in God, I put all my misgivings aside, moved over one lane and didn't hear any crunching of metal. I didn't even hear any honking horns or screeching of brakes. I pulled on to the shoulder and stopped to catch my breath. Thank you, Jesus, and you too, Susie.

I used another page of the Santa Fe section to temporarily fix the mirror and moved on.

An apparent Immigration problem.

Hatch, New Mexico billed itself as the "Chile capital of the world". I wanted to know more about those little devils since spending the previous evening with the chiles in Santa Fe. We pulled into the parking lot of one of the chile stands lining highway 26 and looked at all the bright red peppers hanging from every available hanging spot.

"You sure have a lot of peppers here." I said to the lady behind the counter.

That's all it took to get her started. I had hit some kind of button with that remark.

"We used to have a lot more until the Goddamn federal government let all the pickers stay in the U.S.." She said, almost breathing fire. "They gave them welfare and food stamps and now they won't do any more picking so everybody had to cut back on their crop."

Soapboxes weren't my forte and I didn't want to press her for more information or question any of her statistics because she was obviously quite agitated. Instead, I asked her for a good place to eat.

"Try the B and E café down the road a piece." She said, calming down a little and gesturing west.

"You'll have to watch because 'E café' is missing."

"I beg your pardon?" I said.

"A while back a drunk truck driver whopped the sign with his trailer and knocked out the E part."

We drove a quarter-mile west on the highway and there it was. The "B and" sign was hanging at an awkward angle from a rusty pole and the shattered glass of the E café was still lying on the gravel parking lot. The building itself was not very big and more than likely had been a one car garage in some previous life. It had a flat roof and had recently been whitewashed. It looked clean so we thought we'd take a chance.

Inside, there were only a couple of tables for the customers. There was no wait person in sight, instead we spied a little window where, assumedly, the clientele walked up to place food orders. The menu had only Mexican food items. Susie had tacos with green chile on the side and I had enchiladas smothered in the red chile. Rice and beans also came with the meal. I'm not a food editor or anything so I can't tell you how they fixed this stuff but it was delicious. I'm sure it was an authentic recipe because the cook/owner and the cook/dishwasher both spoke Spanish. In addition, the Mexican border was about 30 miles south. How could it not be authentic? I know I had never tasted anything like it at Taco Bell.

We each downed two large glasses of water. We needed the water. The chiles were great going down but you need something to cool your innards after eating that stuff. Beer would have been good but they didn't offer it. I considered asking if I could bring my own but thought better of it.

We left the town with a full belly and headed west. We went through the Dragoon mountains east of Tucson after dark and got quite of a view of the lit up city off in the distance. It was my first exposure to seeing vast distances in the desert. I had scheduled us to be in Quartzsite at this hour but we hadn't made it. I started to complain.

"So What?" Susie said. "What's the rush? "

I started to answer her and then realized I didn't have an answer. She's right, what's the rush? What's your big hurry? I asked myself but I didn't have an answer for that either. We had driven six hundred miles today, damn near killed ourselves in Albuquerque and eaten chile until it was coming out of our ears, all in fourteen hours. We could have done half that and still had a good time. I had a lot to learn about being retired.

We stopped for the night in a Flying J parking lot about forty miles west of Tucson. I didn't want to go through Phoenix in the evening with no turn signals. We decided to get up early and get through the city before people got up and clogged the roads.

We did get up at three but the highways of Phoenix were anything but empty. There were all kinds of people out there, either coming or going. Still, I was able to go all the way through the city without changing lanes.

Eighty miles later, we pulled into the Wagon West RV Park located in the Sonora or Mojave desert. The map isn't very clear about where one desert ends and another begins, so I'm not sure which it was. However, We were 90 miles north of Yuma, 300 miles east of Los Angeles and about 90 miles south of Lake Havasu.

We drove 2110 miles in five days to get here. We spent about 45 hours of those five days in the truck. It was not an unpleasant experience at all but if I had to do it over and over again, however, it might be. I have decided to cross truck driver off my list of new occupations.

We got the camper set up and the lawn chairs in place. I got a cold beer out of the cooler, Susie poured a glass of wine and we sat down to enjoy the scenery and to make a toast for our new found freedom. We even said a little prayer thanking God for our safe arrival.

There was lots of scenery for us to see; vast expanses of desert with tall cactus plants sticking up here and there, breaking up the monotony of the surrounding sameness. Small scrubby plants dotted the landscape and I imagined that they probably end up being the sagebrush that blows across the desert floor in Gene Autry movies.

I took a sip of my beer, already growing warm in the morning sun and leaned back in my lawn chair. A mental cornucopia of pictures went running through my head. My office cubicle, now occupied by somebody else, a company functioning without me, our kids back in Indiana getting along without us and the 2110 miles between all that.

I suddenly realized this was not a vacation. This was our life now and all I could think was "What in God's name are we doing out here?"

Quartzsite, Arizona

An article in National Geographic provided us with our initial acquaintance with Quartzsite. That article and the accompanying pictures convinced us that we should visit the place as part of our indoctrination into living on the road in our RV. Quartzsite is a town of 3000 permanent residents but when you drive around the place, there doesn't seem to be enough buildings to support that kind of population. Maybe that count includes some of the RV'ers.

I wouldn't consider Quartzsite an attractive town like one would see in the Midwest. Of course, it's in the desert but even given that, it still has an unkempt look about it. Making sand look attractive is probably more work than it's worth.

On the surface, it seems to be a very ordinary desert town, There are places to buy the staples of living; a grocery store, a hardware store and a couple of places to get things for your automobile. Most people go on to Blythe, California, another fifteen miles west, to do any serious shopping. Another favorite shopping place of the locals is Parker, Arizona on the Colorado river. It's about thirty five miles north. Beyond Parker is the city of Lake Havasu if you're looking for a mega-mart. It's about a two hour drive. I hesitated to drive that far just to shop but out here, a drive like that seems to be like crossing the street to the people who live here year round. Phoenix shopping is also available about eighty miles east if you can stand the traffic and the congestion but don't look for us there. We got into camping to get away from crowds. Of course, Quartzsite isn't exactly deserted.

All in all, Quartzsite seems to be it's an unlikely place for an event such as the one we came to see. In January of every year, the World Series of RV rallies is held here. It seems as if every producer of RV's, RV products and RV services gather here to display their wares. In addition, anyone who has something to sell that an RV'er might be interested in has a booth here. There are a couple of thousand vendor tents that line both sdes of Interstate 10 for a mile or more. If you want to hang around long enough, there is also a gem and rock show, a classic car show and a craft show.

All this stuff attracts about a million visitors over a two month span. The biggest share of them arrive in an RV and lacking anywhere else to go, just pull their rig off the road and out into the nearest flat, empty spot in the desert. The land is owned by the Federal Government and the Bureau of Land Management (The BLM to those in the know.) serves as the overseer of the area.

Motor homes, garishly painted VW buses, Travel trailers, truck campers, fifth wheels and converted school buses all share the landscape. Their owners have anywhere from a few hundred dollars up to a million or more invested but the price of the unit doesn't seem to get you a better parking spot. This democracy among the RV set makes for strange bedfellows among the people of all descriptions who inhabit these homes on wheels. I had led a relatively sheltered life in Indiana and didn't venture far from my cultural, religious and financial peers. This trip quickly exposed me to all the different kinds of people there are out there on the road. The different ideas put forth on politics, religion or lack of it and social norms also opened up our horizons. It probably didn't change anything but at least we knew there were differences out there.

It would not be too far fetched to say that every vagabond west of the Mississippi will turn up in this town at one time or another and most of them will be toting a dog or two. Man's best friend comes in as many shapes and sizes as their owners. But one oddity seems to persist. It seems as if the larger the owner, the smaller the dog and vice versa. A six foot, beer-bellied tattooed guy wearing a Harley Davidson tee-shirt should have a snarling German Shepherd at the end of the dog leash he's clutching. Instead he has one of those prancing little fu-fu dogs with a pink ribbon in its hair. It's a bit disconcerting when a long haired, bearded, earring wearing guy clad in a Hell's Angels Tee-shirt talks like a baby to his doggie.

"Is my ittle cutsee wootsy thirsty-wirsty?"

Ga! I wanted to shake the man and get him to come to his senses but he had about 20 pounds on me.

Quartzsite, like any place where you find a gathering of people, has food vendors by the dozen. The food offerings run pretty much true to form for a gathering of this kind. Lots of barbeque, corn on the cob, biscuits and gravy, and hamburgers and deep fried everything. Our personal favorite came from a booth called Billy Bob's and to borrow a phrase from Dave Barry, I am not making this up.

Billy had cut a couple of barrels in half and rigged the four halves up on saw horses. Piled beside them was a huge stack of mesquite wood and in the barrel halves, he had more mesquite burnt down to charcoal. He was smoking meat of some kind and serving the finished stuff on a bun. Balanced on the corner of one of the cookers was a big black pot filled with barbeque sauce made by Billy Bob's own hands. A big dose of that sauce on a sandwich piled high with meat was worth going back for.

The traffic is the last thing that needs to be mentioned about Quartzsite. It's always backed up. There are two four way stops in town. One is at the intersection of Highway 95 and the main east-west street and the other is this same east-west street and the entrance to Interstate 10. There's usually a 10 minute backlog of cars at either of the intersections but no one is very concerned. Oh, there's a few impatient cusses out there that like to lean on their horns. What the hell's their hurry? I'm tempted to tell these fellows to slow down and smell the roses. Everyone is retired and not supposed to be in a hurry anymore. Hell, sitting in traffic gives us all something to do.

Just go behind that cactus!

We've been told that no visit to the southwest is complete without a visit to a Mexican town. This was not high on my list of things to do because leaving American soil always makes me a little apprehensive. Being a naïve Hoosier who grew up on cowboy movies, I was a little concerned about meeting up with some overweight Mexican bandito needing a shave, wearing a sombrero and looking for a gringo to rob.

That's me. Gringo by birth. They could spot me from a mile away with my white legs sticking out of a pair of jean shorts and wearing tennis shoes with white gym socks. I'm not talking about those little sissified socks that barely cover your ankles, either. I'm talking white tube socks with a red band; The kind that reach to your knees and provide a little protection from snakes and other varmints.

Susie, of course, never worries about varmints or bandits. We had been in the campground less than a day when our neighboring camper, Theo, and his wife started filling her head with stories of great meals, good dentists and cheap prescriptions just across the border and with easy access on foot. She began to badger me that day about making the trip.

I talked to Theo and he told me that the town of Algodones seemed to be the most popular spot for people camping around Quartzsite. It is southwest of Yuma and just across the border in Baja California. The Highway to Yuma is an easy 80 mile drive from Quartzsite through the Mojave desert with views of the Castle Dome and the Chocolate mountains, so called because of their dark brown color.

"Plan on taking all day." Theo told me. "There's a passel of things to cover."

We were up early the next morning and on our way. Once Quartzsite is left behind, so is civilization. There are no towns until you reach Yuma. The Yuma Proving Grounds occupies the west side of the highway for the entire trip and the KOFA wildlife refuge borders the east side. KOFA is an acronym for the former 'King of Arizona' gold mine and that's all I know about it. There are several scenic and historical markers along the way but most of them require you strike out into the desert on a sandy roadway consisting of two pathways in the sand.

Susie, once again, is ready to do this. Every time we would pass one of these markers, I had to remind her that sightseeing was not our objective. In truth, I have read several things about what you should do if you get stuck in the sand or get lost in the desert and they all imply that you can die if you don't know what you're doing. Since I have no idea what I'm doing, that alone keeps me on the paved roads. Then you throw in the fact that part of the countryside is called a WILDLIFE refuge and you got another reason for me to stay on the pavement. That's wildlife as in Wildlife. I'm not sure what kind of wildlife they're talking about. For all I know, it could be mountain goats or lizards but the word wild is enough.

I don't mention any of this reasoning to Susie because she possesses an adventurous soul and would not understand my misgivings. I ignore her pleas to stop and assure her that we'll check it out on the way back.

The highway has a lot of dips in it necessary to handle the water runoff when there's a rainstorm. There are no bridges. The road goes down one side into the gully and back up the other. There are also signs that say "do not enter when flooded.' Being one of those people who obey all traffic laws, I proceed cautiously even though there is not a cloud in the sky and the humidity reading is recording a negative number.

Besides the risk of flood, if you go through the dips at a high rate of speed, you don't need to do very many of them before nausea sets in and a couple of hard dips will jolt your kidneys into action.

About thirty miles out of Quartzsite, Susie tells me to find a bathroom because she has to go. I look around and there's nothing but desert sand as far as my eye can see, with an occasional cactus or creosote bush sticking up to break the flat plain. Distant dark colored mountains on both sides of the road frame the highway disappearing on the southern horizon. We have the whole road to ourselves so I suggest we just pull over to the side to relieve ourselves.

Susie is having none of that because for all her adventurous nature, she is still a prim and modest female when it comes to using the Necessary. I continued driving south for another five or so miles and we pass by a sign that says "Yuma 48 miles". I hear a little sigh of dismay from Susie and so I tell her once again that we'll pull off the road because the last dip in the road had jolted my own kidneys into action.

I slowed down and pulled off the road in a hard packed sandy area. There were two huge Saguaro Cacti with wannabe sagebrush bushes growing around them about fifty yards off the road and I walked back there to find a place to relieve myself, ever mindful of rattlesnakes. Susie follows me mumbling "I can't do this, I can't do this."

The urge to go outweighed her fear of being seen so she picked the bigger of the two cacti and started to assume the position when a huge motor home came over a little rise in the highway and flew noisily past us. That was enough for Susie. Up she came with a howl, still fully clothed.

"They saw me." She said.

"There's no way anybody saw you. They were too far away and they were going too fast."

She headed for the truck, saying, "I don't care. I can't do this. We have got to find a bathroom."

About ten miles later, she said "How much further?" It was the same question our kids used to ask when we were on the road and they were bored but it wasn't boredom prompting her to ask.

"Maybe twenty or twenty five minutes." I told her.

"I won't make it." She said, her left leg jiggling at about 500 RPM. Sometimes, when she's bugging me about stopping for a restroom, I can put my hand out, extend all five digits and set them into a squeezing motion. It just drives her wacky. It's one of the little ways that I use to tell her that I love her. I normally do it out of good heartedness and with a sense of playfulness but the agony in her face as we head southward tells me I better not move my hand.

"Okay, find a place to pull over." Her agony has outweighed her modesty.

I immediately start to slow down because I see a gravel covered area alongside the road. Two dusty wheel tracks to the west are leading the way into the desert. A sign proclaiming this to be Yuma Proving Grounds property sits to the side of the roadway.

"Just exactly what the hell do they think they're trying to prove?" Susie asks and the exasperation in her voice tells me not to say anything. Instead, I pulled off the highway and drove down the dusty tracks about a hundred yards. What appears to be a military plane flies over at an altitude of two or three thousand feet. Susie is half way out of the truck and looks up at the plane.

"What was that?"

"Probably part of a team practicing a bombing run." I said, half to myself although I had no idea. I had seen a sign a few miles back about the "Yuma bombing Range" and figured that this must be it.

"You mean that there are more planes out there?"

"I suppose" I said. "But they're a long way up there and they're probably flying five hundred miles an hour. I doubt that they will be able to see your cute little behind from up there."

"Right." was all she said as she climbed back into the truck. "Drive."

It looked like she was going to have to wait until I found an actual restroom and not just any old restroom, either. Susie likes those full service type of service stations; the clean well lit establishments where you can get milk or snacks and maybe even a latte. The restrooms in these places were usually clean and sanitary. There surely would be something like that in Yuma.

We reached the outskirts of Yuma a few minutes later and I knew I had better find something fast. Susie was sitting with legs crossed, rocking back and forth. I thought I could even hear remnants of the Rosary escaping her lips.

A gas station loomed in the distance. As we got a little closer, I could see that that this place would not be a good choice. It was a little dirty looking with lots of old cars sitting around. Two old fashioned looking gas pumps stood out front. They appeared to be inoperable. A home made "Mechanic on duty" sign leaned against the one closest to the road. It was a filling station in every sense of the word. No bright lights, no snacks. Just a couple of old guys sitting out front, legs crossed, studying the oil stains in the blacktop like they had just discovered a portfolio of Rorschach ink blots. I started to drive on by.

"Stop there", Susie said, pointing excitedly .

"But,Susie, I don't know how sani—"

"Just stop the damn truck before I break your arm." I made a hard right and she was out of the truck and disappearing inside before it stopped rolling. The old guys looked up from their ink blot guessing games but all they saw was a blur in pink bermuda shorts.

Susie was back in five minutes, hands dripping wet and climbed into the truck. "No towels."

"Okay." I replied.

"Do not let me drink anything the rest of the day. I don't care how hard I beg."

"Not a problem." I said and pointed the truck towards Mexico.

Where do I find the U-bolts?

We left Wagons west RV park outside of Quartzsite the same way we came in, with the same bunch of old guys who stood around and watched us setting up camp, now standing around watching us getting ready to go. A couple offered words of wisdom as we scurried around putting things away but most of them just watched. Thank God none of them offered to help.

Our neighbor, a GM retiree, wandered over to where I stood in the middle of a pile of stuff.

"Ya know, me and the wife, we don't hold much truck with hauling a bunch of stuff around with us." He said, leaving me to ponder the meaning of 'much truck'. "Yessir, when we break camp, it's just snap, snap and we're on our way." He snapped his fingers for emphasis.

It was not the right thing to say to me at the moment. I was already an hour into this breaking camp business, standing in the middle of our stuff; two bikes, two coolers, Susie's rock polisher, three plastic storage containers, a twelve pack of Corona that I had bought in Mexico, a propane grill and about a hundred pounds of various rocks that Susie had picked up in our walks. I had no idea where I was going to put all this stuff and this guy was beginning to irritate me with his snapping fingers.

I was already upset with him because he was 5 years younger than me and had been retired almost six years. Of course, it wasn't his fault that I had not worked for a big company that would take care of me for the rest of my life. I only thought it was.

I grabbed one of the coolers and with no regard for my fragile spinal cord, gave it a mighty heave-ho into the truck bed.

"Is that right?" I think the note of sarcasm in my voice went right over his head because he just smiled.

"Yep. Snap, Snap."

Theo, the old gentlemen across the street who had been a mechanic at the same California Chevrolet dealership for 46 years stopped by as I was loading the last of the rocks in the back. Our only previous conversation had concerned his longevity at the dealership.

"I outlasted 5 different owners. Only job I ever had." He had told me. When he told me that, I had a hard time imagining doing something like that. I thought back to the 10 or 15 jobs I went through before I finally settled into the last one and wondered how things might have been had I stuck with one of the earlier jobs. I have been doing a lot of that that 'what if' stuff lately. I think it has something to do with getting old and examining your past mistakes. Whatever it might be, it drives Susie nuts so I try not to do it anymore.

Theo's topic on this day was not about his work history but instead concerned horror stories of trailers breaking loose from their fifth wheel hitch. One story involved some teen age kids unhooking the hitch while he and his wife were taking a restroom break.

"Little sonsabitches. I saw 'em waiting down the road on their bikes when we came out but I didn't think nothin' about it." He said. "I moved the truck and down came the fifth wheel. Three thousand dollars damage." He shook his head. "I tried to catch the bastards but they was on them bicycles."

"That's terrible." I said sympathetically while vowing to always check the pin before moving the truck. I turned to pick up another rock but he grabbed my arm.

"One other time, I hit a huge chuckhole and ripped the axle right off the camper. U-bolts was wore out, I reckon."

U-bolts. I needed to check my U-bolts even though I wasn't a hundred percent certain of where they were. Better put that on the list of things to do before breaking camp.

Theo shook his head and spit something dark that quickly stained the desert sand where it landed. It was tobacco juice, I hoped, because if it wasn't, he had some serious problem in the nether regions of his chest cavity.

"I don't mean to worry ya or anything." He said, walking back to his camper.

Ha! He didn't know that I had instantly filed the stories away in the worry section of my brain. There they would lay until I needed to drag them out; say when I'm crossing a huge bridge or climbing a mountain pass on a tiny two lane road. I knew with some certainty that the next time I was in a perilous situation, the picture of a U-bolt, strained to the point of shattering, would occupy my mind front and center.

We spent a total of two and half hours from the time we started till the time we pulled out of the campground. This included stops for coffee, our morning toilette and forty five minutes for Susie to fix her hair as well as the aforementioned interruptions from the watchers. I had originally budgeted an hour for this operation but I realize that once again I was entirely too optimistic. I am either going to have to stop budgeting time or else do a better job of estimating.

The Salton Sea

Our first stop after Quartzsite was Blythe, Ca. where I had made an appointment to get the turn signals and the rear view mirror repaired. I had been trying to find time to do it since we had arrived in Arizona and this was the first real opportunity to get it done.

While we were waiting, Susie and I wandered through the dealership's inventory and found a nice Dodge convertible. I sat down in the driver's seat and through the windshield I saw a small Mexican restaurant across the street with a whitewashed sign on the window advertising something called Menudo.

"What's Menudo?" I asked the guy washing one of the cars.

"A terrible soup. It tastes like the sweat of a horse." he said.

"Ah, maybe so, but it is very good for a hangover." said his partner in charge of the water hose. "Too much Dos Equis on Saturday can be cured by eating Menudo on Sunday." He grinned widely and winked at me.

That little conversation around the car wash made us reluctant to try it. As a matter of fact, after hearing the 'sweat' comment, Susie would not have eaten it if she'd been offered a thousand dollars. I filed the information away for future reference.

After our repairs were done, we headed west on Interstate 10. We were on the move and I realized this was the part of traveling I like best; the journey itself. Another part is exploring the less traveled roadways. We were able to do just that when we left the Interstate and headed south on Highway 86.

Our ultimate destination was San Diego but for this day we were aiming for the Salton Sea in South central California. We had read about it in our Smithsonian guide to California-Nevada and it sounded like an interesting place to see. It's a huge body of water (about 380 square miles) that is 280 feet below sea level and is 25 times saltier than the Pacific ocean. It was created in 1905 when an irrigation project went awry and let the Colorado River run unchecked into this area. It took two years to stop the flow of water and there were several salt mining operations that were flooded. Now the lake is fed by runoff from irrigation.

We planned to stop in the town of Coachella to get some groceries because there was no real town around the lake. Coachella is located in a valley between the Santa Rosa, the Orocopia and the Little San Bernardino mountains. I don't know who decided they were little. They looked pretty big to me.

The region is known for the produce grown here; lots of grapefruit, oranges and grapes. Most of the populace is Hispanic and I assume that the huge produce farms are the reason. The insensitive part of my upbringing tells me that it is.

It is also called 'The date capitol of the USA'. I wasn't aware we had a date capitol in the United States but then I'm learning something new every day. We stopped at a roadside market where an overly friendly grower sold us a pound of dates. It was my first exposure to dates. This lack of experience with the fruit caused me to remark to the grower that they looked like prunes. I think it insulted him. There may be some deep seated resentment about prunes amongst the date grower community because this guy's demeanor changed from nice to surly immediately.

"They taste nothing like prunes. Much sweeter with more texture." He growled. I looked at his face, heavy with a 3 day growth of hair. Not knowing if he had a weapon, I tasted one and decided it was the better part of valor to agree with him. In truth, I found dates to be a little chewy and more than a little expensive. Three dollars a pound right off the palm tree.

We drove through most of Coachella before we found a supermarket. It was a very interesting store for a couple of midwesterners. All the signs were in Spanish, the cashiers spoke Spanish and all the stock was directed toward the Hispanic culture. The meat case had whole goat heads, including the eyes and other kinds of meat that, seeing as how I was a flatland mid-westerner who had led a sheltered life as far as the culinary arts go, looked a little suspicious to me. I tried to get Susie to buy us one of those goat heads but she wasn't having any of that. She wouldn't get within ten feet of that meat case.

I wanted to get some bagels and couldn't find any. I looked around the bakery area and found only corn tortillas and other baked goods popular in the Hispanic culture. I was fascinated by the tortilla making machine in the bakery. It was cranking those tortillas out by the hundreds but still, I wanted bagels.

I went to the bakery counter and asked where I might find them. The girl behind the counter gave me this quizzical look that told me immediately that we weren't going to find any bagels in this store.

We did however, find a green chile salsa in a big pot in the deli area. Using my best pidgen english, I asked the deli clerk what was in it. After about three tries of my best 'me Tarzan, you Jane' conversing, we figured out that it is made with tomatillos and jalapeno peppers. It was also hot as fire but delicious when eaten with freshly baked nachos that we bought with the stuff. It wasn't bagels with cream cheese but as we found out a little later, it did go good with a Corona.

We went on south to the Salton City Spa and RV resort. The resort where we found a place to camp was very nice but it is another place that calls itself an RV park when it's really a retirement community. Most of the Campers were permanently anchored and only a few spots were left for people passing through.

We rode our bikes the two blocks to the lake and tried to identify some of the different kinds of birds that were gathered around the shore. Great quantities of White pelicans, gulls and terns made it easy to pick them out but that was about the limit of my bird knowledge.

Back in the 1960's, an effort was made to develop the Salton Sea as a resort area but that had not worked. Roads half grown over were laid out in a grid among the empty landscape. There were acres and acres of empty space divided by blacktopped streets that were covered with sand and vegetation. An occasional house could be seen jutting up from the barren scenery. It was readily apparent why the place never developed. There was a rank odor of fish and the shoreline was mushy with small shells and fish bones. The bottom was kind of slimy and had a green tint that made the whole place unattractive. There were several fishermen in their boats out on the lake so the good fishing story must be true.

We spent an uneventful night there and got up early to explore the area a little more before heading for San Diego. We had been told that we needed to go see the box canyons and the Borrego Springs in the Anza - Borrego state park west of town. That tip turned out to be a good one. We had only gone a mile or so on state road 22 when we got into an area that was like the badlands of South Dakota only more desolate. I was kind of concerned because I was pulling the camper, the road was narrow and there was no shoulder. Loose sand lapped over the asphalt and I could see us getting stuck in that stuff. Our cell phone had a little 'no service' message in the display area so I doubted that we could use it.

I was ready to turn around but there was no place to do that so we just kept going. The landscape seemed to change every few hundred yards. Deep canyons on both sides of the road then sand as far as you could see and then huge rocks piled into hills. We couldn't keep up with the wonders in front of us. We stopped several times for pictures but it's impossible to capture that kind of scenery with a camera.

We eventually got to Borrego Springs, a town of about three thousand, after a thirty mile drive. The springs, which we never saw, made the town an oasis in all that brown landscape. There was a mountain range just to the west of town that dominated the surroundings. We stopped for fuel even though I had three quarters of a tank. I kept the tank full because I was leery of running out of gas in that desert. I asked the guy who took my money for the best way to get to San Diego from there. He told me that the shortest way was over the mountains but it would be a little difficult to go that way pulling a camper.

That just about cinched it for me. I dislike driving in the mountains anyway so I decided to take a safe and flatter route. The only thing about this was that I would have to backtrack that same thirty miles I had just traveled and take Highway 86 south to Interstate 8. That was about an extra eighty or ninety miles. I didn't want to do that so I started seeking reassurances from other patrons that I could indeed make it over the mountains.

"I know campers go over the mountains every day because I usually get stuck behind one of the damn things." One lady told me.

I decided to go ahead, scared or not, because of something that happened over thirty years ago. This was an incident involving the Chesapeake Bay Bridge where the fear of heights got the better of me on a trip that I took with

Susie and both of our mothers. We were outside of Annapolis, MD and on our way to Baltimore when we came upon the bridge. It scared the daylights out of me. The thing seemed to stretch forever across the water and it looked like it disappeared into the clouds somewhere out over the bay. I refused to go across it. My mother was relieved because she had a bigger fear of heights than I did. I turned around and went a different direction. Neither Susie nor her mom said anything but I knew they wanted to go across. I was horribly ashamed but there was no way I was venturing out over that water. I have carried that moment with me ever since.

If I had known what I was getting myself into with that particular bunch of mountains, I would have probably have done the extra eighty miles. Of course, I would have missed quite an experience. We drove eighteen miles to get to the top and it took just over an hour to get there. It was one switchback after another, some with guardrails and some with nothing to keep you from plunging over the edge. The view was fantastic. The whole desert for maybe a hundred miles or more was visible right there at your feet but I didn't look at it very much. Even Susie was unusually quiet. I did notice that I wasn't really scared once we started up but still we were both pretty tense when we finally got to the top. But we made it and had my mom still been alive, I would have called her on the spot.

We found a place to pull over and only then did I notice that the landscape had changed again. Now we had trees and grass. I hate to keep saying 'amazing' but it was. We were in Eastern San Diego County which is very picturesque with little towns, small lakes and rolling hills. We went through towns with names like Ranchita and Santa Ysabel on our way into San Diego. I was beginning to wish we had stayed up there in the hills because San Diego is such a busy place. For many years, I dreamed of living there but I guess age must have gotten the better of me because when we arrived, all I wanted to do was leave. The weather was terrible; cold and rainy and the traffic was horrendous. Every bone in my body was aching and all of a sudden, I was tired of traveling.

Who you calling maggot shit?

It was still drizzling rain when we pulled into the RV park in San Diego. It had been a long day of driving made even longer when we couldn't find the park. The rain had become kind of a welcome relief after all the dryness we had left behind in the desert.

It was after five on a Sunday so the park office was closed but there was an envelope taped to the front door. "Grebstat - 75' was scribbled on it and I assumed that was us. Grebstat was closer to Grindstaff than a lot of spellings we've seen so it was a good bet that it was for us.

The '75' turned out to be the site in the rear of the park where we were supposed to set up camp. It was a back-in spot with trees on both sides and while it was a little tight, I had by now gotten comfortable with maneuvering the camper so I wasn't really concerned about getting it in there. I got out of the truck and walked around in the drizzle inspecting the spot where the trailer would hopefully end up. At about that time, a small Chevy pickup pulled up in the next spot and a little guy climbed out of the pickup and walked towards me. He stood about five feet tall and based upon his dark complexion and our location, probably of Mexican descent. He was wearing a Mechanic's type of uniform with the name of the RV park above his shirt pocket. He turned out to be the head maintenance guy at the park.

He introduced himself and I promptly forgot his name although in days to come, thanks to Susie, I took to referring to him as B. H.. Susie, who is much more adept at noticing a person's personal appearance than I and who, being the culturally insensitive member of our party, called him "the guy with the blackheads on his nose." She never ceases to amaze me. I wouldn't have noticed those blackheads in a million years. Naturally, I checked the load range on his truck tires but never noticed his nose.

B. H. said that he had come to help me park the trailer. I thought at first he was joking but then I realized he wasn't. Public speaking makes me sweat but I get really nervous when complete strangers are watching me maneuver the trailer around. I told him that I could manage and hoped that he would go away. He was very nice and explained that it was his job to help. I have since figured out that since the sites were kind of small, he didn't want any encroachment by me or anyone else on someone else's site. Probably prevented a lot of arguments that way. I also noticed when I looked down the street that all the trailers were lined up so the guy was apparently some sort of neat freak. He was here to keep me from doing some kind of a sloppy parking job.

I was ready to protest again except a couple of things stopped me. I didn't have a lot of daylight left to get things done and I hate setting up the camper in the dark. The second thing was that the guy reminded me of a Hispanic drill instructor I had when I was a Marine Corps recruit in this very same city. Good God, I realized, this little man standing in front of my truck could even be related to that ramrod straight marine who made my life miserable for three months back in the summer of 1958.

My drill instructor was also only a bit over five feet tall but to a scared boy from southern Indiana, he was evil incarnate, Nothing I did was good enough for him and he kept me in a constant state of anxiety. .

"You piece of maggot shit" was his favorite greeting. It still makes me queasy to think of it. My instructor had a little swagger when he walked and here was the maintenance man, the swagger in his step almost a duplicate of Sergeant Cavasos. It was enough to make me break into a sweat. B.H. also had a baseball cap perched on the back of his head with 'Maintenance' inscribed across the front. That completed the picture of authority for me.

With visions of "maggot shit" in my head, I said "okay, what do we do?".

B. H. walked about six feet to the west, stood by one of the trees, motioned to me and said something like "bring her through here, put the nose there, kick it that a-way and follow the box right back."

I heard what he said but I didn't have the foggiest idea what he was talking about. I just got back in the truck and started backing up. The instant the truck moved, it was like I had flipped some internal switch in the maintenance man and he started scurrying around that trailer like a sheepdog whose flock had just been frightened by a wolf. The truck inched the camper into the spot as B. H. jumped back and forth, shouting those unintelligible orders and waving his arms this way and that. He was wearing me out.

My back was aching as I turned the wheel and twisted in the seat trying to watch him, the trees, the trailer and Susie who stood to the side with an amused look on her face. I know she dreads giving me parking directions so any chance she gets to watch is a treat for her. She gave me a little Queen Elizabeth wave and continued her smiling..

Suddenly, B. H. signaled for me to stop. "Kick the nose a little and we'll have it."

Still not having any idea what he meant, never the less I backed up a little more and stopped. He walked first to one side of the truck and then the other, peering down the length of the trailer. He gave me a thumbs up and a big smile, apparently satisfied with the work we had done. He walked over, patted the hood of my truck, gave me a big wave, climbed into his truck and drove away.

I sat in the truck, wondering what had just happened. All I was really sure of was that I had just gotten a thumbs up from this little guy, something I had never gotten from the guy I suspected was his cousin. I had let him order me around just because his appearance had invoked an unpleasant memory from the late 1950's. But here he was happy with me. Apparently I was no longer just a "piece of maggot shit " to five foot tall Hispanics. That fact alone made this trip worthwhile.

San Diego

We had only five days to spend in San Diego before we were due to be in Casa Grande, Arizona where I had put a deposit on a campsite. San Diego is such a beautiful city with all kinds of places to visit and five days is not enough to do it justice but neither of us wanted to lose the Arizona deposit so our plan was just to hit the highlights and come back another day.

That plan went out the window because we had to spend the next two days in the camper. It was raining, the first rain San Diego had seen in several months and in addition, I had come down with the flu. I was convinced that I had caught a cold from getting wet and chilled the day before but Susie told me that is an old wives' tale. It was quite a coincidence that I got sick after getting wet (of course, Susie didn't get sick and she was right there with me) and I would have argued with her but I was too miserable.

We had not considered getting sick in our plan to hit the road and when I did get sick, I found myself questioning our decision to be quasi full-time Rv'ers. I suddenly missed our home in Indiana. It's not pleasant being sick in the first place and then being confined in a small area makes it worse. Even though I'm very brave, I'm still the kind of person who requires a lot of nursing care. Susie is just the opposite so she doesn't believe in so much as holding my hand when I'm feeling bad. I should have checked on that aspect of our relationship before we got married but I didn't so I had to suffer by myself. I did do a lot of moaning during the day trying to get a little sympathy but I might as well have been groaning for the dog.

On our third day in town, I bravely got up out of my sick bed and we drove to Coronado Island across the bay from San Diego. We took the toll bridge, one of those artistic bridges that only about halfway terrifies me. It is constructed with concrete and rests on pillars standing in the waters of the bay. The bridge soars high into the air to allow room for the Navy to get its ships out of the Harbor and there are none of those comforting steel girders on the side that would keep you from plunging into the bay should you blow a tire or lose control in some other manner. Fortunately, it was not very long so I was able to hold my breath all the way across. It is always reassuring for me to hold my breath when in tense situations. It drives Susie crazy for she is not afraid of anything and when I expel the air from my pent-up lungs, I get no sympathy, only a look of derision.

Coronado Island is the home of the Del Coronado Hotel. It was built around the turn of the 20th Century and is a huge, luxurious, wooden structure that looks out over the Pacific Ocean beach. I seem to remember reading that it's the largest wooden structure in the world but don't quote me on that. The interior is dark wood and very rich. The grounds have some of the most beautiful landscaping we have ever seen. We walked around the gardens and Susie identified some of the beautiful plants for me. She has never had any formal training, but she never ceases to amaze me with her floral knowledge. Not me. Within ten minutes, I had forgotten everything she had told me.

The Hotel was beautiful and we decided we'd spend the night there the next time we had a few hundred bucks to spare. Our original plan was to eat dinner in the hotel but after we looked at the menu and did a quick calculation, we figured out we could probably put a couple of tires on the truck for the same money.

Putting the menu away, we decided to find some fresh seafood that we could grill back at the RV park. We drove on south towards Imperial Beach figuring that the "Beach" in the town's name might lead us to a place that sold fresh seafood. No such luck. We drove the entire length of town and didn't find anything that even resembled a seafood market. I asked a lady in a gas station and she directed me towards the city pier because she had heard that fresh fish was sold in a little market at the end of the pier. She was only partially correct. There was a small business at the end of the pier but it wasn't a market, it was a restaurant that served fish.

The long haired young man behind the counter was chopping lemon peels into a hot skillet and had a little pile of fish beside it that he was preparing to sauté. His dark curly hair, baggy pants and snake tattoo on his arm made him look more like a skateboarder than a cook but he told us we should forget about taking fish back to the RV and just eat there in his restaurant instead. He guaranteed that we would like the food.

When I asked about locally caught fish, He shook his head in the negative.

"You wouldn't want to eat anything caught in this area."

"Why's that?"

"Tijuana." He answered with an air of authority. "It's only a few miles down the road."

I didn't ask what that meant because he turned around to his grill. I'm assuming the guy meant that the water was polluted although maybe he meant something else.

The more I looked at that snake tattoo on the guy's arm, the more skeptical I became. I couldn't equate snake tattoos and good food but it was late and it had started raining again. Our clothes were damp from our walk out to the end of the pier. I was shivering and my nose was still running. I probably had pneumonia but don't tell Susie I said that. We decided to take him up on his offer.

It turned out to be a good decision. His specialty was a homemade seafood stew that was steaming on the stove behind him. I ordered a bowl of the stew, hoping to cure my ills. Ever the cautious one, Susie asked what was in the stew and found out that it contained scallops so she backed away from ordering it. She's never been one to eat things that squeak when they're bitten into so she ended up with a fish sandwich. The food was just as he had promised. It was good and like any food in these out of the way places, unique to that establishment. The skateboarder guy added a little extra hot sauce to my stew after I told him of my nasal affliction. Halfway through the bowl of stew, I stopped shivering as the warmth of the liquid radiated outward from my stomach and opened my plugged up nose.

"Susie, you have to try this stuff. It's delicious." I told her, trying my damndest to get her to try the stew but to no avail. I used every trick that I knew but once her mind's made up....

Still, I handed her a spoonful of the soup but she closed up like a clam. She pressed her lips tightly together in an act that reminded me of rhe times when I'd tried to give her liquid cold medicine. She hates that stuff.

"I'mmmmmm nnnnotttt eatnggg any of thattttt dammmmnn stttfff," There was no opening her mouth so I gave up trying to make her eat the stew, having been down that road before. I once saw her spit a raw oyster halfway across the main dining room in an Orlando, Florida lobster house after I sneaked one of those slimy little fellers into her chowder. I didn't really want a repeat of that. It was hilarious but she didn't speak to me for three days.

The rain was coming down again when we headed for the truck. I had a warm feeling in my stomach and things were beginning to look up.

We were up early on our last day in San Diego. The temperature was still on the cool side so I bundled up against catching a worse cold because we had decided to go to the zoo before we left town. The ticket prices were pretty steep but it was, after all, world famous.

"What the hell," we said, "damn the expense." As soon as the words were out of our mouth, I realized we've started cussing a lot in our old age. This trip was the second good decision we had made in as many days. The zoo was everything we had heard about plus a little more. The animal exhibits were extraordinary and the physical surroundings practically transported us to the Serengeti, contributing greatly to our experience. We saw every animal imaginable including two pandas and several koala bears, all of whom were sound asleep. It sort of reminded me of my last days at work.

Our last stop at the zoo was the reptile house. Snakes fascinate me and I'm scared to death around them but as long as they're behind a big piece of glass, I can watch them. Susie, on the other hand, will not even look at a reptile of any size. I said earlier that she wasn't afraid of anything. That's not entirely true. Snakes terrify her. She will pluck spiders out of the air and swat wasps with a broom but get a snake around her and she turns to mush.

I had to take her by the arm and drag her into the exhibit. There were snakes of all kinds, including several types of constrictors and brilliantly colored, deadly poisonous snakes from all over the world. Susie was dragging me through the room while I was trying to make her stop long enough to read the little information cards on the windows.

We came to a huge cage that contained a yellow boa constrictor that was surely twenty feet long. It was slithering over a limb that reached from one side of the cage to the other. I jerked loose from Susie and stood next to the window, mesmerized by the size of that thing. When I looked around a few minutes later, Susie was nowhere to be found. I walked around the whole building and couldn't find her. She had just disappeared. I know what you're thinking. The snake ate her. Nope. I found her on a bench outside by the ice cream stand licking on an ice cream cone.

"Susie," I yelled, "Come see this snake."

"Not on your life, Buster." (Buster is a pet name she sometimes uses when she's upset with me.) 'I think it's time to leave," she said, heading for the exit sign.

We left the zoo and San Diego after four days of record cold, a couple of rainy days and a little snow in the higher elevations. We seem to have a lot of bad luck with weather, having seen in the last year at least three events that rated the title of 'Storm of the century.' Either we're extremely unlucky or else the forecasters are overly proud of their atmospheric disturbances.

Area 51 or a reasonable facsimile

We left San Diego with the hot sun warming the truck as we headed east towards Casa Grande, Arizona. Ahead of us was 350 miles of Interstate 8 snaking its way through a couple of deserts and a mountain range or two. I was on top of the world. My bout with the flu was behind me and I was cruising through Southern California, an area that I had dreamed of seeing for thirty years.

The Rocky, craggy landscape soon took on the appearance of a place for a moon landing just about the time we passed a sign informing us we were entering the Manzanita Indian reservation.

"Boy, we didn't do them any favors." Susie said, looking out at the vast expanse of Brown.

"Who?"

"The Manzanita Indians is who. How were they supposed to live in this?" She swept her arm out toward the horizon.

"I don't know." I told her. I was a little astonished myself at this example of what passed for Government largesse. She just shook her head.

Our original plan was to drive a couple of hundred miles and find a campground and spend the night. We stopped shortly after dark on the outskirts of Yuma for a cup of coffee. The pot must have been boiling since early morning because about 3 sips of the stuff had me wide awake. I wasn't ready for any campground so we decided to keep going.

Not far out of Yuma, we noticed a light in the sky that at first glance appeared to be a plane but as we drove on, it didn't move. Maybe it's a house or something on a mountaintop, I told myself, but as we put miles between us and Yuma, the light stayed roughly in the same spot just ahead of us. It was beginning to make me a little uneasy and it was definitely bothering Susie. She propped the road atlas up in the passenger door window and put the sun visor down so she wouldn't have to look at it. Traffic was sparse as we crossed the desert terrain and it was pitch dark except for the glowing light.

"You know what?" I said to Susie.

"What?" she answered, her voice cracking ever so slightly.

"I think we're pretty close to Roswell and area 51." I had no idea where Roswell was but I knew it was in the southwest. I was only off by one state.

"What are you talking about?"

"I'm talking about the place where all the space ships have been seen. Maybe that's what we're seeing." I was half scaring myself and the subject of possible alien infestation was more than a little unsettling for her.

"Just quit talking about it." She said, burrowing down into the seat.

I didn't hardly mention it anymore. In retrospect, I later wished I hadn't mentioned it at all.

We approached Gila Bend around 11 in the evening and the light disappeared. It had been with us for 75 miles and poof, it was gone. I have no idea where it went. One minute it was up there and the next, it wasn't. A slight shiver made its way up my spine as I heard Susie breathe a sigh of relief.

I was getting tired so we decided to stop for a few hours and rest. I didn't see any point in paying for a campground site just so we could sleep for a few hours so I pulled off the highway at the next interchange and on to what turned out to be a gravel road. There were a couple of tractor trailer rigs and a motor home pulled off on the hard packed sand of the desert so I figured it would be alright even though it was pitch dark. I eased off the road into the sand and shut the engine off.

In the dark, I could make out a sign stuck on a fence post. I grabbed a flashlight and shone the beam on the sign.

'Property of the Gila River Indian Reservation.' It said. I forgot about the flying saucer because my mind was suddenly occupied with memories of those long ago Saturday afternoons when every kid in town would go to the movies and cheer on Gene or Roy or Lash Larue against those bloodthirsty Indian savages. I knew they were only movies but after seeing what my forefathers had done to them with the resettling on barren reservations, I could see why they might not like us palefaces.

I pointed out my misgivings to Susie as we got ready for bed and I got another one of those looks from her that are reserved for my more idiotic ravings. I put the Indians out of my mind and tried to go to sleep. Unfortunately, I was still keyed up from that coffee and couldn't doze off. I was playing a continuous newsreel in my brain of all the scenarios of things that could happen to us when it occurred to me that we were only a few miles from Mexico. We could be right in the path of a bunch of Mexicans running from the border police. Naturally, it also occurred to me that they would probably be the bloodthirsty kind. I got up to get dressed and Susie rolled over and sat up.

"What in God's name are you doing now?" she said in exasperation.

"I just realized that a band of Mexican marauders could be lurking out there."

"Good God, where do you come up with this stuff," she asked. "Get back in bed and go to sleep."

I climbed back into bed, leaving my pants on in case we had to get going in a hurry. Susie went right to sleep but I did a lot of tossing and turning before finally drifting off.

The scream came out of nowhere. "AAAAAAAAAGHGHGGHGHG HHGHG, get them off of me!!" The words screamed out of Susie's mouth, penetrated through my sleeping brain and went directly into my already overworked and fear induced inner warning system. I sat straight up, banging my head on the cabinet mounted over the bed. My heart was pounding as I looked around for something to defend us from….., from whatever it was that was attacking Susie. Snakes, aliens, Mexicans or even Native Americans. I had no idea.

"Get it off!" She yelled, as she flailed her arms around, still half asleep, grabbing at an invisible something. I quickly realized with my superior powers of observation that she was having a nightmare.

Not wanting to do any permanent damage, I grabbed her arm and gently said,

"Wake up, Little Susie. Wake up."

She opened her eyes and looked around,

"It was a snake, a huge snake and it was wrapping itself around my neck." She gasped, trying to get her breath. It made the hair on the back of my neck stand up. I was rubbing my scalp, feeling around for blood soaked hair or at least a knot from the meeting of my head with the cabinet. I was pretty sure I was injured but nothing was readily apparent.

"Jeez, Susie, you scared the water out of me." It seems like I had been telling her that with increasing frequency these past few weeks. As a matter of fact, I was beginning to think I should have included that phrase in our wedding vows. "For richer, for poorer, for having the water scared out of you…"

She stared at me for a second, then punched me right in the stomach.

"It's YOUR fault," she said, gasping for air. "You made me go in that damn snake house and then you had the aliens getting us.

"I'm sorry." I stammered.

"But you weren't satisfied. No Sir. You had to bring in the wild Indians and that story about some Pedro guy murdering us in our sleep."

"I was just being cautious."

"Cautious, my hind end. You're a lunatic and I want it stopped right now."

"Okay." I calmed her and got her to lay back down but I was done sleeping for the night. I tried several times to go back to sleep, but I would start snickering almost as fast as my eyes closed. I couldn't help it but all that did was make Susie more annoyed with me. After she punched me in the arm for the third time, I gave up. I rolled out of bed, pulled on my shirt and went outside to warm up the truck. Casa Grande was our next stop.

Part Three
The Birth of Riley Marie.

This story requires a bit of explanation because it doesn't really fit with the format of the rest of this book but without this piece, the book would have a gaping hole in the timeline of our adventures.

The story is almost a book in itself, albeit a short one. It's my account of an event that spanned three days of the most intense activity we have ever participated in.

If you read the table of contents, then you have an idea of what the story is about. If you didn't read the contents page, the story concerns potentially fatal complications in our daughter's pregnancy while we were 2000 miles away.. We found out about her pregnancy a couple of months before we set off for our first winter of retirement. We planned to be home in time for the early June birth and beyond that, we hadn't really given it much thought. We didn't have any experience with grandchildren and just assumed our life would go on as we had envisioned.

The birth of Riley Marie was a major event not only in her parents lives, but in ours as well. Even though we were nowhere near where it took place, The first appearance of the baby was life-altering in every sense of the word..

I'm going to stop here because I don't want to get ahead of myself. I'll just be quiet and let you read on.

Chapter One

Retirement was turning out to be everything we'd dreamed of and more. The 'lived happily ever after' tag line ending many fairy tales could have been written just for us and we were beginning to believe it was. Of course, we would have done well to remember that line was only used in fairy tales and the cell phone bouncing off my noggin should have told me something was amiss. It was no more than a sudden bonk but unbeknownst to me, it signaled the beginning of another one of Mother Nature's random acts of contrariness; one of those acts that produce turmoil in the lives of anyone who happens to get in her way. We'd had some experience with one of these acts when our son John was born with Cerebral Palsy but we had still managed to get through thirty eight years of marriage and into retirement before we got in her way again. This time, it ended up with us spilling a little blood, producing a fair amount of sweat, crying a lot of tears and taking an unexpected hair raising ride across the country. It started small enough; just that bonk on my head from the cell phone. Before it was over, however, our carefully conceived retirement plans would be revised in ways we had not even dreamed about.

I pulled out of the drugstore parking lot and was driving back to our winter home, a resort campground just north of Casa Grande, AZ. The sun was going down behind the mountains and the sky, thanks to the ever present desert haze, was turning a gleaming shade of orange. For the moment, I considered stopping the truck and taking yet another picture but I resisted the temptation because I already had a hundred just like it.

Instead, I shifted the sun visor to shield my eyes from the brilliant colors, taking care not to dislodge the dangling cell phone case from it's attached roost.

Of course, that didn't work and the phone came tumbling out of its case and onto my head. "Bonk."

There was a missed call message on the display screen when I picked up the phone. The caller ID display indicated it was from Susie's sister, Jenny. I'm not crazy about using the phone while driving the truck but I'm also a curious soul. Susie doesn't consider it curiousness, though. She tends to call it by its real name; nosy-ass. My sensible side said to wait until arriving at the camper but my curiosity buried that argument. I dialed the voice-mail and got the short message that Jenny had intended for her sister.

"Susie, call me. I've got some news about Julie."

A tiny alarm went off in my head but only a very tiny one. Julie is our only daughter, five years out of the University, five years married to Rick and pregnant with her first child and our first grandchild. Her pregnancy had been to this point one of the textbook variety, twenty five weeks into it with no problems. She had been taking very good care of herself, eating all the right things, taking pre-natal vitamins and following the doctor's orders to the letter. She would not even do a champagne toast at her cousin's wedding for fear of harming the baby. It didn't seem possible that the call had anything to do with a pregnancy problem. Probably a baby shower. There wasn't any reason for me to call, it was best to just have Susie call from the camper.

Before I could even put the phone back on the visor, it began to play its rendition of reveille to let me know that someone was calling.

Once again, I debated about not answering but ... you know, what with the curiosity thing and all, I pressed the answer button.

"I want you to know first of all that Julie is one hundred percent okay. This is all just a precautionary thing." My son Jason's voice, slightly quavering and lacking any hint of his usual light hearted manner came at me at about a hundred miles an hour..

"What precautionary thing are you talking about?" I said, trying to concentrate on the cars coming at me and at the same time fight back a rising uneasiness.

"Well shit, you mean nobody's talked to you yet.?" he said in an irritated voice.

"Talked to me about what?" I said, trying to swallow the large knot that was taking shape in the middle of my chest.

"Julie's in the hospital with some minor problem. I don't know what it is except her blood pressure's up". He paused long enough to catch his breath. "I don't think it's anything to be worried about".

I talked myself out of hyper-ventilating, taking deep slow breaths and at the same time managing to tell Jason we were okay.

Jason had called to reassure me because I was famous in family circles for my worrying abilities. Besides the normal litany of concerns, I carried a vast catalogue of worries in my brain concerning the kids and thirty seconds after answering the phone, I began mentally racing through the entries. The worst part was that we were two thousand miles from Indianapolis and something bad was happening back home. How bad we didn't know but it made me very nervous. I talked myself out of hyper-ventilating, took a few deep breaths and at the same time managed to tell Jason we were okay.

"Keep us posted." I told him.

I hurried on to the camp ground where I found Susie and our two visitors in the swimming pool. Mary and Trese were visiting us from Indiana. The two are associates from the Handicapable Hands workshop, an endeavor for mentally challenged adults. Susie had been the director of the program before we retired. Both of us were very attached to the kids who worked there and we had invited the girls to spend some time with us because the two were especially close to Susie. They had been with us for a week and were due to fly home the next day.

I pulled Susie aside and she called Jenny immediately after my explanation. Jenny teaches nursing at the university so she was able to explain what was happening with Julie and the baby.

It was more than just some elevated blood pressure. Julie had a condition called pre-Eclampsia that could be serious if not watched and that was why she was in the hospital and at this point, it really was just a precautionary move. One part of this predicament was that she would not be able to work. She would need to stay at home, off her feet and get a lot of rest.

I knew of, or at least, had heard stories of expectant mothers who had to do the same thing so this helped to reassure me.

Jenny gave us Julie's number at the hospital and Susie called her.

"Hey, three months of not working. I can handle that." Julie said in a very upbeat and cheerful manner.

"Your dad and I think maybe we should come home." Susie said, completely surprising me. It was still winter back home and there wasn't anywhere to stay in Indiana in February. We lived full time in our R.V. and cold weather wasn't part of this lifestyle. Our schedule, such as it was, had us getting back to Indiana in early May, a month before Julie's due date.

"Uh-h-h, Susie." I said to her, tugging on her sleeve to get her attention so I could ask her about this going home business.

"Hush." She said, pulling her arm out of my grasp and continuing her conversation with Julie.

"No, you're not coming home." Julie told her. "That would be silly. We can handle this. You guys just stay out there."

The whole idea still worried me and I wanted to tell Julie this but Susie had already hung up the phone.

Chapter Two

"I wanted to talk to her." I told Susie. I wanted a little more information if we were talking about going home.

"You can talk to her later. Besides we can't do anything today." She said to me. "Let's get Mary and Trese settled first and then we can talk about it."

Even though Mary and Trese were lacking in mental skills, they had listened to the conversation with Julie. They both picked up on our concern and Susie had to convince them that everything was okay. They soon forgot about it and went to bed complaining about having to go home. They had hoped to meet some cowboys while out west and had not yet done so.

Indianapolis was two hours ahead of us so Susie set the alarm for five a.m. when Julie would be up. We made our bed on the fold-out couch and listened to Mary and Trese in the other room talking about cowboys and we soon fell asleep.

Susie was out of bed before the alarm went off. She didn't want to wake the girls so she went outside to call Julie.

"Staying in bed isn't going to be enough. Now they want her to stay in the hospital till the baby's born." She said to me when she came back into the camper.

"Three months in a hospital?" That sounded damn serious to me.

"Julie said it's just a precaution. She still doesn't want us to come home."

"Why don't we call Jenny and see what she has to say about it?"

"I'll call her after eight. She's probably on her way to work now." Susie said, climbing back into bed.

When we got Jenny on the phone, she had more information to give us.

"It's Pre-eclampsia right now. It just pops up in some pregnancies. Neither Julie or the baby brought it on. Keeping her in bed is one way to slow it down and give the baby a chance to develop."

She did not mention that the full blown version is sometimes fatal to the mother, the child or both. Her voice was calm as she spoke and that made me feel much better except for one thing. All medical Professionals I have ever talked to have a calm detached and sometimes, uninterested voice when they're talking medicine. I guess they do this to keep from sounding involved. I knew that Jenny was very involved in this situation and if she was calm, it probably meant that things were okay, but still, I thought, she is a medical professional.

We both felt better after talking to Jenny. We were also busy getting Mary and Trese ready to go so we didn't have a lot of time to dwell on any more unpleasant possibilities. The forty mile trip to the Phoenix airport went quickly as Susie used the cell phone to get what updates we could get.

We had a problem at the airport when Susie couldn't find her driver's license.

"I'm sorry mamm, but you cannot go any farther without a picture ID." I heard this from the lady standing guard at the entrance to the concourse. I was busy at the time removing my shoes at the request of another lady guard and I started to protest but I knew enough to keep my mouth shut. Since the 9/11 WTC tragedy, I never joke with anyone in a uniform.

"It's okay, Susie." I said. "I'll take the girls to the gate."

Mary and Trese immediately burst into tears at the prospect of having to part with Susie. They hugged her till her face turned red, then the three of us headed down the concourse for gate 24. Susie sat outside the security barriers and waited on the plane to depart. This gave her time to phone all six of her sisters who convinced her that everything was going to be okay with Julie. Three of the six were nurses and two of them had been to see Julie.

"Did any of them assure you everything would be okay?" I asked as I rejoined her after the plane left. I was looking desperately for something that would get rid of the little dark cloud hanging around my head.

"Jenny promised me that she would keep on top of things and let us know if there's any change."

"Okay. Let's get out of this place."

We spent the remainder of the afternoon in Phoenix at a mining museum that had several displays on minerals and gemstones. Susie was becoming quite a rock hound and this museum was on her list of things to do. It turned out to be an enjoyable experience. You would think that walking around looking at rocks in glass cases would be boring for someone like me and you would be right.

We were up at six on Thursday morning and Susie called Julie. She had only a minute to talk.

"Everything's okay but I can't talk right now." she reported. "The doctor is here. Call back in a little while. I'm actually feeling much better, my urine even looked normal this morning".

I felt a lot better after that. We had a cup of coffee and I was looking through the Road Atlas pondering our next trip while Susie looked for her driver's license. We were planning on spending a couple of weeks in Tucson and I was researching things to see in the area.

"I can't find it anywhere." She told me, going through her wallet for the tenth time.

"When did you last see it?"

"I had it out when we went to Mexico. Did I put it back?"

. "I don't know."

Somewhere around noon the phone rang. Susie picked it up and cheerily said "Grindstaff's".

"Hi Rick, how's everything?" were her next words. I sat up and looked at Susie. Rick was not one to call and make idle chatter so a call from him was not a good sign. The small expanse of time it took for Susie to greet Rick was the last calm moment we were going to have for the next several days.

Susie listened for about ten seconds and then sat up straight, motioned for me to be quiet, even though I wasn't saying anything, and listened intently. I could see the concern and near panic in her face as the little dark cloud that had been hanging around in the back of my mind was starting to expand into a full blown storm. I tried to interrupt her to see what was happening and got only another furious hand waving motion to shut up.

She listened for another minute or so (maybe it was an hour) and then she said, "Okay Rick, we're on our way home. We'll be there as soon as we can." She turned to me, laying the phone down in the same motion.

I didn't get a chance to ask her what was happening. I'm not sure if I could have talked anyway. She just started in explaining:

"Julie is getting worse and they've decided to transfer her to University hospital where they have more experience with Eclampsia."

"Who is they and where are they transferring her from?" I said, suddenly realizing I didn't even know what hospital she was in.

I was frantically trying to find some socks to put on while fighting off the anguish that was welling up in my throat.

"She's at St Francis and her O.B. is moving her."

"What else is happening?" "Why are we going home?" "what do you mean, 'worse'?" I was firing questions at her as fast as they would come out of my mouth.

At this point, things really got confusing and damn near sent me over the edge The doctors had told Rick that they were going to give her something that would sedate her and also would bring her blood pressure down. Somehow, in the anxiety laden moment, Susie interpreted this to mean something different.

"They're putting Julie into a coma."

"A COMA??" I screamed. I remembered an episode of the television show ER where Dr Green (or maybe Dr John Carter) put a lady into a coma one night and it was some serious stuff so when I heard "COMA", I quit breathing for a minute or so. I couldn't think about what to do. All I really knew was that my daughter was laying out there unconscious and we had to get home.

"I'll call and get us a flight." I told her, taking the phone from her.

"I can't fly anywhere, remember. I don't have a picture ID.". She said calmly. No ID. Damn. We would have to drive.

"We better get on the road, then." I said, trying to think where to start.

I went outside, shoes untied, and started throwing stuff into the back of the truck. We had meticulously assembled a check list for breaking camp and I considered getting it out but then I thought "screw that." There was no time to do this in an orderly manner. We needed to get out of there and the faster the better. I did put the TV antenna down because you don't get a second chance if you go under a bridge with it up. Panicked or not, I still obsessed over that antenna. All four tires could be flat but if the antenna is down, I figured we're ready to go.

Susie had been collecting rocks to take home and my original plan was to pack them away in the pickup bed so they wouldn't roll around. Instead, they ended up being pitched into the back along with the cooler, one of the bicycles and some flowers that we had meticously planted in clay pots. Dirt flew everywhere when the pots landed on the rocks.

Susie was putting things away on the inside of the camper and as I backed the truck up to the trailer, I realized the bicycle didn't belong in the pickup bed.

"Damnit." I said, suddenly realizing I still hadn't bought that bike carrier. We had stored the bicycles inside the camper on the trip out but it was too cumbersome when we needed to get to something. I had seen a bicycle carrier in Quartzsite but didn't buy it, figuring I could pick one up a little cheaper later. Too late now.

I grabbed the bike, tossed it out of the back of the truck and Susie wrestled it into the trailer. Within an hour of the phone call, we were ready to go. I double checked the pin on the fifth wheel hitch (another obsession), pulled out onto the street and headed for Interstate 10 and eventually, Indianapolis.

Chapter Three

We pulled out of Casa Grande on the last day of February. The temperature was already in the mid eighties. We drove by the K-mart and their great selection of garden supplies. We had originally planned on buying tomato plants as well as several varieties of pepper plants and cultivating them as we leisurely worked our way east. Our intent was to have these plants ready to bear fruit once we got home for the summer but we didn't even give that project a second thought as we went past the place.

I really hadn't taken time yet to figure out what highways we should take back to Indiana. My gut was telling me to stay as far south as possible as we made our way east but that would add miles and time. The closest route was to go north to Flagstaff, take Interstate 40 east to Oklahoma City and then head northeast on the Will Rogers Parkway. I had already ruled out at least the Flagstaff part because it was cold up there and the weather was unpredictable.

I figured I could still turn north towards Oklahoma City farther down the road if the weather was okay. Susie called Jason, told him about the worsening crisis with Julie and asked him to get us as much information on the roads as he could. Then we headed east towards Tucson.

Jason called back shortly after we got on the road but before I could ask him about the weather, he told us that he had spoken to Julie.

"They gave her something to prevent seizures so she's feeling a little woozy, but she sounds okay." he reported.

"Wait a minute" I said. "She's supposed to be in a coma."

"A coma?" he asked. "What in the hell are you talking about?"

"A doctor induced coma.." I told him. "They're supposed to put her out so she won't move."

"I -um hadn't heard about that one." he said slowly as if he was talking to some lunatic on the other end and in reality, I guess he was.

"Your mom said… never mind." I growled, trying to figure out what the hell the coma story was all about.

"Where did you talk to Julie?"

"She's in her room at Saint Francis." was his reply.

"Okay, we'll call her." I said, ending the call and handing the phone to Susie.

"Well crap," I thought, "I forgot to ask him about the weather."

Susie quickly dialed Julie's room at St. Francis. and the phone rang several times before Julie answered.

"Julie, are you okay?" The words came shooting out of Susie's mouth.

I only heard some of what Susie said to Julie but it was apparent that there was no coma nor, as it turned out, would there be. None of that made any difference to me, though. I needed to know NOW what the story was and Susie was taking too long to find out. I poked at her arm trying to find out what was being said. She paid no attention.

"What's she saying?" I asked. "What's she saying?"

No reply. She was listening intently and paid no attention to me.

"Susie, what's happening?

"JUST A MINUTE." she roared. "Be quiet, for God's sake. I can't hear with you making all that damn noise. "

I quieted down and in a few moments, she finished the conversation. she hung up and started explaining to me what was going on.

"They're moving her to University hospital pretty soon. Her blood pressure is up and toxins are giving her problems. Also they've got her on Mag Sulfate, whatever the hell that is." All this medical crap came flying at me. I was too crazy to apprehend all that was happening to Julie but while it was serious, it certainly wasn't the coma thing that had been talked about early that morning.

I took several deep breaths and tried to relax a little. Relief that there was no coma in the picture flooded through me. I still felt like crying but no tears were in the offing since I am one of those Neanderthal men who cannot cry. There were no tears when my mom passed away and none when our son John died, although, God knows, they weren't far from the surface. I must have cried as a little kid, but I don't remember it.

Fifty five years ago a priest walked in my parent's front door and told my mom that my dad had ran a motorcycle off the road, over a hillside and had gotten killed in the process.

I vaguely recall my younger brother, Ronnie and I standing half dressed in the kitchen trying to figure out what had happened to our dad as people started crowding into the house. My brother had this scared look on his face because everyone was crying, He was picking at his nose to hide his tears. Two of my aunts were pacing back and forth, crying. My mom was sitting at the kitchen table, hands covering her face. Her friend, Mrs. Hawkins, was patting her on the back and crying as well. I decided then I would have to be strong and not cry. I don't remember crying either, but then again, I was only six years old and my memory could be a little fuzzy.

When Susie hung up that phone, I was feeling helpless and probably closer to tears than I had ever been. If She had shed one tear at that point, I think I would have cried for the next hundred miles.

Chapter Four

We reached Las Cruces around six in the evening. By this time, Julie had been transferred to the other hospital. Jason called us from her room. Julie was sleeping and Rick was talking to the new doctor.

"Are you sure it's not a coma?" I asked Jason, half seriously.

"No, dad, she's just sleeping. I called to give you her new phone number. They turn the phones off at ten so call her in the morning."

"Okay, but if anything comes up, you call us."

We hung up and pulled into Wendy's to get a sandwich. Even in a crisis, us retired folk like that 99 cent menu. While we were eating we tried to make a decision on which way we needed to go. The quickest way from here was to go North on I-25 to Albuquerque and east from there. North possibly meant snow and we didn't want that. We decided to go east to El Paso and postpone going north for a while.

We got back in the truck and turned the dial on the radio looking for a forecast. Down south and out west, when folks talk about the weather, they will say "They're calling for rain" or "they're calling for snow." That "calling" business was one of my pet peeves and it always rubbed me the wrong way. Of course, the weather lady I found on the truck radio said that they were calling for snow in the mountains around Albuquerque.

I yelled at the radio "Who? Who is it that's doing this calling, you crazy son of a bitch???"

Susie tugged on my arm to bring me back to reality.

Snow, no matter how it was being predicted, eliminated going north. We pulled out of Wendy's, got back on I-10 and headed for El Paso.

We were not very far out of Las Cruces when we decided we should talk to Julie before much more time had passed. We were conscious of the time because it was important what time it was when we used our cell phone. At that time, We had one of those nationwide calling plans with no extra charges as long as you're communicating through an AT&T cell phone tower and as long as you don't use more than 500 minutes a month. Five hundred minutes is a lot unless you have a very sick daughter, you're a couple of thousand miles from home and you need to find out everything you can about what's going on.

Luckily, there is a caveat to that restriction on minutes. If we called after eight PM and before seven AM, the minutes did not count toward the 500 total. The AM and PM times apply to whatever time zone we might happen to be in. Don't ask me to explain how the damn phone knows what time zone we're in when we don't know ourselves most of the time. We spent much of our time on this trip trying to guess what time it was at the moment so we could figure out what time it was where we were calling. (although now, as I write this, It occurs to me that we should have set a clock set on hospital time and saved ourselves all this trouble).

There is also a caveat to the "no extra charges" on AT&T's towers. Apparently, cell phone towers can be owned by just about any Tom, Dick or Harry and if they happen to plop one in the vicinity of where you are, they're going to lock on to your signal and take your money.

The only way you know this is when you see a little 'Roaming' message in the window of the phone.

I complained to AT&T earlier about this and the guy there told me to turn the phone off when I see this "roaming" message and maybe they'll let go of the signal.

"Cloudy weather could also be a factor. The signal might bounce off the clouds." he had mentioned as an afterthought.

"Could be." I told him. "They ARE calling for rain."

The phone display indicated that we were not in an AT&T territory. "Maybe we'd better talk to her anyway." I said as we wound our way east out of New Mexico

"What time is it here and what time is at the hospital?"

This was a legitimate question from Susie because of the ten o'clock restriction on the hospital phones. Susie and I, like most people, struggled when converting from Central to Mountain to Eastern time. We hadn't done anything to help the situation. The clock in the truck was still on Arizona time and six minutes fast. It was too much trouble trying to figure out how to set a digital clock correctly using the radio buttons. When I set it originally, I got within six minutes and figured, 'close enough'.

The battery in my watch had been dead since before Christmas and Susie's was laying on the sink in the camper. By and large, retired people don't really care what time it is.

Adding to the confusion was the fact that we had no idea what time zone we were in. This time zone thing was the first order of business because we needed to use the free minutes. I suggested to Susie that she get the atlas and figure out where the dividing line between mountain and central time was. It could have been the Texas state line but I wasn't sure.

I attempted to explain to Susie how to find the time zone on the map.

"Get the road atlas and turn to the front. There's a map of all the states."

Susie thumbed through the pages looking for the United States map and I grew a little impatient with her browsing. Expert Map reading requires more than just a little testosterone. In other words, it's a man kind of thing and lacking this, she is not a map expert and doesn't want to be one. More than once, Susie has made some pointed remark about my choice of bathroom reading material, the road atlas being one of my favorites.

Slightly exasperated, I started to say "Susie dear, it's at the fr...."

"Well, this is interesting." She interrupted. "I always thought the Grand Canyon was at the top of Arizona."

"I believe it is." I said in my most patient manner.

She adjusted the overhead map lights and showed me the pages. She was looking at a detail map of the Grand Canyon area. It was printed below, but on the same page of the Arizona map.

"Well, I'll be damned!" I said very seriously. "Some son of a bitch has moved the Grand Canyon."

She punched me in the arm and said "Don't give me that stuff. Why would they put it down there?"

Laughing at Susie can bring severe consequences so I stifled that inclination and instead, explained a little of the art of map reading.

Turning to the map of the United States and trying not to run off the road at the same time, I told her "If you'll find the clocks on the map, You'll see the little dotted lines that show the time zones." "Find the one for Mountain time."

She scanned the page. "Got it. It's right in the middle of New Mexico." She pointed to the line running south just west of Albuquerque.

I knew that couldn't be right. Steering with my knees, holding the map and glancing at both the road and the atlas (Kids, don't try this at home), I saw the problem.

"No Hon, that's the continental divide." (I kept the little terms of endearment coming to keep from sounding irritated.) "As a matter of fact, we crossed it a little ways back. Don't you remember me pointing it out?".

"Well damn." she muttered, going back to the map.

After a minute, she said "Okay, it's the red line on the other side of El Paso."

Once again, I did my balancing act and looked at the pages. She was right. The line was a about a hundred miles into Texas and we still hadn't left New Mexico.

"It's five minutes till seven o'clock here so it's almost nine o'clock at the hospital." I said. "Call her anyway, before they turn off her phone ."

Chapter Five

I took the phone from Susie long enough to say hi and ask Julie how she was doing. "I'm okay." She told me, but she didn't sound very convincing.

I handed Susie the phone and listened as she started talking, trying to interpret her mood as she talked to Julie. It was hard to do because she did little more than listen intently, nod her head and ask a question or two. When she hung up, she turned to me with a quivering chin and a scared sort of look that made the hair on the back of my neck stand up.

"They want to try to hold off delivery for another week. If they can do that, the baby will have a ninety percent chance of survival. If they have to take it now, it's about eighty percent."

"Another week." I yelled. "What happened to the three months?"

It was time to stop this foolishness.

"They can have other babies." I thought. "Get that baby out of there." I didn't really have any say in a decision like that but it didn't keep me from thinking it. Rick and Julie were well equipped to make their own decisions. We had to let go and let them do what was right. This child of ours had turned into an adult, regardless of how hard it was for me to accept that.

We decided to say the rosary again. I haven't mentioned it before but after every phone call, we said the rosary. We were wearing those beads out as we drove through the night.

One rosary and several panic attacks later, We pulled into the Flying J truck stop on the west side of El Paso.

We had driven about four hundred miles since we left and we were both pretty well pooped out. The Flying J provides an area for RV's to park overnight so we decided to do that. I drank a beer while Susie warmed up some soup. We ate our dinner and went into the truck stop to brush our teeth and use the restroom.

When we got back, we climbed the two steps into the camper bedroom. I noticed the TV set that resided on a shelf in the bedroom was laying at an odd angle on the carpet. The antenna cable was still attached to the overhead fixture with a strange looking little doo-dad dangling from the end of it. On closer inspection, the doo-dad turned out to be the end of the antenna connection that normally resided in the back of the TV. I remembered then that I had not taken the TV down from it's shelf, one of our breaking camp duties. Somewhere along the way, it had bounced off and jerked it's guts out as it headed for the bedroom floor.

"I never liked that cantankerous Korean son of a bitch, anyway." I said to myself, assigning the now useless appliance an Asian personality it never had when it worked. I turned it over and propped it against the side of the bed where it should have been when we were traveling.

I lay there in bed wondering what I would have to do to dissolve this oversize grapefruit jumping up and down in my esophagus. It had been there for the last few hours and the damn thing wouldn't hold still, rebounding off the sides of my throat and down into my stomach. Jesus, I thought, we can't lose another child. Julie doesn't deserve this and neither do we.

Chapter Six

Eight hours of driving while pulling a 9000 thousand pound trailer should have been enough to help get a good night's sleep. It didn't help us. Worry about Julie along with the lights of the El Paso Flying J contributed to our lack of rest on that February evening. The noise coming from the generator in the motor home parked next to us also made it impossible to get any real sleep. We had a few snatches of unconsciousness but mostly we laid in the fifth wheel bedroom in a groggy stupor. During a moment of temporary awareness, I phoned my brother in Sacramento. He now knew about our crisis.

'Did I tell him? I thought. 'I don't remember'.

He had been watching the Weather Channel so he could help us find a way home.

"Every thing looks okay as far as Dallas. There's some snow north of there and rain over in Louisiana." He told me. No ice, at least. I remembered reading about ice storms that seemed to visit Dallas at least once every winter and we couldn't afford to get caught in one of those. Pulling a thirty foot trailer on a slick interstate highway didn't sound the least bit appealing.

"Call me if anything changes with the weather." I told him and went back to tossing and turning until two in the morning. That was enough. It was time to hit the road. Rolling out of bed and putting my clothes on, I considered leaving Susie asleep but she would for sure get a little crazy if she woke up and we were moving.

Shaking her gently, I said "Susie, Wake up. We're gonna get going."

Her voice sounded exhausted as she whispered "Okay. I'm awake. I was just about to ask you to get us out of here anyway."

It beats me why she was whispering because no one could hear us. It was just that kind of night.

The coffee in the Flying J truck stops is generally pretty good but the cup I sipped on as we pulled out of the parking lot was terrible. It tasted like it had been left out all night and dumped back into the pot as an afterthought. It took one gulp of water for every drink of the stuff just to get some of it down.

Interstate 10 winds through the middle of El Paso. The lights of the city helped me to adjust my sleepy eyes and wake up a little. The scenery was very familiar even though I had never been to El Paso in my life. It's funny how, at three in the morning, one city looks pretty much like any other. Four and five story buildings of various shapes fill in the gaps between the taller buildings dominating the backdrop. Some of the structures are only dark silhouettes with an occasional light glowing from an office window. Others are lit up like they were in a contest with the power company headquarters. Neon lights at street level blinked their message out to a world where no one was awake and we were the only ones receiving it. The truck's headlights bounced off the overpasses and across six empty lanes of highway. It was kind of surreal, like watching an old detective movie. I half expected to see Humphrey Bogart prowling the streets in a mid 40's police car.

El Paso was a much bigger city than I thought. When Marty Robbins sang his mournful tale about this 'West Texas town', it sounded like a one horse burg with dusty streets and clapboard houses. It was anything but that. I was also under the mistaken impression that former Indiana coach Bobby Knight lived here in El Paso and I wondered if he'd like to hear a friendly Hoosier voice. My God, I must have been going crazy.

It took us an hour of driving before we left the city behind. Not far to the south, the lights of Juarez illuminated the horizon, individual beacons blinking on and off warning whatever might be in the sky to stay away. Once again, it appeared to be something out of that same detective movie. My obsolete notions of Mexico did not include modern cities lighting up the night skies so it was hard to think of those lights in the south as being in another country.

"That's probably Mexico over there." I said, pointing out the lights to a sleepy Susie. I was trying to take her mind and mine as well, off what might be happening in Indiana.

She wasn't interested in geography lessons. Ignoring my ramblings, she asked "What time is it at the hospital?"

"A little after six." I answered.

She picked up the phone and dialed Julie's room using the speed dial memory she had recorded the night before. The phone made a funny 'beepbeepbeep' similar to the noise that a busy signal makes but it wasn't that. We must have been in some kind of dead spot because we couldn't make a connection. She tried several more times without success.

Finally, in a fit of frustration, she dialed the AT&T customer service number. She listened for a moment and then said into the phone "Oh, Por Favor, your ass".

She turned to me, her voice shaking, and said "the damn phone is connected to the Mexicans. I don't have any idea what they're saying."

"It's okay." I said, mentally cursing the phone company. "We'll go a while longer and try it again."

We had no luck with the phone. Either we had 'the Mexicans', No service or the ominous 'roaming' message in the little display window.

About three hours after leaving El Paso, we could begin to make out the horizon as the eastern sky was displaying that familiar dim light that precedes the rising sun. We pulled into a rest stop to use the pay phone and to wash our faces in an effort to wake up. Susie called the hospital and talked to Rick. The conversation didn't last long because Julie was asleep. The hospital staff was testing her liver enzymes every other hour. We had no idea what liver enzymes were, but Rick said "If the count doesn't come down, they'll have to deliver the baby."

"We're hoping they can hold off for another week to give the baby a fighting chance." He said.

That was enough for me. "A week? Get that baby out of there now. They can have other babies."

"Will you shut up abut that?" Susie said in a falsetto whisper while covering the phone. They've got enough to worry about right now."

Susie turned back to the phone and said goodbye to Rick. We could begin to make out the horizon as the sun inched it's way upward. We climbed into the camper to eat a bowl of cereal before taking off again. Susie's head hurt and my back was aching so we both took some Tylenol and sat down on the bed. That's all it took.

Chapter Seven

We slept for three hours. The combination of the bright sunlight and the smell of coffee along with the noisy little perking of the coffeepot woke me up.

"What time is it? I asked, sitting up and looking around.

Susie replied "It's either nine or ten but since I don't know what time zone we're in, you can take your pick."

We left the rest stop trying to keep two coffee mugs in the cup holders on the dash. It was an impossible task. Every bump in the road splashed a little coffee onto the road Atlas laying on the transmission hump. Normally, this would be worth a tormenting growl from me. My heart wasn't in it and Susie certainly wasn't in any shape to be taking harassment.

We had driven only a few miles when a sign mounted across the highway announced that the Interstate 20 interchange was just ahead. Another crucial decision awaited us. I-20 would turn us Northeast towards Dallas but it could also result in some colder weather. Staying on I-10 would take us southeast to San Antonio and continuing warm weather but it would also add several hundred miles to our trip. I had misgivings about the Northeastern route but we had to go into the cold weather eventually anyway, so we took the I-20 interchange and headed for Dallas.

The three hours of sleep in the rest stop had rejuvenated me. It was five hundred miles and ten hours to Dallas and that sounded like a reasonable goal for the day, especially since there wasn't any thing to do but drive and eat.

It even looked like we could be in Indianapolis by early Sunday morning with a little bit of hard driving and some luck with the weather. It was hard to imagine cold temperatures in the north giving us any problem. The temperature was in the low 80's and not a cloud was in the sky as we headed across Texas.

Susie picked up the cell phone and saw that we still had the evil "roam" display which meant that we would be paying a dollar a minute or so to talk.

"Call 'em." I said. We hadn't talked to anyone for three hours and we needed to know what was happening.

The news wasn't good. The last count of liver enzymes was higher than the one before. Rick explained that the hope now was to retain the pregnancy until Monday. Julie was being given steroids to help speed up the baby's lung development.

Monday! Good God, we had to hurry.

"Let's put you on a plane when we get to Dallas." I told Susie.

"We could try. But it seems like we could waste a lot of time waiting on a flight, not to mention pulling this thing into a busy airport. We'd better keep driving."

The hours went by as we passed through West Texas towns and landmarks with familiar names. The Pecos river and the "West of the Pecos" museum came and went without even a thought of stopping. Odessa with it's oil wells wasn't worth a second look. Midland and it's "home of President George W Bush" billboard came into view. Susie checked the cell phone as we went by the billboard and we still did not have any AT&T service.

"What the hell kind of company is that? I asked Susie, as if she had the answer. "They should at least have a tower in the president's home town, for Christ sake."

We stopped in Abilene to get something to eat and to use the pay phone again. Susie was crying when she placed the phone back in it's cradle.

"It's getting worse." She told me, stopping to catch her breath and wipe her eyes. . "They can't get her blood pressure down and they're afraid to give her anything that might harm the baby."

I remembered having these discussions in high school religion classes about the church law that said "save the baby and let the mom die" in cases where there had to be a choice. At the time, when Father Doyle explained the reasons, it sounded plausible.

But not in real life. That's my daughter, not some textbook case. How asinine could a priest get, for God's sake?

"Forget the baby. Take care of Julie." I said aloud to a priest who had been dead forty years.

Taking me by the arm and bringing me back to the present, Susie said "C'mon, let's get going."

We stopped to get fuel before getting back on the interstate. As an afterthought, I pulled the camper up by the service bay and borrowed the air hose used to fill truck tires. Draining all the fresh water from the tank, I blew all the water lines clear of moisture. There weren't any freezing temperatures in the forecast, at least not in Abilene, but there wasn't any point in taking chances. We wouldn't be using any water on this trip, anyway.

As the Abilene traffic began to thin out, we topped a rise in the highway and noticed a thin black line that stretched across the horizon off in the distance.

"What's that?" Susie asked as if I knew the answer.

"It could be a cloud." I told her even though there was still none in the sky. "Maybe somebody's burning something."

My biggest fear, even though I said nothing to Susie, was that it could be a violent thunderstorm. You could see for miles in this part of Texas and there was no landscape like that in Indiana so I had no experience to suggest what it might be. "There's no lightning." I told myself. "It's probably not a tornado".

We continued our northeastern heading, keeping a nervous eye on the black looking thing out there. We had decided to stop for a few hours to get a little sleep and take a shower in the Dallas area but it was still a hundred and eighty miles away and it didn't seem like we would get there before dark. Susie got our campground book out from under the pile of supplies behind her seat.

"Look in the Fort Worth listings." I told her. We both knew that all we needed was a place to clean up and rest a little while." The campground also had to be near an interchange. I didn't want to be driving around country roads trying to find it. She found an inexpensive park about fifty miles west of Dallas that was just off the highway.

I picked up the phone to call the place, hoping by now to see the familiar AT&T logo in the display and once again saw the nasty "Roam". "What the hell, I thought, dialing the number that Susie was reading off to me.

"Sure, we got a spot." the lady told me. "Sixteen dollars."

"How about AARP or AAA?" I queried, not wanting to barter too long. It was stupid to try and save one dollar while spending two dollars on the phone call.

"Okay, fourteen fifty with an AARP card."

"You got plenty of hot water for the showers?"

"Yes sir." She replied, sounding extremely proud of their water heating capabilities.

"We'll be there about seven thirty. How's the weather?"

"It's raining and I'm closing at seven." She said. "Just pick an empty spot and put your money in the envelope in the mail box. It's hanging by the front door of the office. We'll see you in the morning." There was no chance to tell her we wouldn't be staying that long.

"Raining?" I thought. That must have been the dark stuff on the horizon. It had grown much larger and now occupied more than half the sky ahead of us. It was definitely a cloud. We continued on towards it as the sun moved lower and lower in my rear view mirror.

It turned out to be more than just a cloud. Texans have a name for a weather system such as this. They call it a 'Blue Norther'.

It was a cold front like none we'd seen before. One minute, the thermometer in the truck cab said seventy-five degrees and as we passed under the cloud out of the sunlight and into semi-darkness, it dropped to fifty-four degrees.

The sudden change fogged up the windshield. "Good Lord." Susie said, reaching over to switch from air conditioning to the defroster.

The rain started then and continued on to the campground. The windshield wipers tried mightily to rid themselves of the west Texas dust but all they did was make mud streaks that obscured our view. We pulled off I-20 and saw the sign for the RV park. There was a Chinese take-out restaurant on the corner so we pulled in there.

"Some hot and sour soup would be good." Susie said.

"Right." While I was at it, I ordered some Hunan chicken and rice.

It was dark when we pulled into the RV Park. The few lights around the place cast their glow on a bunch of dilapidated trailers.

Crap! We've been had. It was a trailer park in sheep's clothing. I drove by the office and down between two rows of the trailers. Most of the beat up cars or trucks parked around the mobile homes appeared to have just left the 'buy here, pay here' lot in disgrace.

"I'm not staying in this god forsaken place.' I said to Susie.

"Where are we going to go? She said. "It's dark, it's raining, I'm tired and hungry. I need to go to the bathroom and I really need to take a shower. Find a place to park."

Chapter Eight

We found an empty, level site and pulled in without any problems. I didn't bother to unhook the camper from the truck because we were only going to stay a few hours. The electrical hookup was standing in a puddle of water and hoping electrocution wasn't in the cards, I took a deep breath and plugged the trailer connection into the wet outlet. The lights in the camper came on and I was still standing so I went to the office mailbox and found an envelope to stuff the money in. By the time I got all this completed and climbed into the camper, I was soaking wet.

Susie had already called the hospital and looked up at me as she was putting the phone down. She explained that the duty nurse had answered the phone in Julie's room.

"Rick isn't there and the nurse thinks that the baby will be delivered before the weekend is over. Julie's kidney's aren't working right and the doctor doesn't want to wait much longer." She looked up at me, despair in her eyes. "Oh God, Gordie. We've got to get there."

There has never been a more helpless feeling in my life than there was at that moment. My wife needed me to make things right with the world and all I could do was stand there dripping water on the carpet, shivering like a wet dog and wondering what to do next.

I gave Susie a comforting hug and made some lame joke about the Chinese food still in the little white cartons. Neither of us were hungry but we tried to eat. The food tasted like sawdust so most of it went into the trash, little white cartons and all.

"I want to go home." Susie sobbed.

"We're going." I told her. "but we gotta get some sleep. "Let's lay down for a while and then we'll get up, take a shower and get on the road."

"I gotta go to the bathroom. I'm about to wet my pants now." She told me as she grabbed an umbrella out of the closet.

"It's pouring down rain, Susie. Just go in that yellow bucket in the bathroom and I'll empty it for you."

"I'm not peeing in any bucket. Let's go." She said, acting as if I'd just told her to make water in the middle of Downtown Indianapolis.

We ran through what was now a cold rain to the bathroom, dodging puddles as best as we could in the semi-darkness.

The news was on by the time I found the remote and got the television powered up. We listened but we couldn't watch because the TV set was behind the wall of the camper slide out. The slide was in it's traveling position and I didn't want to set it up because of the time that it took to get it accomplished. There was also the matter of the rain. There would be a terrible mess if we put out the slide and then brought it back in with water all over the roof.

The weather people on TV were predicting a wet night with temperatures in the low forties.

I hated driving in the dark in the rain but it looked like that's what we'd be doing. It was eleven thirty Dallas time when we got to bed. We set the alarm for four so we could get up and be on our way.

The phone played it's version of Yankee doodle dandy at one in the morning. Susie was wiping at her eyes, trying to wake up so she could find the phone. It was already in my hand and up to my ear.

"They're not going to wait any longer." Rick said. "Julie's kidneys have quit functioning and they have to deliver the baby now." There was a note of fear in his voice but he was calm.

"Who else is there?" I asked him.

"No one. Jason went home to take a shower."

"Okay, Rick. Hug Julie for us and tell her we love her. We'll be there as soon as we can get there."

I punched the button to end the call and used the memory dial for Jason's house. I waited one, two, three rings.

"Hello." A sleepy voice said.

"Jason, you're gonna have to get back over to the hospital now." I hoped I didn't sound as frantic as I felt. "The baby is coming now. Those two need all the support they can get and we're not there. Rick's parents obviously aren't coming so you're it."

"God dad, what should I do? Julie doesn't need to see me panic stricken and I don't think I can hide it."

"You don't need to worry about it. I don't think Julie's going to see you at all for a while. Just go sit with Rick and keep us informed about what's happening. Call us when you get there."

Thirty minutes later, he called back. Susie answered and Jason started talking before she could say hello.

"They're just waiting for a doctor who can do a C-section." He told us. "Rick has gone to the delivery room with Julie."

Our sleep, what little we'd had, was done for the night. It was too late for us to get there so we decided to stay until we heard more news.

Susie called Jenny. She would get to the hospital as soon as she could. Barbara, another sister and also a nurse, was already at work in another hospital in the huge medical complex.

"We'll call her." Jenny promised.

It was getting cold in the camper so I plugged in the electric heater we kept under the bed. I could have turned on the furnace but Susie did not like the Propane burning when we were in bed. We held hands and said a rosary for Julie. I included the baby as an afterthought. We knew, thanks to Ultrasound, that the baby was a girl but to me she still wasn't real. It was only a swollen belly on Julie, and not very swollen, at that. A pregnant Julie didn't seem real because this couldn't be a woman ready to give birth. This was my daughter who had just been out playing in the back yard. How in the hell was she getting ready to start a new generation?

"Rose Mary" I prayed to my dead mother just in case God was busy elsewhere. "Make sure everybody's okay."

We paced the four feet of trailer that we could move around in. The rain tapping on the roof set a cadence for us. I needed to go to the bathroom but there was no leaving that trailer. Back and forth we went, the rain's patter changing to a drumming clamor. The noise would have made it hard to hear the phone ring if it had not already been in my hand.

We both said "hello."

"It's me." Jason said as if we were expecting someone else. Our heads were pressed together as we maneuvered the phone to hear.

"She's here and she's tiny. I saw her. Holy crap, she's little, but she's all there. Every finger and toe." Jason told us. "A pound and change. She'd fit in the palm of your hand if they'd let us touch her. We've got ourselves a miracle baby here. I mean a real miracle baby."

He was almost babbling, practically singing the words and the relief he felt practically rolled out of the phone.

I interrupted his sing-song verse. "What about Julie? How is she?"

"Rick's with her. She'll be okay. She's so strong. I think she was the only one who thought this was gonna work. She never doubted it for a minute. My God, if I had half her resolve…." The words trailed off and his voice was beginning to crack and I could sense the tears were close to flowing. Susie was gripping my arm, squeezing her fingers so tight, I almost dropped the phone.

"I know the baby's name too." He said, in an instant going from almost tears to almost laughing. "But I'm not gonna tell you what it is. Rick and Julie can tell you that."

Susie shouted into the phone and my ear as well, since the two were glued together. "Tell them we're on our way."

We put the phone down. Susie grinned and said "Okay Gramps. You want to say a prayer?"

"Do what?" Her words were almost drowned out by the rain. She picked up the rosary and gestured towards me.

"No more rosaries, it's time to pee."

Opening the camper door, I looked towards the bathroom, trying to gauge how wet I was gonna get on my trip. The lights of the bathroom were difficult to make out through the rain. Squeezing my eyes to get a better look, I saw a reflection of what looked like white stuff accumulating in the circle of light cast by the overhead bulb. I stepped out of the trailer and fell right on my butt. I looked around, my hind end getting wetter and colder by the second. The camper steps were coated with ice. As a matter of fact, everything in sight was coated with ice.

This was supposed to be rain. "You son of a bitch!" I said, cursing who ever the weatherman was that missed this. "Susie." I yelled, struggling to get up. We got a problem."

Chapter Nine

The ice put an exclamation point on the situation that we found ourselves in. There was nothing about the storm on television. Of course it was Two A.M., we could only get reception on one channel and all it had on were infomercials.

"Three easy payments of forty......" the wavy haired man on the TV managed to get out before Susie picked up the remote and shut him up. We tried the radio and after sorting through several pre- recorded programs, we found a station playing jazz music. An announcer's voice came on when the music ended.

"Well, Dallas" he said, in that soft bebop voice that all jazz lovers seemed to have, "In case you haven't looked outside, that rain we were getting has turned to ice."

"No shit." I said to the radio.

"If you're planning on going anywhere, the roads are covered from Abilene all the way to Longview." His quiet soothing drawl, completely unperturbed, told me.

"I know about Abilene but where in the hell is Longview?" I asked Susie, one of the last people in the world who would know the answer to that question. .

"I don't know but there's no point in worrying about it. We're stuck for now."

In a way, the storm was a relief. The baby had arrived and we couldn't move. There was nothing we could do so we decided it would be a good time to get some rest. I turned off the electric heater so it wouldn't burn us up while we were sleeping.

We went to bed, taking a couple of Wal-Mart's fake Tylenol P.M. tablets to help us sleep. Somewhere around six A.M. the noise of the phone penetrated the darkness in the camper.

"I got it. It's my turn." Susie reached for it, much more awake that I was. She listened for a minute and then said "Thank God. Thank you too, Rick."

She turned to me. "Julie's in recovery, she's awake and everything looks good. The baby's vital signs are okay and she's holding her own. She's been moved to Riley Hospital."

She turned back to the phone. "Rick, we're caught in the middle of an ice storm so I don't know when we'll get there but we'll be there. God bless you.." Her voice broke, she shook her head and her eyes filled with tears as she handed me the phone.

"What kind of storm?" I heard Rick ask.

"Ice." I told him. "We're stuck and I don't know how long it's going to be before we get out of here."

"Just take your time, we're okay here. Julie already looks a hundred percent better. I just talked to her and she's doing great. The baby's doing okay too. They've got her rigged up with oxygen to help her breathe." He paused to catch his breath. "And by the way, her name is Riley Marie."

Riley Marie. That was perfect. I had not even seen this baby but the name fit her to a tee. I somehow felt, no, knew that should be her name. It was really weird. In that instant, she was no longer a threat to my daughter's well being, no longer something that had us driving to Indiana like maniacs or even just an abstract being occupying space in Julie's womb. She was a little person who had the same blood as Susie and I coursing through her veins. I loved her immediately and knew instinctively that we wouldn't venture very far from her for the next few years. Here was a member of our next generation, weighing no more than a box of Morton salt, and she had just altered our whole retirement plan.

"God." I thought, "you better take care of that little girl".

"That's perfect, Rick." I said, coming back to my senses. "It's a great name. Give them both a kiss for us."

I heard Jason in the background saying something about food as Rick hung up the phone.

"What was that about her name?" Susie asked.

"Her name is Riley Marie." I told her. "I couldn't have come up with a better one myself."

The ice was still coming down as we put the phone away. The most exciting thing to happen to our family in the last twenty five years was over and we had missed it. No matter, though. Things were looking better by the minute.

We considered getting up and getting dressed but decided against that. Pulling the covers up, our heads hit the pillows and we slept.

Chapter Ten

We woke up about nine and exchanged grandma and grandpa greetings. Looking out the window, we could see that the ice had stopped accumulating, at least for the moment. Susie started the coffeepot as I switched on the radio to get a weather report.

"Ja-e-sus loves Central Texas, he loves Dallas and of course, He loves you." The radio voice said. For the most part, I had never for a minute doubted that although that belief was on shaky ground right at the moment.

I twisted the dial. "Corinthians, my children of God, says that...'

One more twist. "Repent, or your soul's on it's way to eternal damn...."

Twist again. "And Ja-esus said..."

"What the hell?" I said, talking to myself. "Where's the weather?"

Twist. "God so loved the wor...!

"Son of a bitch", I said to Susie. "This is Saturday, isn't it?"

We had obviously strayed into some pocket of the bible belt. There was nothing but religion on the air. I grabbed the phone and called my brother. Jason had called him so he had the whole story. Having no grandchildren, he was almost as excited as us.

"The weather channel is covering the storm." He told me. "The ice is on I-35 way up into Arkansas. There's no going that way. There's some ice to the east but only as far as Longview."

"Longview?" an irritated tone was in my voice. "Longview what and where in the hell is it?"

"It's over around the Louisiana border. If you can get that far, you can go to Alabama and get around the storm. They're calling for thirty five degrees this afternoon in Dallas so it should get better."

"Who's calling for thirty five degrees?"

"What?"

"Never mind. Keep us posted."

"I'll do that, Grampa."

Susie had gotten us towels and clean clothes. We walked gingerly across the campground to the showers. The ice had coated the building and the ladies room door was frozen shut. Susie yelled at me to help so I banged on the door and got it to open.

The men's room door was already half open when I got to that side of the building. I sat my shaving kit on the sink and noticed that the basin was shaped in the outline of Texas.

"Pretty tacky." I mumbled.

The Urinal had an 'out of order' sign dangling from the handle so I stepped into an empty toilet stall. Along the bottom of the door someone had scratched "tap toe for BJ" into the paint.

"Tap toe for BJ. What in the hell is that", unconsciously tapping my foot to some unrecognizable tune running thru my head. Who is BJ?

Before I could figure it our, a voice came from behind the occupied stall next to me.

"Hey Bud, you got any toilet paper over there? Some body stole everything out of this one."

The request shocked me. Down where I came from, men didn't talk in bathrooms. They just did their business and got out.

"Uh…. Sure." I said, lowering my tone of voice an octave or so, trying to sound as manly as possible.

My God. How much should I give him? A few sheets, the whole roll? My mind was scrambling. I tried to recall any studies that had been done on the average consumption of toilet paper per activity. Would he be insulted if I passed him a big wad?

Half in a panic, I tore off a handful and handed it under the wall.

"Thanks, Pal." The disembodied voice came at me. "Where you from?"

Arkansas. Tell him Arkansas. Before I could formulate a lie to tell this guy, a female voice came from the general direction of the door.

"Is everything all right in here?

"Hell no it ain't alright, Pearlene." My next door neighbor said. "Some idiot stole the toilet paper in here again."

"Dad gum it, Leroy." The voice said, coming much closer. "I told you to bring your own, then you wouldn't have no problem.".

'Ja-esus." I thought, suddenly remembering the surroundings we had pulled into the previous night. The term 'trailer trash' leaped into my mind as the sound of footsteps approached our end of the bathroom. The thought occurred to me that this woman might be coming into the stall with me.

I looked around for an escape route but none was to be found. I was preparing to make a run for it when a roll of toilet paper, apparently tossed by the lady, bounced off my foot and under the wall to the next stall.

"You need anything in there, Mister?" I guessed she was talking to me.

"No mamm. Everything's fine." My voice cracked like a thirteen year old who had just been caught fondling himself.

"Well, alrighty, then." she said. "You just holler if you need something."

A sound like the door scraping the floor echoed her words. I didn't know if she had left or if someone else had come in. All inclinations of doing my business had disappeared the moment that female voice had penetrated our little male sanctuary. All I wanted was to get out of there. I waited a minute or so and didn't hear anyone moving around. Leroy next door was now making guttural noises that frightened me. He was either having a very good or a very bad time in there. Even though it went against my most basic of beliefs, I interrupted Leroy's morning toilette.

"Is she gone?" There was now so much bass in the tone of my voice that I sounded like one of the Foggy Mountain boys.

"Yep." He said "All clear."

Taking the word of a man I had not yet, nor would I ever, see face to face, I left the stall, crossed the room and tried shaving. The Texas shaped sink made this endeavor impossible. The faucet poured water into the panhandle around Amarillo and the area was too small to get my hands in there to do anything. Abandoning the shaving idea, I jumped in the shower before Pearlene showed up again.

Chapter Eleven

Water was melting off the ice covered and gutterless roof of the office building when we headed back to the camper. This was a good sign. I started to tell her of my experience.

"You wouldn't have believed it, Susie."

Susie was incredulous and interrupted me before I even got to the Pearlene part.

"What's wrong with men talking in bathrooms? Women do it all the time. What are you supposed to do if you need toilet paper?"

"Well, I don't know but...." I was going to explain the rules of bathroom behavior to Susie but knew that it would do no good. She held little sympathy for men's macho peculiarities.

By noon, we could hear trucks moving around on the interstate. I got out my campground book and started calling places north and east of Dallas to find out how the weather was in their area. After talking to five or six people, it looked like the weather channel had been correct. We would have trouble trying to go North or northeast. There was no ice in Shreveport and although they were expecting record cold, the sky was clear. It was going to add about three hundred miles to our trip but we decided to go that way.

The Interstate had one slushy lane open as we made our way up the icy onramp. It was not a steep incline but I was holding my breath, hoping that nothing would stop in front of us. Our truck with that heavy trailer on the back would never get rolling on that slush filled ramp if we had to stop.

Susie flipped on the CB radio to see if we could get any details on road conditions. It was full of chatter but not much real information.

The highway maintenance people had seemed content to let Mother Nature and the traffic clean off the ice. It worked for the most part. The underpasses were a different story, though. Sunlight could not reach those areas so the roadway under the bridges was still coated with ice. The first icy underpass we encountered had the rear end of the truck trying to slide sideways and after that, we quickly learned to slow down, hold our breath and not do anything rash when we went under a bridge. Many truck drivers had obviously failed to learn that lesson. We inched our way through several underpasses where overturned trucks were blocking one or more lanes.

The road atlas predicted about a four hour trip to Shreveport. I was figuring on eight and it took just over six. Once we cleared Dallas and all of its icy underpasses, the driving became easier and when we passed by the Longview exit, we were traveling at the speed limit.

We talked to Julie and she insured us that she was okay.

"I haven't seen the baby yet but Rick has pictures on the internet." We got the address of the web site with the idea of logging on somewhere and looking at the pictures.

We also gave up the idea of making a mad dash home. It was going to be Monday before we arrived at the hospital and it seemed futile at this point to drive like maniacs. We found a nice campground when we reached Shreveport. There was no internet access available but we decided to stay anyway. I needed a drink after the icy highways and other events of the day. It took only a short time to unhook the trailer and unload the bicycles so we had some room to move around.

We decided to celebrate the baby's birth so when we finished getting everything set up, we drove to dinner at a place that the campground host recommended. We had some excellent fresh catfish and a nice cold beer. One thing notable about the meal was that the fish was served with large thick slices of white onion. We asked the waitress what to do with the onion and in her best southern drawl, she replied

"Why, y'all eat it with your fish. It's goo-ooo-ood."

And it was. A forkful of fish and a forkful of onion washed down with sweet tea, an invention we need to bring up north, really hit the spot. It was the first real meal we had eaten in three days. I went through four slices of onion and asked for more.

I stood about four feet away from the cashier when we were leaving, afraid that my breath might knock her down.

"How was everything? She said in a jolly manner. "Did y'all enjoy the catfish?"

"Yes Mamm." I said in my best southern accent. "It was jest fine. Real good. What's the damage?"

I looked up from my wallet in time to see her eyes blinking rapidly as she tried to reply. It was probably a reaction to the onions, I thought, but then again, she might have been flirting with me.

It did get very cold in Shreveport that night. As a matter of fact, it was a record cold. Our electric heater did a credible job of keeping us warm. Against my better judgement, I let it run all night, hoping it wouldn't catch fire. There was no reason to believe that it would. I was just being cautious.

Somewhere, during the night, I woke up, suddenly figuring out something that been bothering me all day. "B.J.! tap toe for for B.J." Crap. Had I been tapping my foot?

"What did you say?" Susie asked.

"Nothing. Go back to sleep."

Chapter Twelve

Sunday morning found me headed for the showers with my toothbrush to try and scrub away the onion taste that coated my tongue. An acrid smoke was rolling out of the camper doorway when I returned. Susie stood in the camper waving a towel at the television set that had fallen off its shelf a couple of days earlier. It was perched on the table and black smoke was pouring somewhere out of its guts.

"I thought we should see if it worked." She said. Susie had always fancied herself a TV repair person although she had no idea how anything electronic worked. We had been through this several times over the years so I wasn't at all surprised to see her trying to fix this one. It was impossible to be mad at her, though. Hell, she was a brand new grandmother.

We got the camper ready to go and I took the TV set to the dumpster. I was walking back from the trash area and watching Susie trying to maneuver my bicycle into the camper.

"Hang on. I'll help you." But before I could get there, her foot slipped off the camper step and she fell forward, banging her nose hard on the bicycle frame. She fell to her knees, grabbing her nose with her hands. The blood was gushing through her fingers when I reached her. I helped her inside, sat her down at the kitchen table and ran to the showers to get a dishpan full of cold water.

I applied cold wet washcloths across the bridge of her nose and the bleeding slowed to a trickle after several applications of the homemade compress. I helped her to the bathrooms where she put more cold water on it.

"We need to get you to a hospital to see if anything's broken."

"We're nod goding to any hospidal. We're goding to see that baby." she said, holding the cloth to her face. "I'll be fine."

Her nose had started to swell as I got her in the truck and gave her an ice filled towel to apply. She leaned her head back, put the towel on her nose and we headed for home.

Susie slept for the next eight hours as we drove through Louisiana and Mississippi. We had never spent any time in either state and this day wasn't any different. We began turning Northeast as we crossed into Alabama. We stopped for the night outside of Birmingham in a State Park. The young park ranger was very sympathetic to Susie's injury. The area under both her eyes was turning black and her nose was taking on Jimmy Durante proportions. I felt certain it was broken but the ranger who had a little first aid training, gingerly examined it and assured us that it wasn't. He found us an ice pack and then, since it was dark, he helped us to get the camper parked.

"You folks fixin to go to Florida?" He asked.

"No, we're headed north."

We told him of the excitement of our last few days and when he heard about the internet pictures, he took us into his office and retrieved them from the web site. There was Riley Marie, her legs no bigger than a nurses finger.

We looked at this little bird like creature with tiny tubes in her nose and mouth and other tubes attached to her stomach and her toes.

"My Goodness", the ranger said. "She's a cutie."

This was probably an out and out lie but it made our day. It was our very first compliment on our new grandbaby and it couldn't have come at a better time. The ranger, whose name I never got, copied the pictures onto our laptop computer so we could look at them at our leisure.

We arrived at University Hospital at 1:00 in the afternoon on Monday. The trip had taken ninety eight hours of fright, frustration, pain and occasional elation. It was all worth it though when we finally got to Julie's room and saw that she was okay. She was in good spirits because Rick had wheeled her over to see the baby earlier in the day.

"Oh my gosh. Your poor nose." Julie said to Susie

"Her nose is fine." I told Julie. "How are you feeling, Miss? I asked her, using the name I had called her since she was a little girl.

"I'm doing great. My blood pressure is up a little but that's only supposed to be temporary."

"Who does she look like?" Susie asked with a nasally inflection. .

"It's kind of hard to tell." Julie said. "She has a lot of tubes in her nose and mouth. When Rick takes you over to see her, maybe you can get an idea."

That was Susie's cue. "Okay Rick, can we go see the baby now?" she asked, dancing around like a woman who had just become a grandmother.

"I thought you'd never ask."

The baby was in Riley Children's hospital, on the medical campus but a ten minute walk through a maze of tunnels. On the way, Rick gave us instructions on what to do when we got to the preemie area.

There were strict hand washing procedures that had to be followed and limits on the number of visitors. Only one of us at a time could go in with Rick. Susie went first. There was no keeping her out of there.

I looked over her shoulder as she went through the door. There were three isolettes along each of two walls. They were surrounded by several stainless steel machines each of which had an array of blinking lights. A tiny arm and a cap covered head were visible in the nearest of the cribs. That was our granddaughter. Blue light emanated from beneath the blanket covering her.

I went to the waiting room and sat with a dozen other folks who were there to see premature babies. Over the next three months, we were to get to know many of these people well as Riley Marie struggled to live. We shared news of advances and setbacks and shed tears with some of them as they prepared to go home empty handed.

But that was in the future. Thankfully we were blissfully ignorant of all this on that first day. Susie came in the waiting room with a grin on her face that almost matched the size of her swollen nose.

"Well….?" I said.

"The ranger was right. She's a cutie."

Epilogue:

Riley Marie spent the first three months of her life at James Whitcomb Riley Hospital where her parents, grandparents, other relatives and friends were taken on almost daily roller coaster rides of elation one minute and despair the next. There was a heart operation, lung problems, possible eye and ear problems, blood problems and twice a week scans for excessive brain bleeding. Julie and Rick remained calm and very involved in all the decision making processes.

Today Riley continues to make progress. Her oxygen tube was removed at four months of age and she breathed normally from the get go. At this writing, she is just over four years old. Her weight is in excess of thirty-one pounds She is pretty much a regular four year old, albeit a little small and the outlook of everyone involved is that she will lead a normal life.

Now, her grandparents, though, that's a different story. It was a blessing that we were on the road and ignorant of much that was going on. Susie is a rock and would have been a great help had we been here but I doubt that I would have survived knowing of the threats of real danger to my daughter and her child.

One's thing for sure. Riley Marie's presence in our lives is something we could not do without. Our lives have never been the same and our harrowing trip home is now a fading memory. Still, now that everything turned out okay, it's safe to say that we wouldn't trade one minute of that trip for anything.

Punkin? What punkin you talkin' about?

Riley Marie was released from the hospital on her original due date and came home to begin her life with her mom and dad. She still had the oxygen tube and her feedings were exercises in patience but overall, she was doing much better than any of us expected. Our daughter, Julie, took a three month leave of absence from her job to spend Riley's first summer with her at home. There was no way that Susie was going to stray too far so we decided that we would abandon our travels temporarily and give Susie the chance to care for Riley for the remainder of 2002.

Our decision to postpone our travel plans gave me the chance to put out a vegetable garden. I had put out a garden for the last 25 years of my working life and had reluctantly given up that hobby when we decided to travel. Early June was a little late to get seeds in the ground but I still could have home grown produce if I bought plants from the nursery.

Gardening was one of the things that seemed to just come naturally to me. After we moved out to the country, I started buying the 'Mother Earth News', a magazine that touted self sufficiency and a movement back to simpler living. Many of their suggestions were beyond my capabilities; home generated electricity with windmills and homemade wood burning furnaces come to mind but one thing they talked about enthusiastically was something I could attempt. I could plant a vegetable garden.

I started tentatively by ordering a gardening catalogue from the magazine. I ordered a few things out of the catalogue and that opened the floodgates.

Before you could say Zucchini, my mailbox was full of catalogues that had anything even remotely to do with outdoor living. And it wasn't just that one time, either. Once I was on the mailing list, I never got off.

In subsequent years, the arrival of these things served as a barometer of the weather for me. I knew the worst of winter was over when the garden catalogues started arriving. Catalogues for trees and plants, vegetable seeds, various gardening implements and lawn furniture overflowed our mailbox. I would pore over the pages for hours during the long winter nights, making lists of items to buy and drawing detailed plans of my garden plot, trying to squeeze in everything on my ever increasing list of edible plant life.

The seed companies were always prompt in their shipments and tomato seeds of all varieties arrived in little boxes as did the asparagus and onion sets, the strawberry plants and the seed potatoes. The seeds went into dirt filled egg cartons that I had been accumulating all winter. They were all lined up on shelves by the kitchen windows. I thinned the little shoots religiously as they popped out of the dirt. I lusted after a Troy Bilt rear tine tiller but could never see my way clear to withholding enough food from the kids to allow me to buy one. I had to make do with an old tiller that just about beat me to death every time I went into the garden with it. It flopped around in that dirt like a recently beheaded chicken and I vowed that someday I would have one of those tillers that allow eighty year old ladies to plow five acres with one manicured hand; the kind that made the cover of the Mother Earth News.

I waited anxiously for Good Friday to plant my potatoes and used the farmers almanac to pick the days that my strawberries, onions and asparagus went in the ground. I marked the days off the calendar waiting for the last possible frost date to get the tomatoes and peppers planted. I also invariably ended up throwing away the plants I had lovingly cultivated from seed because the plant farm had much better looking specimens. Of course, this drove Susie crazy and I tried explaining Darwin's theory to her but I'm not sure she bought it.

I've tried growing about everything over the years. I grew peanuts when President Jimmy Carter was elected and then I grew broccoli after President Bush made light of it. I had been experimenting with organically grown vegetables and this broccoli turned out beautifully. Suddenly, I realized I no longer had to be a slave to the profiteering rat race, making my daily commute to the city like some task driven king sized ant. I could make our fortune selling organic broccoli to the burgeoning masses who were begging for healthy foods. I plucked several stalks and took it in the house for Susie to prepare. She dropped them in a pan of boiling water and these little green things quickly came to the surface.

"What is that?" she asked suspiciously.

She picked one out of the water and let out a scream.

"Aaa-aa-gh! It's a worm. It's full of worms." She grabbed the pan now filled with squirming green worms, ran outside and dumped the lot onto my compost heap. That was the end of the organic farming. It was also the end of growing broccoli.

My last endeavor in growing vegetables for profit came about the year I grew the giant pumpkin. I had managed to acquire some pumpkin seeds from a gypsy lady on the eastside who had a shop next to a little diner where I ate my lunch. She sold exotic seeds and also read palms and tea leaves. She was very mysterious about the origin of these pumpkin seeds but finally admitted that she got them from a group of Mediterranean gypsies on her last visit home. I didn't know whether to believe her or not but I planted the seeds in a pile of three year old cow manure. The vine that grew out of that pile was tremendous. It overwhelmed the garden but it didn't bear much fruit. As a matter of fact, a single pumpkin was the only offspring but as the summer wore on, it kept growing until it overwhelmed my garden. All the neighbors came to visit and view my huge pumpkin.

I kept turning it as it grew trying to maintain some semblance of pumpkin shape until the day when it got too big to budge. I knew I had something special then. I had visions of winning pumpkin contests all over the Midwest and I was making plans to have one of those giant pumpkin pie fests that would get me into the Guinness book of world records. I envisioned a picture of myself in my flannel shirt and jeans, wearing my John Deere cap, leaning on my hoe and standing next to this leviathan of the vegetable world.

One cool fall morning, I went out to get a picture of the sunrise over my pumpkin and it was gone. It had disappeared. I noticed a trail of mashed down weeds and grass where it had been drug from my garden thru the neighbors yard and out to the road. The trail picked up on the other side of the road and led directly to the house on the hill. I didn't need to bring in Sherlock Holmes to find out where my pumpkin went. I was never able to pin it on them but the twin teenage boys who lived in that house are now grown men with families. They are respected members of the community and while I could never get them to confess, I expect some day they'll step forward and own up to the heist of my pumpkin.

She had me there.
I couldn't insult the Pope.

A couple of months after Riley arrived home, her oxygen tubes were removed, making it much easier for her to travel. To celebrate, Susie and I took Riley Marie and her mother to Southern Indiana to visit my home town. I was ready to show her off.

When we got there, we drove by the cemetery where several of the gravestones, including the one for my parents, still had small American Flags flying next to them, placed there for the Independence Day celebration.

My Father was a world war two veteran and although he survived the war unhurt, he died in an accident less than a year after returning home. I was six years old, the middle child between an older sister and a younger brother. Another child was imminent, my mother being 8 months pregnant at the time of the accident.

A week after my father died, my mother delivered a stillborn baby boy. I attended, at six years old, another funeral service that has stayed with me since that day. I stood in the cemetery on one side of my Uncle holding his left hand while my sister was on the other side holding his right. My mother and my younger brother stayed at home.

The baby was buried beside his father, making one short mound of dirt next to a still fresh, but much longer one.

There wasn't a lot of money to go around so the Military headstone of my father sufficed to mark his grave. The Funeral home provided a flat, aluminum grave marker etched with 'Baby Grindstaff' on the flat surface. It was placed at ground level next to my father's marker where over the years, the grass inched its way over the surface until you had to dig to find it. Once, at the cemetery, I asked my mother why the baby didn't have a name and she sighed. "It was such a sad, hectic time. I didn't think about it. Baby was a good name because that's what he was; a baby."

Life went on and from time to time, I would think about that baby and wonder what he might have been like. There were two boys in our neighborhood who were born around the time the baby was and anytime an event of any importance took place for them, I took notice since he would have also been participating. At their First communion, I saw Baby in his little white outfit with his hands folded in prayer. Then there was Eighth grade graduation with his first suit and a burr haircut. His High School graduation was in 1964, the same year I got married. He could have been a groomsman, I remember thinking.

The baby faded from my thoughts as time went on and my own family grew.

One morning in 1976, my sister called my office.

"You better sit down," she told me and I did as she had told me. "Mother died last night." She said, her voice fading away into a sob.

A few days after the funeral, my brother, Ronnie and I sat with my sister going through our mother's stuff.

"We need to get a headstone." My sister told us. "I'll take care of ordering it and you two pitch in on the cost."

A few months later, The phone rang. It was my sister.

"The headstone's in." she said. "You need to come down and see it."

That Saturday morning, I made the hundred mile trip where I picked up my sister, Vera Rose. I normally just call her Vera but the use of a middle name is a phenomenon that happens when you hit the city limits of my home town. It can't be helped. You just automatically start calling people by both of their Christian names.

We drove to the cemetery, parked the car and I helped her to the grave plot where a beautiful piece of granite sat. I looked at the headstone where my Father and mother's names and their wedding date were inscribed. It was very nice and I told her so.

"Come look at the other side." she said.

There on the back was the inscription 'Our Children: Vera Rose, Gordon Lee, Ronald Dale, Peter Bernard." I stared at it for a minute, knowing something was not right but not knowing immediately what it was. Then it hit me.

"Peter Bernard?" I said incredulously. "Who the hell is Peter Bernard? "

"He's our baby brother."

"That wasn't his name." I said, disbelief in my voice. "He didn't have a name."

"Well, he's got one now." She told me with the petulance that only an older sister can have.

"Vera Rose, you can't just name that baby."

"Why not?"

"Well, I don't know, but you just can't."

"Well, I did." She said, in that stubborn manner that had been driving me crazy since I was old enough to remember.

"There's probably a law against it, for one thing. " I told her. "Besides that, I don't like the name Peter Bernard." The thought of her hanging a moniker like that on my precious brother had me livid.

"There's no law against it." She said as if she really knew. "And why don't you like that name?"

"For one thing, Do you even know anybody named Peter."

"Only the first Pope, Smartass. And as for Bernard, there's our Uncle, our mother's brother." She retorted.

She had me there. The Pope? My uncle? I couldn't think of anything to say.

"You got a better name?" She continued.

"No. But, but….." I stammered, knowing from years of experience it was fruitless to argue with my sister.

"Okay. Peter Bernard it is, then" she told me.

I threw in the towel. It was already on the headstone. No point in telling her I already gave him a name years ago. I shook my head and slowly walked back to my car.

Sorry, Jimmy Ray. I tried.

PART FOUR
Winter in the sunshine state.

Bring 'er on back.

The end of the year came at us in a hurry and I was busy with two major projects: Trying to smooth our separation from our granddaughter and preparing for our departure to Florida for the remainder of the winter.

The Christmas trees and the outdoor lights were taken down and wadded into tangled messes that will be impossible to sort out next November. This year, just like the past 30 years, I have resolved that next year they will be put away neatly. The other New Years resolutions on weight, thriftiness, cheerfulness and orderliness were all made, broken and the holiday spirit was boxed up and put away for another 11 months. The days were slowly getting longer after passing the winter solstice and we were plunging headlong into the worst part of winter. Now that I could leave it behind, it didn't bother me unlike previous years, when I used to dread the long dreary days.

I spent the previous twenty five winters looking forward to an eagerly awaited February 2[nd,] hoping that a rodent in Pennsylvania could tell me if we had another six weeks of freezing weather or whether we could look forward to an early spring. I'm not exactly a rube. I knew that groundhog couldn't really predict the weather but it was just one of the many ways I used to get myself through those long Indiana winters.

Of course, now that I was retired, I didn't have to spend any time anticipating the prediction of Pauxatonie Phil because cold weather was a thing of the past for us. Our winter was going to be spent in the sun laying on a beach somewhere.

We had to wait until the snow had melted enough to let us get out of our driveway and when it had, we hooked up our fifth wheel camper and headed for I-65 south.

The trip to Florida was pretty uneventful with a few exceptions. We had the usual number of eighteen wheelers passing us, an unnerving event when you have a thirty foot camper, even a fifth wheel, in tow. Every time one would come by, I would try frantically to stay in my lane, not wanting to get sideswiped.

During one of these encounters, Susie turned to me and said "Why don't you just get behind one of them and get sucked like the race cars do?"

"Susie dear," I told her in my best Jeff Gordon imitation, "I believe that 'drafting' is the correct terminology. Please don't ever say 'sucked along' around anyone other than me." She had no other driving advice for me this trip.

Our destination on this part of the trip was the Southwestern part of Florida. We've spent several Spring break periods there and most of the time when we made the trip, we turned left in Nashville and then when we got to Chattanooga, we turned right and headed south through Atlanta. It's the most direct route but since we were no longer in a hurry, we decided to try a different direction. This meant traveling south through a couple of Alabama's cities that figured prominently in the Civil Rights battles of the nineteen sixties. I thought it might be interesting to visit some of the more historical stuff but we passed through Birmingham on Interstate 65 without even slowing down. I was surprised by the hills surrounding the city but I don't know why. I just figured it was flat.

Montgomery was another story. It was flat and we did get off the Interstate. I was busy looking for Highway 231 south and didn't see anything historical. I saw a sign saying that Selma, Alabama, one of the important civil rights sites, was some 60 miles away. I was under the impression it was much closer although I don't know why I thought that. Aside from that, all I saw were the same kinds of businesses that we had in Indiana lining both sides of highway 231; the road that would take us to Panama City, Florida. From there, we were going to our campground where we had reservations in a state park on St. George Island just east of Apalachicola.

The island is not easy to get to. In fact, they advertise it as part of the 'forgotten coast'. It's a beautiful drive from Panama City Beach on Highway 98. The water laps right at the edge of the roadway for part of the drive and I expect it would be an exciting ride during a storm.

A causeway and bridge have been built to provide access to the island where the park and campground occupy the east end of the land. It has level camping spots, a great beach and most of the topography is sand dunes. The best thing about this area is the seafood. We bought a pound of shrimp and a pint of oysters at one of the fishing boat docks and cooked them on the beach. I had the oysters all to myself Susie's aversion to oysters is already well known so I won't bring it up again.

Leaving St. George after a two night stay, we drove east on around the bay until we reached Highway 19 where we headed south to meet up with Interstate 75 north of Tampa. Highway 19 passes through several small towns and the drive gave us a glimpse into what Old Florida looked like before everybody in the country moved there. We stopped in Chiefland, Florida and visited a fresh produce stand. I was in heaven; fresh vegetables in January. We also stopped alongside the road where a fellow was smoking mullet in his front yard. We had not had this before, It being an old Florida treat.

We arrived at our home for the next two months in Punta Gorda, Florida with the snow shovel still in the back of the truck. The Florida natives were not sure what this big flat thing with the handle might be. Some even thought it could be a weapon. I tried to explain the concept of snow and how you have to move it around but I'm not sure I got through to them.

We landed in a campground for people fifty five and older and when you pull into one of these, you can expect plenty of help parking your rig unless there's a bingo game going on in the recreation hall. The minute I put the truck in reverse and started inching the camper towards our assigned spot, fifteen or twenty old geezers popped out of their campers and started motioning me to turn this way and that. It's a little unsettling the first few times you experience this but you soon get used to it. I guess some of them don't have enough to do.

It didn't take long to settle in to a routine. A daily trip to the grocery, the art center and the library kept us quite busy. I'd tell you more about it but I gotta go now. Some new people have just pulled in and from the looks of that rig they're driving, they're gonna need help getting that baby in their spot.

I swear I'm not a pervert.

A few days after we arrived, I stood in our tiny camper bathroom getting dressed and tugging on my jockey shorts to get them arranged the way I like. Susie was sitting on the bed studying me and she said

"Do they make underwear for left handed men"?

That stopped me in my tracks. "Say What?"

"Look at the flap. It should be the other way for lefties." She said.

"Get out of town." I told her.

"No, I'm serious."

"Susie, trust me, lefties just have to suffer because there's no such thing as left handed underwear."

I finished dressing, picked up my wallet and headed out the door to Walmart to get some stuff for the camper.

"Why don't you look for that underwear while you're there? Susie said as I climbed into the truck.

"Right." I said, backing out of the campsite, being careful not to hit any of the old geezers piling out the front doors of their campers. There were about twenty of these guys and at any one time, five to ten of them were on unofficial duty serving as the guardians of the Southern Florida campground where we were staying. The rest were out reconnoitering the day's early bird dining specials. There is not always a lot of things to occupy their time so they made themselves useful by helping everyone maneuver their vehicles on the narrow roadways.

Every time I started that diesel engine in my truck, out they came, hoping that the driver of a large diesel pusher would need some help. Some times I wish I didn't have that diesel. Maybe I could sneak out without them hearing me. The disappointment in their eyes as they saw it was only me was evident as they turned around and headed back inside while I drove away.

The Walmart greeter smiled at me as I went in. Not a bad job, I thought. Maybe someday......

I was heading for the automotive section when I passed a lady wearing the familiar blue vest. She was straightening up a stack of levi's in the men's department.

"What the heck." I said to myself. *"Maybe they do have them."*

"Excuse me, mamm." I said, walking up to her. "Do you happen to know if you carry jockey shorts for left handed men?"

She turned her head and looked at me with a stare that practically shouted "I SAW THIS GUY ON AMERICA'S MOST WANTED.

"My God", I thought, *I've picked a woman who thinks men are perverts and I'm going to jail.*

"I beg your pardon." She said "Did you say left handed......"

"No. No. That's all right. It was nothing." I was stammering and backing away simultaneously from the woman. Any second now, I expected her to yell "Code Red" or whatever it is the help broadcasts when they want the authorities.

I hurried away, got the stuff I needed and headed for the checkout. I avoided the men's department and kept an eye out for the lady as I put my purchases on the belt.

The young guy on the register looked me over.

"Them ol' Packer boys of yours didn't do to well last week, did they?" He said, smiling.

I figured he was talking about the football team but I didn't see my connection with them. Still I said "No, they didn't."

He continued ringing up items.

"How 'bout them Falcons?" He said again, the big grin on his face getting even bigger while dragging my new wire grill brush over the scanner. "Them At-lanta boys of mine sure made them Packer boys look bad."

I smiled back at him.

"Yes, they did." I said, wanting to tell him that I didn't even like professional football.

He pushed the last item on the belt through the scanner.

"Seventeen dollars and eight cents." He said. "Maybe your Packer boys 'll have better luck next year."

That was enough for me. I handed him a twenty and said "What makes you think I'm a Packer fan?"

He kind of nodded his head up and down, moving his eyebrows towards the top of his head.

"What…?" I said.

He raised his hand and touched his forehead.

I got it. My hat. I took it off, looked at it and turned to him. "That says PACERS." They're a basketball team up in Indiana.

He looked at me like I'd just shot him in the chest as he realized his mistake. An unintelligible noise that sounded like "Ooooooh…pnnn." came out of his mouth and his face took on the hue of an over ripe sugar beet.

I was as embarrassed as he was. I said "It's an easy mistake to make. The K could have fallen off the h……"

This was only making it worse. It was too late. His head was down and he was bent over the register furiously counting money.

"You were right, though. Them Packer boys did take it on the chin." I said to him as he handed me my change. I hoped it was right because there was no way I was gonna embarrass him any further by counting the money in front of him.

"Well???" Susie asked me shortly after I returned. "What did you find out? Do they make left handed …."

"I can't believe I let you talk me into that." I interrupted. "I almost got arrested for being a pervert."

"Ha." She said. "Don't give me that. You didn't even ask."

"No," I said, "I did ask. They don't have left handed underwear but I did stop a guy who was writing a check with his left hand and asked him about it."

"And what did he say? She asked me.

"He told me that it's no problem. You just need to wear your briefs inside out."

I'm not going a penny more.

The national pastime in Southwest Florida is visiting garage sales and flea markets. I know they have the same thing in Indiana but there's always something else to do at home so flea markets were all new to me. Susie, however, is an expert on these home made entrepreneurships so she talked me into making the rounds.

We set out from our campground one Saturday morning to arrive at a field full of cars parked haphazardly amidst tables piled high with everything imaginable. We needed a toaster but I was a little leery about buying anything. Not Susie. She was in her element and almost seemed to be glowing as she wasted no time taking off for the middle of this pandemonium, leaving me standing there.

I wandered down a row of booths and stopped in front of a dilapidated camper. A little old lady was arranging a few items of what I perceived to be junk on a makeshift table that leaned precipitously to the left. This thing also served as her sales counter. An old gentleman whom I guessed was her husband was backing out of the camper with an armload of other trash.... er .... Treasure.

"Be careful, Harold." The little old lady said. "Don't break that mirror. It's almost priceless."

The only mirror I saw in Harold's pile of stuff looked like something recently pried from a wall at the Motel six. These poor people were obviously confused about the value of their stuff but I thought maybe I should buy something from them anyway. One look at them and I had some how gotten the idea that their next meal might depend on what they sold on this particular Saturday.

I picked up a coffee mug. I'd seen some at the previous booth that were a quarter and I figure I could go that much to help them out.

"How much?" I said to the lady, bent over most likely from the onset of Osteoporosis. She squinted at the cup and said "I've got the macular degeneration, honey, but I believe that one is four dollars. That cup goes way back in our family. I think my Uncle Albert, no...., it was my Uncle Lester gave us that cup for a wedding present over forty years ago."

I looked at the mug. A printed picture of a shrimp occupied one side and the words '2001 - Gulf Shores Shrimp Festival.' took up the other.

I could see I was in trouble. I was not about to tell this almost blind lady that the cup wasn't even four years old, much less forty. I didn't want the cup but I did want her to be able to eat.

"I'll give you two dollars." I said.

"Well, I don't know, honey" she said, sounding a lot like Maude Frickert. "I've got the macular degeneration, you know."

"Yes...," I said. "I believe you told me."

"I can let it go for two fifty but only because Uncle Lester has passed." she said and her voice seemed to crack. "He'd turn over in his grave if he knew I was selling family heirlooms."

I wanted to turn around and walk away but a lifetime of helping old ladies across the street; I was a boy scout, you know, would not let me. I was hooked.

"Okay." I fished in my pocket and pulled out a crumpled five dollar bill and a handful of change.

'Say honey, is that the new Illinois quarter you got there?" Maude says, reaching into the little pile of coins I had in my hand. "I've been looking everywhere for one."

I watched as she nimbly worked her way around my palm through the pennies to extricate the Illinois quarter, two dimes, a nickel and the five dollar bill. She reached into the little nail apron tied around her waist and pulled out a wad of money that would have bailed Robert Blake out of the L.A. lockup.

She licked her thumb, peeled off three bills, handed them to me and said "Thank you, honey. You take good care of Uncle Lester's mug."

I wandered on down the lane with my Gulf Shores Shrimp Festival mug to a table loaded with paper back books. A hand lettered sign taped to the front of the table said 'Romance — twenty five cents.'

I pointed to the sign and said to the frizzy blond lady behind the table;
"You're a pretty cheap date."

She looked up, cigarette dangling from the corner of her mouth, peered through the cloud rising from the smoldering tobacco and closed her left eye to fend off the smoke. She stared at me with the remaining eye, shook her head and decided I must be some simpleton just escaped from police custody.

"Get outta here before I call a cop." She said.

I was fumbling around, still trying to think of a witty retort, when Susie walked up and got me off the hook.

"No good stuff here. Let's do the garage sales."

We drove a couple of miles and parked across the road from a huge home with an orange tile roof. The back yard sloped down to a canal where a yacht as long as the house rested in the water.

The place was beautiful but I didn't notice much about it. Instead, the part of the place that caught my eye was a four slice toaster resting on a table in the middle of the sculptured, multi colored driveway. It was marked down from two dollars to seventy five cents. I smelled BARGAIN.

"Does it work? I asked the guy behind the table.

"It did when I brought it out here," He said, taking off his yacht club hat and smoothing back his silvery hair.

There's something bizarre about dickering over pocket change with the owner of a half million dollar boat parked behind a three quarter million dollar house but I persevered.

"I'll give you fifty cents."

"I don't know," he says. "I paid thirty dollars new."

I found myself starting to feel bad for this guy whose monthly boat fuel bill was probably more than my social security check but I was also still smarting from my encounter with Maude Frickert and needed to recoup my losses. I moved in for the kill.

"Fifty cents. That's my final offer."

"You're stealing it." He said, pushing the toaster towards me.

I paid the man and headed for the campground with Susie protesting all the way.

"I wasn't finished." She said.

"We'll go back next week."

Arriving at the camper, I made a pot of coffee, grabbed the bread and popped two slices into my new toaster. A minute later, I was eating toast and drinking coffee from my new two dollar and fifty cents Gulf Shores shrimp festival mug.

Life is good.

Who you calling an old geezer?

I've been trying to play some golf while I'm down here in Florida, if you can call what I do, golf. The only problem I'm having is that I don't have a lot of golf playing built into our entertainment budget. Because there are eight jillion people who made the trip down here specifically to play golf, it can easily cost seventy five dollars or more to tee it up.

Luckily, There's a golf course just down the street from where we're camping and I have been trying to find time to go over there and play a round. It's just a nine hole par three course but it would be fine for me to hit the ball around. It's about ten dollars to play but I came up with a way to save even that. I got this really brilliant idea one day as I watched the young guy mowing the greens.

I walked over and waited patiently while he parked the mower.

"May I help you?" he said politely when he noticed me watching him.

"I got a proposition for you." I told the guy. "I'll come over here every day and help you out. I don't want any pay, I'll just play a round of golf for every couple hours that I work."

There was no way he could turn down a deal like that. He looked me over real good and his polite demeanor turned ugly.

"Get outta here." He said. He had a look on his face that made me think he was gonna spit at me. "Do you have any idea how many of you old geezers wander over here every day to make me that offer? Don't any of you have anything to do?"

At this point, he might as well have quit talking. He was just wasting his breath. I had quit listening at 'you old geezers."

Me? An old geezer. I've got news for him. That's impossible.

Okay, maybe I did listen to Harry Truman's inauguration because there wasn't any television to watch it on and maybe trying to call General Eisenhower 'President' was a little unnatural but that doesn't make me an old man.

I know it hasn't been that long ago when my hand was pried from my mother's fingers by Sister Mary Ellen as she tried to coax me into her first grade classroom. Old geezers don't remember that kind of stuff.

I'll admit that, when I was young, our house didn't have door locks and locking the keys in the car was unheard of. Why? Because the doors were never locked and the keys were always left in the car. Why would you take them out? Today we lock car doors, buy expensive alarm systems, put 'The Club' on the steering wheel, keep a pit bull in the back seat and paste a sticker on the bumper that says "This car protected by Smith and Wesson". Even if I remember better days, it doesn't make me old.

I know time goes by but it doesn't seem like more than a few months ago that I met Susie and it couldn't have been many more months after that when I watched her walk down the aisle of the church toward me. She had a wonderful grin on her face as she hung on to her dad's arm and the wedding dress she wore as we stepped up to the main altar of St. Patrick's is still under our bed in a big old cardboard box. That ought to prove I'm not old.

Sure, I remember standing in the middle of Ritter Avenue at two in the morning on a blustery December night. I had stopped my chain smoking and my pacing up and down the street long enough to blow warm air into my frozen hands. I was also praying for all I was worth as Susie lay in a room at Community hospital trying her best to deliver our first child. Why wasn't I with her? Husbands weren't allowed in the room in those days. I couldn't remember all that if it didn't just happen, could I?

Many of my high school friends are watching their great grandchildren play soccer or basketball but that doesn't make them old. Well, maybe it does but I don't have any great grandchildren. I barely have a grandchild. Who's that guy think he is?

Good Lord, I haven't even decided yet if Richard Nixon was guilty and I'm just now realizing the horrible mistakes we made in Vietnam. I still get goose bumps remembering how Susie and I waited, along with the rest of the country, for Three Mile Island to blow up and poison us all with radioactive particles.. But that couldn't have been more than a couple of years ago, just like Mount St. Helens and landing a man on the moon.

I can still hear almost everything Susie says and I may have a little gray hair but for the most part, it's still all there. I'm certainly not one of those forty mile an hour guys in the high speed lane and driving after dark is no problem for me. What's this guy doing calling me old?

I'm alive, aren't I? So what if half the Beatles and two thirds of the Bee-Gees are dead? I'm not and I'm not positive that Elvis is dead either. That young whippersnapper on the golf course has his nerve.

Me? An old Geezer? I don't think so.

Don't look down, whatever you do.

My name is Gordon and I'm afraid of heights, especially really tall bridges. There, the secret is out and I feel better now. I'm pretty good with bridges that are flat but the ones where the roadway rises to a steep incline scare me half to death. Having said this, though, the most frightening bridge I was ever on was a flat one down in Appalachia probably forty five years ago.

My mom, my brother and I were on or way to visit my sister in North Carolina and we were winding our way through the mountains on two lane roads that didn't seem wide enough for one car, let alone two. I had only recently learned to drive and was half out of my mind with fright at the severe drop offs on the edges of the road. I rounded one of the passes to confront a bridge hung from one mountain side to another. It wasn't particularly long and by itself, it was no more scary than any bridge I'd been across but something about this one was different. A banner starting above the entrance to the bridge and wrapped around the corner clear across the chasm proclaimed in scarlet red letters at least twenty feet tall that "Jesus Saves."

I had not ever doubted that for a minute but at that particular moment in my life, I needed no reminding of it. I went under that sign hoping that eternity wasn't just ahead and resisting the temptation to close my eyes.

The second worst bridge is one I've been over several times and I hate it every trip. It's called the Sunshine Skyway and we drive across it when we go to Saint Petersburg from our southern Florida campground. It's the quickest way there and the only way to avoid it is to go around the bay through Tampa and add fifty or so miles to the trip. For those of you not familiar with it, the skyway traverses the water where Tampa Bay meets the Gulf of Mexico.

It's a beautiful drive but somewhat unnerving for someone like myself. Much of the trip of ten miles or so is a causeway and conventional bridges fifteen or twenty feet above the water.

The skyway part of the trip is a suspension structure that rises a couple of hundred feet above the water to allow shipping traffic access to the bay. Over the years, I have made an effort to cure myself of bridge fear but not with this baby. It's either because it's too high or else it's because of what happened on the original version of this bridge. The center section was knocked down some years ago by a runaway barge and several people perished when they drove out on the bridge in the fog and plunged into the water. That story always makes me a little queasy and has been the source of more than one nightmare.

What's left of the original bridge is now advertised as the 'world's longest fishing pier' and it's presence to me is a constant reminder of what could happen to this thing I'm driving across. Susie was not concerned at all. Heights have never bothered her and in more than one of my stressful instances of high altitude driving, she has expressed her appreciation of some bit of far off scenery, scaring the daylights out of me. I like complete quiet when I'm more than a few feet off of old terra firma.

The first glimpse of the suspension towers comes from several miles away. From this vantage point, the large tractor-trailers crawling up the structure look like little ants struggling to make their way to the top. Cars are not visible from this distance but can be detected by the glint of sunlight off their tiny little windshields.

We started across the causeway and I gave Susie her usual warning to keep quiet when we get up there. I never go very fast on this bridge and always stick to the right lane so that the faster traffic can pass me. A nice wide shoulder gives some measure of comfort. It would provide a little room to maneuver in case a sudden gust of hurricane force winds would knock me towards the sheer drop and certain death. On this day, however, they were working on the roadbed and the slow lane had been moved onto the shoulder and right up against the EDGE!!!

I wouldn't get in that lane if my life depended on it and at that point, I believed that it did. The speedier drivers were just out of luck until I got off that bridge. I moved into the left lane and started up this first cousin to a ski slope.

My breathing was approaching hyper-ventilation speed and my eyes were looking straight ahead as I concentrated on getting to the top. I risked a glance in the rear view mirror at the long line of traffic piling up behind me. This made me even more nervous so I squeezed the steering wheel to the point where I thought it might actually break. It took only a second to loosen my death grip when I got this mental picture of the wheel shattering into a thousand pieces. Just as we reached the summit, Susie, contrary to my orders, yelled out.

"Oh God, look down there."

I'd look. In a pigs eye. My gaze didn't move one iota from the road ahead. I don't know what she saw but I was not about to look. If the whole side of that thing had just collapsed, too bad. I was not looking.

"The sailboats. Aren't they beautiful?" she said.

"Jeez, Susie, You scared the water out of me and just to tell me there's sailboats out there. It is the damn ocean, you know. What'd you expect?" I told her thru gritted teeth.

The ride down the other side went smoothly and as we reached the bottom, I took a deep breath to get my heart rate down.

"That wasn't so bad." I said.

"Right." Susie said. "Don't forget we have to go back."

Anyone know if alligators eat Yankees?

We almost had a disaster in our Florida campground a few days after we settled into our routine. A newly arrived motor home started backing up the road towards the only empty campsite on our road. Immediately all the old geezers bailed out of their campers and into the road to direct the guy into his spot. They all stopped almost in unison and stared at the RV as if it had a tail-gunner with a machine gun sitting on the top ready to mow them down.

It turned out to be more terrifying than that. A woman was sitting behind the wheel and her husband was outside guiding her towards the campsite.

"It's a woman driver." Leroy across the way said as if he was announcing the arrival of Rosemary's baby.

Then the strangest thing happened. It was almost as if we had entered a parallel universe. Upon the announcement of the female driver, all the women in the campground immediately shot out of their camper doors and into the road where they began waving their arms this way and that. Susie, much to her credit, stayed put.

I don't know if it was the driver or the women helping her but the lady did a very credible job of parking the rig.

As I stood watching this apparition from some parallel universe, one of my friends here at the RV park joined me. He is retired from the Indiana Department of Natural Resources and is quite a naturalist. He and his wife have taught Susie and I some things about bird watching. Now he had another idea.

"Would you like to go kayaking?" He asked me. "We could go out by the harbor and look at the wildlife." He is an avid outdoors person and has obviously mistaken me for some sort of sportsman.

"I don't have a kayak." I told him, relieved at that moment that I didn't. Water, especially an ocean, puts me outside out of my comfort zone because buoyancy isn't one of my strong points. Besides that, Susie and I went on a tour in a two-person kayak in Key West last spring and that almost landed us in divorce court. Susie guided the front-end and I took care of the back-end. It required some know-how and an extreme amount of cooperation to operate that thing and we had neither. Needless to say, it was a disaster. We ended up tangled in a mangrove outcropping and had to be rescued by our guide. So I was a more than a little hesitant about another trip.

"Who's gonna steer?" I asked him.

"I have two kayaks. You steer your own." He replied.

I right away had visions of me in the middle of Charlotte Harbor a mile from shore trying to paddle my way to land and losing the battle with the tide.

"Oh no." he said when I expressed my fear of open water. "We won't go out into the Gulf. I thought we could just go up Alligator creek to the dam and then back to the harbor. We won't be gone more a couple of hours."

Immediately, two words from that conversation jumped out at me. Dam and alligator.

I was mentally trying to figure out how high a dam in sea level Florida could be as I said: "I bet they call it Alligator Creek because it probably looks like an alligator from the air."

"No-ooo-o." he said. "They call it Alligator creek because there are alligators in it."

"Not to worry, though." He continued. "It's too cold for them to be very active."

I stood there in the nearly seventy five degree temperature and asked "How warm does it have to be before they start eating kayakers…. I mean… before they get active?"

"What we normally do.." He explained. "is find one of those little foo-foo dogs and throw him in the creek. If he gets back to shore, we know it's still to cold for 'em."

I stared at him incredulously. "You've got to be kidding me."

He grinned. "I'm just funning you."

"Funning you, my ass." I thought, reluctantly agreeing to go with him.

I dressed in shorts and a tee shirt to avoid having heavy clothes drag me down if I had to abandon ship. I also carried my pocketknife in case I ended up in a deadly struggle with a gator.

When that mental picture hit me, I suddenly wished I would have watched more of that idiot that shows up on TV every few days wrestling a crocodile. I know crocs aren't alligators but I would assume that the techniques of wrestling would be similar. If I would have paid more attention, I might have had a fighting chance if I'm attacked by a gator.

The trip to Alligator creek was without mishap and I fervently prayed that the trip on the water would be the same. I managed to get in the kayak without tipping it over and we headed up the creek with me on the lookout for alligators. Initially, every limb and leaf floating on top of the water looked like alligator eyes and I was wary of every ripple that showed up on the 20 yard wide waterway.

It only took a few minutes of paddling and I began to relax. I wish I could tell you that I ended up wrestling a crocodile or having some other adventures but the trip turned out to be very tame as well as very serene. All kinds of birds inhabited the banks of the creek. Egrets, warblers, herons, Pelicans. Even an eagle soared high overhead. The dam turned out to be about three feet high and we were at the bottom so there was no worry about going over it. One small alligator occupied a sunny spot on the bank but he didn't move as we went by. Kayaking turned out to be very relaxing and great fun. I plan to do it again as soon as I can find one of those little foo-foo dogs. .

Boobs at nine O'clock

When Susie and I retired and set out to see the country, our original plans were to spend a few days in an area, absorb some of the local flavor and move on to the next place. We had spent two months in South west Florida and liked it very well but decided we needed to see some more of the state before winter was over. We moved to the Atlantic Coast to set up camp in a state park about twenty miles north of West Palm Beach.

Jonathan Dickinson, the state park we were in, was much wilder than our previous 'old geezer' spot. The campground we had left behind controlled fire ants but here, Susie was bitten by the pesky little buggers several times before we learned to watch for their habitat.

Alligators roam the swamps surrounding the campground and they told us they won't bother you but they lend a sense of danger to our adventures. The no-see-ums, tiny flies that are ninety five percent teeth, will nip at any exposed skin, were also numerous and made it hard to sit outside in the evening unless you used insect repellant. This makes the smell of citronella around a campfire a pretty standard event. The salt air might have rusting the pedals off our bikes but it's very refreshing to breathe. All in all, it's a great place to camp if you want to get back to nature.

The humidity was very high here and when combined with the eighty-degree plus temperatures, everything green grew like crazy. All this growing stuff had me convinced that I was coming down with some obscure disease from the tropics. I had an earache for a couple of days and my lower lip had started to swell up.

I asked Susie to look at it, certain that it was leprosy or some other disfiguring tropical malady.

"Your ear hurts because you spent too much time in the water and your lip...." she squinted as she examined my lip.

"It's just a little fever blister." She said. "You've probably had too much sun."

'Uh-huh.' I thought to myself. *"She'll be sorry when my lip falls off."*

We took a day off from camping to drive the sixty miles to Miami Beach and do some sightseeing. I was a little apprehensive about the criminal element there, having watched several episodes of 'Miami Vice', but decided to go anyway. The traffic southward on I-95 was atrocious and it reached gridlock around Miami, even though it was ten in the morning. All the traffic meant that parking anywhere around the ocean was almost impossible but I did find a spot a couple of blocks from the beach. I had to do some quick maneuvering to get to it so I made a U-turn in the middle of the block and pulled into the spot.

A yellow cab pulled up beside me and the driver, a hispanic guy, rolled down the passenger window.

"Don't choo have turn seegnals een een-diana? He said, sounding just like Ricky Ricardo. I just looked at him, mentally trying to process what he'd just said.

"Use them next time.", he shouted at me as he drove away.

"Yes sir, Mr. Ricardo, sir." I muttered under my breath, knowing now how Lucy must have felt when Ricky chewed her out for doing something dumb. I packed up my wounded pride and we walked to the beach.

As we crossed the sand towards the water, we passed alongside a guy wearing a tiny thong like suit and lying on a lounge chair getting some sun. There was something peculiar about him but I couldn't figure it out. He wasn't overweight but he did seem to be a tad misshapen.

"Susie, did you see that guy." I asked. "What was wrong with him?"

"That wasn't a guy. That was a girl and there's nothing wrong with her."

My mind, exposed only to Mooresville, Indiana dress codes, couldn't register the fact that a topless, half naked female was not ten feet from me.

"That was a girl?? I said to Susie while trying to look back at the figure in the chair. I blabbered on. "And those were ...."

"Yes, Mr. Grindstaff. Boobs." Susie interrupted. "And quit gawking. You look like you just climbed off the turnip truck."

I suddenly realized that people of both sexes were all around us wearing little more than what I could best describe as a wedgie and there I stood like an idiot in my jean shorts, tee shirt and tennis shoes with those dorky little ankle socks that Susie insisted that I wear.

Meanwhile, Susie walked unconcerned at the waterline looking for sea shells. I hurried to catch her, trying not to stare at people and feeling like some bad imitation of Jerry Lewis stumbling along behind Dean Martin. I had also suddenly realized that I was probably the only person on the beach with my camera strapped around my neck.

'Ohmygod.' I thought. *'Do you suppose these people think I'm out here taking pervert pictures?'* Two barely dressed ladies sunning themselves came into view as I was trying to figure out what to do with the camera.

My eyes were focused straight ahead and my hands were as far away from the camera as they could get when we passed by. I had suffered an embarrassing episode with a lady in Wal-mart's men's underwear department a few weeks back and I certainly didn't want another experience like that.

I began to relax after thirty minutes of walking in the sand. The skimpy swimsuits were starting to look normal. Not comfortable, mind you, but normal. We passed a lady with no top on and she probably should have had. She was about our age and was, I would guess, about a thirty four long.

Still……. I tapped Susie's arm as we walked.

"What do you think about this topless stuff?" I asked her. "I bet all that sun probably feels good on the old body."

"And??" she said, the question hanging in the air.

"Oh, nothing." I said, pulling my tee shirt over my head.

"I know what you're thinking, Buster." She told me. "Don't even suggest it unless you want another fat lip."

She smacked me on my ample stomach and said "You're about twenty five pounds and I'm about forty years too late for this stuff."

"Welcome to Old Geezerville." I said to her.

Que Pasa yourself.

Our first extended camping trip several years ago was to the Florida Keys. We went back recently even though State park camping sites down there are hard to come by this time of year. There are only three State owned parks in the Keys that have camping facilities and getting into any one of these is quite an accomplishment. There are plenty of private campground sites available in the Keys but they are much more expensive than the state parks. Eighty to Ninety-five dollars a night is about the going rate for a waterfront spot in a private campground and even with that, very few of them have any vacancies. Our reservation in Key Largo was made last summer and even though only four nights were available we thought the trip would be worth it.

South Florida and the Keys are much different than the Florida a lot of Orlando bound tourists see. If you drive into the state from the north and happen to miss the state line signs, you can't really tell that you've just left Georgia or Alabama. Oh sure, you see the official Florida Welcome Centers but most of them are fake. There's only one real official Florida Welcome center on each interstate and it is easily identifiable because it gives away Florida road maps and orange juice. The fake ones aren't going to give you anything. They're just there to sell you a tee-shirt, a Pecan Log and maybe a dried alligator head.

Southern most Florida is not like that at all. There are the touristy places that will sell you a plastic flamingo but they're not as numerous. This part is also not as accessible as the northern part. You can't get to the Keys from another state. You either drive on Highway 1, fly in, sail in or escape from Cuba on a boat. Susie and I did the first of these, pulling the camper to Key Largo. Along the way, we stopped in Homestead south of Miami to pick up fresh vegetables. There are huge vegetable fields all around the area and it's a good place to stock up on tomatoes or any other vegetable you like.

We have been in this area several times and always stop at the same Mexican restaurant. We were introduced here to Pico de Gallo, a freshly made salsa, some years back and it's also a great place to eat enchiladas and tamales.

"Que Pasa." I said to the waitress as we sat down, throwing out the only two Spanish words I know.

She smiled at me and rattled off a string of words so fast that she sounded like a revved up chain saw. Three fourths of the people in the little room laughed but since I had no idea what she was talking about, I just smiled and nodded my head enthusiastically. I hoped I wasn't agreeing that I was a fathead gringo.

We ate our lunch and headed south. Key Largo is only twenty five or so miles further down the two lane highway. The only way in or out of the Keys by land is on this road. There is a lot of traffic and I could feel a little tinge of panic at the thought of being caught down here with a hurricane approaching. I had a feeling it would be worse than being in Tokyo when Godzilla clambered out of the bay.

"This is winter. They don't have hurricanes in the winter." I said to myself reassuringly while at the same time wondering who had made that no hurricane rule.

John Pennekamp State park was our destination. Much of this park is underwater in the Gulf of Mexico because a large coral reef is part of the park.. This makes the park a favored place with scuba divers from all over the world. Our campsite in the park backed up to a mangrove swamp that had all kinds of wildlife. We had no more than stopped and Susie had her bird book out. Several different types of Ibis, pelicans, herons, teal and a roseate spoonbill were in the trees just behind us. A huge turtle struggled to get through the muck on the bank and back out into the water.

"No wonder it's hard to get in here." I said to Susie.

Part of our trip included a trip to Key West to watch the sunset so we spent one day driving the hundred miles of bridges and islands to the town where Ernest Hemingway spent most of his adult years. My fear of bridges does not apply to the structures in the Keys even though there is one bridge seven miles long.. None of them are very high and the waters they cross have such beautiful colors that fear is out of the question.

Key West sunsets are representative of the purported laid back Key West lifestyle. I say purported because I didn't see anything laid back about it. Thousands of people, tourists and locals alike, milled around downtown's Mallory Square a couple of hours before sunset to eat Nachos with guacamole sauce, have a margarita and watch the street performers. These talented free spirits are a staple of Key West entertainment and can be found performing every afternoon. They have acts ranging from acrobatics to juggling to trained dogs. When they're done, they pass the hat. It's good, inexpensive entertainment.

Sadly enough, some of the street performers including my favorite, Dominique the cat man, aren't out on the square anymore. They've been snapped up by the commercial interests and are now part of the happy hour celebration at a large hotel. I consider myself a street performer purist so I wouldn't go near them. An enormous cruise ship also blocked the sunset view on one end of the docks forcing the crowd to gather in about half the usual space.

Still, it was great fun and the sunset was spectacular. As it dropped lower into the west, it seemed to pick up speed as it started it's slide into the Atlantic Ocean. Sailboats moved back and forth through the shimmering light laid down on the water by the setting sun. It was great. The crowd applauded and raised their margarita glasses in a toast to Mother Nature as the sun disappeared into the watery horizon. Let's see 'em commercialize that.

Say hello to Rodney.

On our way north to Indiana, we decided to spend a few nights on the St. Joe peninsula in northwestern Florida; that same area we had passed through on the way down. The highway near there was lined with campgrounds filled with trucks and fishing boats. We passed by two or three fish camps and then drove past a faded sign saying 'Earlene's Seafood restaurant two miles ahead" and all of a sudden, a meal of fresh fish sounded awfully good. We have had some really good meals in little out of the way places and with it being almost lunchtime, we quickly decided to stop.

A lit up sign on wheels sat out front in the grassy strip between the gravel parking lot and the road. A curved, glowing red arrow with flashing lights topped the sign and pointed directly at the front door of the restaurant. The sign proclaimed 'Today's specials. Fresh Catfish and Grits'. I immediately knew the restaurant was a good one. It had to be since it was serving two of my favorite foods.

"I'll have the catfish and grits special." I said to the waitress after Suzie ordered her usual healthy salad.

"Which is it that y'all want?" she said with an accent from so deep in the south it almost required an interpreter.

"Why both, I reckon." I said, feeling myself starting to slide into my fake southern drawl. I have always fancied myself a southern gentleman so anytime I'm south of the Ohio river, I will lapse into an accent that makes me sound like I grew up in Dothan, Alabama. Suzie detests that twang.

"You sound like a hillbilly, so just quit it." She has told me on several previous instances of my displaying the southern vernacular.

I looked up from the menu towards her and she was glaring at me so I quickly slipped back into hoosier talk.

"That's the special, isn't it, dear?" I asked the waitress so formally that butter wouldn't have melted in my mouth.

"They're both specials," she said. "Y'all can have catfish and hesh puppies or y'all can have Grits and two sides."

"You mean grits is an entrée?" I said.

"Y'all get a big ol' bowl of 'em so if that makes them an en-trey, I reckon they are, sugar."

"Why, shut my mouth." I said, "I'll have the grits."

"What's yer sides, hon?"

"I believe I'll have them turnip greens and some pinto beans." I said, sliding again into my southern accent. I thought I sounded a lot like Robert E. Lee but when I peeked over the top of my glasses at Suzie, she was giving me the little headshake that said "you're treading in dangerous waters, Buster."

I looked away and down at the menu where I noticed the fried pickles appetizer. A friend of mine had fried pickles in Canada and he had raved about them.

'They slice a pickle into spears, dip it in some kind of batter and fry it." He had said, his mouth salivating as he described them. I had wanted to try them ever since. Of course, I should have remembered my friend would eat anything that didn't have the hazmat symbol on it.

"I'll have an order of those fried pickles, as well." I said in my best Indiana voice.

When the pickle order came out, they weren't long slivers of fried pickle spears at all but instead were little breaded round things that probably first saw daylight as hamburger dills.

"You know," I told the waitress innocently as she sat the hot plate of pickles on the table. 'In Canada, they slice 'em longways."

I must have caught her on a bad day or else she'd had an unpleasant experience with something or someone Canadian in the past.

"Well Mister," she said indignantly, 'This here's the hew hess of hay and down here, we eat fried pickles this way and if you don't like it, you probably ought to get on back to Canada with the rest of those Frenchies."

I apologized profusely, showing her my Indiana hat and telling her I liked those pickles just the way she served them. I popped one of them in my mouth and it was so hot, I popped it right back out again.

"I think I burnt a hole in my tongue".

Suzie just smiled her little Queen Elizabeth smile.

The grits arrived in a bowl about the size of one of those crocks that sit on the rooming house washstands in old west movies. It took a while to get them all down but I managed.

After we finished eating, we walked up to the counter where a rack full of moon pies sat next to the cash register. I don't see moon pies much in Indiana anymore so the sight of them took me back to my younger days when my diet consisted primarily of these same moon pies and a long neck bottle full of R.C. Cola.

I couldn't resist. That belly full of grits helped me to slide into my best Rhett Butler imitation.

"Frankly, my dear, I believe I'll have me one of them moo-o-n pies." I told the young cashier with the heart tattoo on her left forearm. The name 'Rodney' was superimposed in a flourishing script over the red heart.

"Would you like a dee-licious Pee-can log to go with your moon pie?" she smiled at me, holding up a foot long pecan bar that must have weighed three pounds.

"No." I replied. "But ah'd surely lak me an R.C. cola.." My words were dripping southern charm by then but Suzie had heard enough.

"C'mon, Jethro." She said. grabbing me by the arm. "We've got to get you back to Beverly Hills. Granny and Jed are probably wondering where you went. "

"You tell Rodney we said 'Hey." I said as Suzie pulled me away from the counter.

"Ellie Mae wants to see you in the truck." She said.

"I'll see y'all, y'all." I shouted over my shoulder as we went out the door.

I'll have those Clearance Lights, Clarence.

There was some big news awaiting us when we returned home. The last payment on our car had come out of our checking account while we were on our way north and the Title was in the huge bundle of mail we picked up at the Post Office.

Paying off that car was quite an event for Suzie and I. It might very well be the first time we have ever paid off a family car before it wore out. During our almost forty years of marriage, it seemed like we'd get within two or three payments of having a car paid for and the odometer would roll over a hundred thousand miles. This was a magic number for me and I would start thinking about getting rid of it before something major broke. The car might still be perfectly okay, but that huge mileage number suddenly placed a pox on it. A new car was out of the question so off we'd go to the used car lot. I hated trading cars because in the old days, car salesmen were not necessarily the honest, God fearing professionals that they are today. Being one of the original 'meek shall inherit the earth' believers, I was a sitting duck for those guys. The first thing the salesman would do is put me on the defensive as soon as we pulled on the lot.

"I saw your car smoking three blocks away." He'd say.

"Smoking????" I would say, my mild mannered voice already trailing off . "It doesn't smoke."

"Use a lot of oil?" he would fire at me.

"Well, maybe a little." I would admit, feeling like the Archbishop of Canterbury had just caught me lying in the confessional.

"Probably a blown frizzen hammer from the looks of it. This car ain't worth much, but I'll talk to the boss and see if we can't get you top dollar for it. We'll treat you right."

"The tires are almost new." I offered.

"I think they sold you retreads." He would say and then continue on before I could defend my tires' honor.

"Not upside down on your payments, are you?"

"It's almost paid off." I would protest, trying to project my John Wayne voice, but sounding more like Barney Fife with a sore adams apple.

"Not paid for? No problem. We'll just roll your payoff right into the new payment." The salesman would say, wiggling his little thin moustache all the while. I suspect that they can't graduate from car salesman school until they've learned that 'rolling the payoff in' business because every salesman we've met since 1965 has been telling us that. That's when we bought our first car, a Chevrolet Corvair. We've been rolling those payoffs in ever since. As a matter of fact, I expect the last bit of bank interest on that long dead Corvair was included in this last payment on our current car.

Yet, for some strange reason, now that this car payment journey was over, I got this urge to buy a new vehicle. Not a car, though. A truck. We still had the truck we bought when we purchased Fionna but it wasn't new when we bought it and it was even less so now.

We could use a new truck, I kept telling myself. "The mirrors could go bad, There was that fiasco in New Mexico with the turn signals." The little devil on my left shoulder was saying.

"But it only has fifty thousand miles on it", the little angel on my right shoulder was whispering in my ear. "And what are you going to tell Susie?"

The little angel was right on that point. My wife, Susie, had not been infected with this new vehicle fever so I thought I would take her shopping with me in the hope that she might catch it as well.

Having never owned a new truck, I took her to see one that I found earlier in the week.

"Do we really have to do this?" She said.

"It will only take a minute." I said, pulling in to the dealership.

"There she is." I pointed at a huge three quarter ton truck. "She's a beauty, isn't she?"

"That color is horrible. It looks like it's been out in the sun too long and beside that, it doesn't match anything we have."

"There are other colors." I started to say as she looked at the window sticker. She pointed at the price. "They're not serious about that, are they?

"Oh, no, no, no." I said. "A guy I know in the service department can get us dealer invoice. End of model year and all that stuff."

A clean shaven young salesman walked up to us. "Can I help you fine folks?"

"We're just looking." I said, hoping he'd go away and let us look. "Don't know yet if we're serious about buying."

"Well, alrighty, then." He said. "Can I answer any questions? "

"Yes you can." Suzie said. "Why is that row of lights across the top of the cab?"

"Those are clearance lights, mamm."

"You mean THAT price is a clearance price?" She said, gesturing towards the sticker. "I don't see anything clearance about it."

"No. No. It's not that kind of clearance." He said hurriedly. "The lights are standard on all the big trucks so people can tell whether the truck will fit under a bridge or something, you know, like the clearance."

I had been wondering why the lights were there myself and he spoke as if he was an expert on these matters so it sounded logical to me but it didn't impress Suzie.

"I don't like them. They'd make us look like we belonged to the carnival. "

I wasn't listening at that point. When the guy said BIG truck, I saw myself pulling into a truck stop somewhere out west with my clearance lights blazing away in every direction and real truckers standing by in admiration and envy. All those early years of having sand kicked in my face by car salesmen were fading from memory as we talked. I suddenly needed to have that truck.

"Suzie," I pleaded, "those lights epitomize tough guys." I walked around the truck in my best John Wayne rolling gait. "I bet every bull rider on the rodeo circuit has clearance lights. We get that truck and everybody will know you're married to a real man."

"Wonder what they think now? " She said, not really expecting an answer. "I still don't like them."

"I guess you know that most guys who have a chain hooked to their wallet drive trucks with clearance lights." I told her, pulling that statistic out of thin air and thinking maybe she would be duly impressed. Wrong.

"You mean if we buy this truck, you're planning on putting a chain on your belt?" she said. "In a pig's eye, Buster."

"Those clearance lights, mamm...." the salesman interrupted, picking up on my lead, "Those clearance lights are saying to the world that the man driving this truck can have any woman he wants."

I could see the buxom blonde waitress in my imaginary Truck Stop pause from her coffee pouring duties in mid pour to watch me through the window as I climbed out of the brightly lit cab of my big truck.

"He doesn't need any more women and we need to do a little more looking." Suzie rolled her eyes in that little way that she has.

"Right." I told the guy. "We don't want this truck. "

The truck fever was abated for the moment but the search goes on.

PART FIVE
Autumn in the east.

Oh God, Susie, please don't say anymore.

By July of 2003, We were itching to get on the road after spending a couple of months in Indiana. Our granddaughter, Riley was now over a year old and out of any danger. Her mother, Julie, and the two of us decided to go to the New York State Fair to accompany our son- in-law, Rick, who was going to perform with the Circle City Sidewalk Stompers brass band at the fair.

We left a few days before Rick and Julie but made plans to meet up in Niagara Falls. We had wanted to go to the Falls since the day we were married in 1964 because that was the destination of choice for honeymooners but due to constraints in time and money, we never made it. Instead, we elected to go with the ambience and the romantic setting of a weekend in Elwood, Indiana. A prominent lodging establishment by the name of 'Brownie's Motel and Wrecker Service' in that area had sent us a discount coupon which fit right into our honeymoon budget.

Looking forward to finally having that honeymoon, we set out. Along the way, we stopped at Greenfield Village outside of Detroit. This was another place we have wanted to visit for many years. It surprised me that it was only about a four and a half hour drive via Interstate 75 through Toledo, Ohio. If I had known that, we would have gone there years ago.

Greenfield Village is a collection of nineteenth and early twentieth century historical buildings. There are also representative modes of transportation from that time period. In addition to the Village, there is the Henry Ford

Museum. Tickets are required for both attractions. We paid the senior citizen rate of thirteen dollars to visit the Ford museum. I used to be a little hesitant to ask for the old people discount figuring that the concessionaire might not believe me but not any more. There can no longer be any doubt that I qualify.

The museum contains some incredibly historical items. We sat in the bus that Rosa Parks was in when she put her foot down and refused to give up her seat. The chair that President Lincoln was sitting in when he was shot is on display as is the car in which President Kennedy was assassinated. A startling fact to me about this car is that it was used by four Presidents after Kennedy before it was retired. I'm surprised they got any of them to ride in it.

We spent about four hours in the building and we could have spent a day. We did not get to visit the village so plan on at least two days when you go. There is more information at http://www.thehenryford.org/

Our plans to drive through Canada almost disappeared before we got started when we had dinner with a friend from the Detroit area who told us that since September 11, it had become much harder to come and go at the Canadian border. We would need passports or at least, birth certificates to leave and re-enter the U.S. We had neither of those with us and since I've made it a practice in life not to deal with Federal officials of any breed, I was ready to forget the Canadian part of the trip until Susie reminded me that we had hotel reservations in Canada that were already paid for.

We stopped at the Windsor, Canada crossing to discuss our predicament with the U.S. Border Patrol. Having been raised in a small town in southern Indiana, my primary exposure to authoritarian figures was a rotund, jolly town policeman who went by the nickname of Popeye so I was unprepared for the seriousness with which the Border people took their jobs.

"If you do not have proper identification, I can't say what will happen when you get to the inspection station." The man told me without so much as a smile. "You may get into Canada but then not be allowed back into this country or they may turn you around and not let you into their country at all. In the worst case, if there are warrants for your arrest in either country, you can be detained."

I tried to think if I was wanted on anything. I had a parking ticket a few years ago and I was pretty sure I'd paid it but all of a sudden, I wasn't absolutely positive.

"Maybe we'd better not go." I told Susie.

"The hotel." She reminded me again.

"You can't turn around now, anyway." The customs officer pitched in. "You have to go forward." I looked behind me at the long line of traffic on the one way thoroughfare and realized I'd gotten myself between a rock and a hard place.

I swallowed the lump in my throat, drove across the bridge and joined the line at the Canadian side.

"Susie, let me do the talking." I told her. I had crossed international borders with her before and knew that her uncompromising honesty as well as her total lack of concern for these types of encounters could give us problems.

"Don't volunteer anything."

"Why are you whispering?" she said.

Before I could answer her, we reached the booth where a stern faced Canadian official wearing sunglasses sat.

"Why are you wanting to enter our country?" He asked.

"We're just visiting." I told him.

"We're on vacation." Susie chimed in.

"Do you have anything to declare?"

"No Sir." I said in a hushed tone.

"What are you bringing into our country?

"Just our clothes."

"How long do you plan to be in our country?

I suddenly realized I had no idea. Susie and her newfound romance with Priceline.com had made all the plans.

"Friday." I lied, not wanting to admit ignorance. "We'll be here until Friday." I figured one little white lie wouldn't hurt.

"No we won't." Susie piped up. "We'll be here until Wednesday morning, then we're going to Syracuse."

"Oh, right." I said to the man, hoping he wouldn't call for reinforcements. "Wednesday. We'll be here until Wednesday."

"Any Alcohol or Tobacco in your vehicle?"

"No Sir. No alcohol, sir." I told him with as much reverence as I could muster.

"What about the wine?" Susie chimed in once again.

"Wine, what wine?" I thought.

Susie leaned over and whispered "You forgot about the wine in the cooler."

"Right. Right." I nodded my head and turned to the ranger. "Yes sir, I forgot, Sir, she has a bottle of wine in the cooler. "

"What cooler is that?" The unamused voice came from the window. "You didn't mention a cooler."

"Ohmygod," I thought, *'Susie, when I get you home....'*

"Yes sir." We have a cooler. I forgot to mention that." I said, my voice cracking as I half expected him to whip out a sidearm and open fire on us.

"What else do you have in that cooler?

I tried to think. "Just some stuff to make sandwiches and some boiled eggs."

"And carrots. We also have that package of those little carrots." the voice from the passenger seat said. "The baby ones."

"Right." I nodded my head up and down at a rate approaching the speed of sound. "We have carrots."

"Do you have any firearms?

I thought about it before answering. Even though we don't even own so much as a BB gun, I also knew that Susie was the ultimate traveler. She was always prepared for any eventuality and a person who packed our bags accordingly. I fervently prayed that she hadn't included some sort of anti-tank device along with my socks and not bothered to tell me.

"Oh God no, sir. We wouldn't have firearms. We come from a long line of peace loving people." I said, trying to sound as much like Mahatma Ghandi as I could.

He ignored me and looked expectantly at Susie, waiting for her to spill her guts but she had nothing to say. He hesitated for what seemed to be an hour and then said:

"Go ahead, Drive carefully and enjoy your stay in Canada."

I took a deep breath and said "Thank you, Sir."

I drove away from the booth and turned to Susie who was busily going through the AAA tour book.

"God, Susie, you could have had me arrested."

She looked up unconcernedly, unaware of our close call. "For what?"

"The wine really wasn't in the cooler, you know. It was just in a sack. You didn't have to mention the cooler."

"Look, Buster. What if he asked you to open the trunk? What do you suppose he would have thought that big silver box was?

"We're lucky he didn't shoot us."

"Shoot us? Where do you come up with that stuff? "

I pulled the car forward, suddenly realizing I didn't know which side of the road people in Canada drive on.

Your frigging what??

It took a few minutes after we left the border for me to calm down. My encounter with the Canadian border guards had left me in a state of agitation, a condition that a few deep breaths cured. We crossed the bridge into Windsor, Canada and drove on to Niagara Falls on Canadian highway 401, a comfortable four hour trip. I was hoping we'd see a lot of Lake Erie along the way but we didn't. The drive was not a particularly scenic drive but still, it was new territory for me so I enjoyed it immensely. The price of gasoline got a little confusing. The Canadians sell it by the liter and trying to convert that to gallons and then do the exchange rate made it impossible to figure out how much I was paying. I gave up trying and while I didn't come up with a number, I knew it was not cheap. Throw in calculating your gas mileage using kilometers and liters and a person could end up talking to themselves.

A harbinger of things to come: We encountered our first sales pitch for man-made attractions around the Niagara area in a rest area about a hundred miles from our destination.

The Niagara River serves as the border between the U.S. and Canada and the best vantage point to see the falls is on the Canadian side. The Falls are awe inspiring and well worth the trip but the many different ways that have been used to coax money out of the tourists is a little discouraging. The Canadian side has an area called Clifton Hill which was about as garish a place as anywhere we've ever been. A building dedicated to Marvel Comics dominated the wax museums, tattoo parlors, video game pavilions and fast food places that lined the street. A large thirty or forty foot tall figure of the Hulk comic book figure hung on the side of this building. Just the sort of thing you'd expect to see at one of the world's greatest natural wonders.

We spent one night there, meeting up with our daughter, her husband and our granddaughter in a hotel on the Canadian side. The next day, we headed for the American side when a near disaster struck. We were approaching the border crossing when I noticed my son in law behind us blinking his headlights. We pulled over and our daughter came flying out of their car.

"I can't find my frigging wallet." She screamed, almost in tears.

Frigging??? I had never heard her use language like that.

"I beg your pardon?" I said

"MY WALLET. My frigging wallet has disappeared." There it was again. Frigging. I was going to have to talk to this girl.

"Calm down. We'll find it." By this time, Rick had the trunk open and was going through the suitcases.

"But Dad, you don't understand? I CANNOT get back into the frigging country without some I.D." She'd gone mad with that frigging stuff. She sounded as if she was convinced that she was doomed to spend the rest of her days wandering the Canadian streets; a woman without a country while her family was safely ensconced in the U.S.A.

I was, of course, sympathetic and understanding.

"Here it is." I heard Rick say. I looked toward the back of their car where he was waving her purse above the opened trunk lid.

"Thank God." Julie said, grabbing the purse and pulling her wallet out. She went through the wallet and produced her driver's license.

"Okay, we can go now." She said, holding up the license triumphantly.

Rick closed the trunk and walked toward the driver's door. Julie screamed. "Ahhhhhhhhh."

"My drivers license. My frigging drivers license." She waved the plastic encased document around like it was on fire.

"What's wrong?" All of us asked in unison.

"It's expired. The frigging thing's expired."

"If I hear the word frigging come out of your mouth one more time..." I told my 30 year old daughter.

"My God, what if they won't let me in the country?"

"They're not going to quarrel over that. It just expired 3 days ago."

Rick listened quietly and then said "C'mon, let's go"

We went through the crossing after a couple of perfunctory questions and we drove a hundred feet where we could pull over. Rick and Julie were right behind us. I watched in the rear view mirror as they sat at the booth. The look of abject terror on Julie's face was enough to prompt a congressional investigation but nothing happened.

Their car came on through the crossing and they came up beside us.

"Well, that wasn't so bad." Julie said after she'd rolled down her window.

"Okay." I said. "Put your frigging license back in your frigging wallet and let's get something to eat."

One of the man made attractions that caught my eye after we crossed the border was the dinner buffet at the Seneca Indian tribe Casino on the U.S. side. Several locals had recommended it and I wanted to go but I have sworn off all-you-can-eat restaurants. The sin of gluttony rears it's ugly head every time I go in one of those places. Instead, we stumbled on a section of town that had a heavily Italian flavor. As a matter of fact, a large wrought iron sign stretching across Pine Avenue proclaimed this area to be Little Italy and it turned out to be just that.

We went into a place called Michael's for dinner. I didn't consider this an especially Italian name but all the people inside, customers and staff alike, sure made it feel Italian. Besides a great meal, we also got an Italian language lesson. It was raining and cool so I was interested in a hot bowl of soup.

'What's your soup today?" I asked the waitress

"Beans and greens and we also have greens and ye-onkey." She said, her nose forced into a crinkling pose by the pronunciation of 'ye-onkey'.

"What is 'yonkey'?" Susie asked.

The girl stared at us incredulously. "You've never heard of ye-onkey? Where are you from?"

"We're from Indiana."

Another waitress went by carrying an empty coffee cup. "Hey Maria." Our waitress said to her. "They don't know about ye-onkey in Indiana."

"Really?" She said in disbelief. "What do you eat out there?"

"Regular stuff." I told her, a bit defensively.

"Ye-onkey is regular stuff."

"What is it?" I asked her.

"It's a potato pasta."

"How do you spell this yonkey?" I asked her.

"Not Yonkey." She corrected me. "Ye-onkey.'

"It's right there on the board." She said, gesturing towards a board filled with the day's menu. "Ye-onkey. G-N-O-C-C-H-I. Ye-onkey" She read it off the board in a manner that brought back memories of long ago spelling bees.

"Oh, 'noch-chey'", Susie said. "we have that in Indiana."

"Not noch-chey. Ye-onkey." Maria patiently said, scrunching up her nose to pronounce it. .

Noch-chey or ye-onkey, it sure hit the spot.

We spent the rest of the day looking at the falls from the U.S. vantage point and decided that we preferred the American side. Perhaps being Americans had something to do with that but still, it was less crowded and not nearly as touristy as the Canadian side. The view is not quite as good but the Niagara Falls state park on the riverbank is a quiet natural setting that provides some wonderful close-up (and I mean, really close up) views of the Falls.

We left Niagara and headed for Syracuse and the New York State Fair. I bagged another site on my unique places to eat list. My current claim to fame is that I've eaten at the original Cracker Barrel restaurant as well as the original Steak and Shake drive-in. And now, I can add to this list the place where Buffalo wings originated. It's a place called the Anchor Bar in a run down section of Buffalo. If you go, just order the wings. They were everything we expected but unfortunately the restaurant has all its eggs in one basket. The soup and sandwiches we had with the wings were terrible. Too bad they didn't serve ye-onkey.

A solemn moment.

I was surprised by how old Syracuse looked when compared to Indianapolis. That fifty or seventy five year head start in history that the former got made quite a difference.

The New York State Fair was pretty much like our own Indiana fair. I was not expecting to find cows and sheep on display. I don't know why. Too much television, I suppose. I expected exhibits on street gangs and middle eastern cab drivers but not so. With one exception, I could have been at the Hooosier land State fair.

That one exception was a big one. Inside one of the display buildings was an area devoted to artifacts of the World Trade center and standing outside the building was a permanent memorial to the nine eleven tragedy.

It had taken almost two years before I finally came to grips with the day we found ourselves in the middle of France watching on television as an airplane flew into the World Trade Center towers. I had pretty well laid the whole thing to rest but it all came rushing back when we walked up to that Memorial.

An upright twenty foot tall steel girder from one of the towers stood in the center of the memorial. Mangled pieces of metal jutted out from the girder at odd angles. The rivets that were meant to hold the tower together for hundreds of years clung to the bent pieces and I looked at them wondering why they hadn't done their job. A wavering flame came out of the ground in front of the steel. Homemade shrines to individual victims were scattered around this flame and about the base of the girder. A garland of dried flowers, pictures of firemen and a policeman, a portrait of a twenty something young lady and a snapshot of a man with two little boys at his side leaned against the rust colored metal.

Handwritten notes with the ink running into unreadable streaks lay on the concrete. All had been placed there, I'm sure, by people walking around with a big hole in their heart. Large blocks of dark polished stones sitting squarely on other huge dark blocks of stone surrounded the girder. There was one stack of these stones for each of the locations of the nine-eleven madness and carved in each stack were the names of the people who perished when nineteen inconceivably evil fanatics destroyed themselves while trying to destroy our civilized world.

I stood at the memorial initially trying to find a good angle for a picture but a crowd of people blocked my way. A conservatively dressed, young lady stood quietly by one of the stacks of stone crying softly and I wondered if she had lost someone in the attack or if she was just crying out for what we all had lost. That was enough for me to put my camera away and forget about taking any pictures. It somehow seemed like an invasion of privacy to record the private moments of these people who came to grieve.

I didn't really need a picture anyway. I've got that image at the fairgrounds, along with at least fifty others of the collapse of those two seemingly indestructible towers. It's all tucked away permanently in that part of my brain reserved for the incomprehensible cruelties that human beings can inflict on their fellow men.

Belt buckle? That looks like a dinner plate.

When I was growing up, there were always jobs available for kids to earn a little money. Mowing grass, a newspaper route, shoveling snow were common things to do and I did all those things but when I turned thirteen, I got a job where I actually drew a paycheck. My position was that of a busboy and part time waiter at a restaurant in my hometown. The restaurant also served as a truck stop for drivers plying the roads between St. Louis, Cincinnati and Louisville.

The place was called the Arrow Café and sat at the edge of Highway fifty in Southern Indiana about midway between St Louis and Cincinnati. This truck stop wasn't like these giant hundred acre places you see at almost every interstate interchange today. There was room for eight or nine trucks if you squeezed 'em in real tight. I loved my job there because I was fascinated by the truck drivers. Of course, in those days, all truckers were men. You were about as likely to see a woman truck driver as you were to see Joe Stalin elected President of the United States.

My dad had died some years earlier and even though I didn't know there was such a thing back then, these guys served as male role models for me. They would come into the restaurant wearing jeans, flannel or western shirts and boots of either the Cowboy, combat or engineer variety. A huge leather wallet always protruded from the back pocket of their jeans, secured to their person by a long silver chain. The chain dangled from a belt that would invariably have an oversize trucker related belt buckle. My favorite was the outline of an all chrome twin stack Diamond T truck. It was about the size of the WWF Championship buckle and it took a real man to wear it.

Such a man was a driver named Leonard who visited the restaurant every couple of weeks. That belt buckle covered three quarters of his stomach area and now that I think back on it, it must have been uncomfortable to wear when he sat down.

There were usually two waitresses on duty and both of them would rush over to bring Leonard coffee and a clean ashtray when he arrived because he looked a lot like Randolph Scott. As a matter of fact, I suspected for some time that he might really be Randolph but could never get up the nerve to ask him. He would take his place at the table reserved for professional truckers and have a lively discussion with any other 'over the road' truckers who happened to be in there.

Most of the regulars who came in drove that St. Louis to Cincinnati route but Leonard was different. He hauled freight from the east coast through Washington, D.C. and on out west somewhere. That sounded adventuresome as all get out to me because in my thirteen years of life, I had not been further than fifteen miles from home. It seems odd to think of that now because Susie and I will drive farther than that today to shop at the day old bread store.

Fifteen miles didn't mean much to Leonard either. He told us tales of driving through Washington, D.C. and seeing the monuments. He had us all listening as he talked of West Virginia and winding through the mountains on the same Highway fifty that ran in front of our restaurant and having to use the truck's 'Grandma' gear in low range to make it to the summit of these leviathans. He spoke of snowstorms where he had to use chains on his tires to fight his way through the drifts. My God, that sounded romantic and heroic to me. I had never seen anything taller than the water tower in the middle of our town and I vowed that one day I'd have my own tractor trailer and I'd wrestle those West Virginia mountains just like Leonard.

After Leonard would leave, I'd walk out to the highway and look eastward and know that if I could somehow travel that way, I could be in the mountains in a day's time. That was as close as I ever came to knowing what I wanted to do with my life. Truck driving was what I wanted to do, but it never came to pass. Don't ask me why. As I got older, I pretty much forgot about it although John Denver would bring those memories to the forefront occasionally with his 'Country Roads, Take me home.'

I told Susie about Leonard more than once and fifty years after I cleaned up tables for those truckers, Susie and I talked about it again and she suggested it was finally time to make that trip through West Virginia. We decided to combine that with a trip to Washington D.C. to do some sight seeing. We have been there a couple of other times but because of time constraints, we always used the Interstate system and the Pennsylvania turnpike. Not this time, though. No more of that plunging pell mell towards our ultimate destination for us. No sir. It was time to slow down and smell the roses. The world is too beautiful to pass by at seventy miles an hour so we left Interstate 70 in Columbus, Ohio and got off that nerve wracking, full of eighteen wheelers, almost grid locked throughway.

Just as we wanted to do, we slowed down right away. As a matter of fact, we came to a dead stop. It was five in the afternoon and we were caught in rush hour traffic. Ninety percent of the population of Columbus must have been using that stop light laden highway to get home. We inched our way southeast of the city while brake lights from the homebound cars lit up the approaching darkness as far as I could see. A stop light at least a half mile away ran through its cycle about a hundred times before it was our turn to go through. I doubted that Leonard had ever had to fight this mayhem or he wouldn't have been as pleasant as he was.

Our rig, while not a tractor and trailer, still made a presence lumbering down the road and it caused more than one person to hurry around me and give me the old universal one finger salute. I wanted to shout at them to slow down and enjoy life but I knew it wouldn't do any good. I'd been there and knew full well what they were going through.

We finally met up with highway Fifty down by the Ohio river in southeastern Ohio and crossed the river into Parkersburg, West Virginia and there we were. The feeling of personal triumph was almost overwhelming even though I hadn't even done anything. The highway of my dreams lay before me and I felt a little like the old pioneers who crossed the country in search of adventure and a better life. But before we started on this adventure, We needed food and at the same time, my doctor prescribed diuretic kicked in and I needed to find a restroom. Any old refuge would do for me, but Susie preferred those that were clean and well lit. Since we were not in the desert and had a chance to actually find one, I left the highway and went in search of such a place.

I need that grandma gear.

Fifty years ago, a cross country truck driver named Leonard got me hooked on driving across West Virginia on highway fifty. The highway went thru my hometown and thanks in part to Leonard's stories, I looked upon it as my own personal yellow brick road to freedom and adventure. As it turned out, the highway didn't figure at all in my adult life so my wife Susie and I decided to explore this highway of my long ago dreams on a trip to the east coast. We started our trip on this highway in a town called Parkersburg that sits on the West Virginia side of the Ohio River. It was almost dark when we crossed the river but still I could make out the narrow, winding Parkersburg streets that were just as Leonard described.

Darkness had fallen by the time we got through town and I could see the outlines of hills but had no real sense of being in the mountains because the highway had widened to four lanes. I was disappointed. What kind of adventure was this going to be? I thought I'd lost my chance to experience the real highway but my disappointment only lasted a little while. The highway went back to two lanes shortly after crossing Interstate Seventy Nine outside of Clarksburg, WV. We spent the night in a Wal-Mart parking lot and the next morning's daylight revealed that we were smack in the middle of the West Virginia mountains. They had cut the top off one or two of them to make a flat spot big enough to build the Wal-mart but the rest of the mountains hadn't been bothered yet.

We drove on into Bridgeport, WV, the kind of town where a man can walk out on his front porch and look down on the roof of his neighbor's residence because the houses marched up the hillsides like blocks stacked on top of one another. It was also another town that had narrow streets and gas stations with tiny driveways which were impossible to maneuver a trailer around in. I badly needed fuel and we ended up backtracking to the Interstate interchange where the gas pumps had roomy access drives.

We continued on eastward and I could see that the mountains were as beautiful as Leonard had said they were even though it was obvious we missed the fall colors by a couple of weeks. The roads were also as curvy and steep as they were fifty years ago. I also didn't need to worry about four lane highways here. The two lanes we had were barely wide enough for our camper and any passing vehicle going the other direction. Two more lanes were out of the question.

Rock ledges jutted out from the carved stone hillsides just waiting to snag the side of the trailer should I venture to close. I hugged the center line fearful of ripping the guts out of our camper as we wound around the landscape. Climbing the mountain grades was even more stressful for a born flatlander like me. The truck engine roared and the transmission kept shifting down, trying to find the torque it needed to get us over the mountain. If my truck, like Leonard's, had been equipped with a 'grandma' gear, I sure would have used it.

Going down the mountainsides was another adventure. The steepness of the downhill grade was posted for the truckers and for idiot amateurs like myself who ventured into these places with a trailer in tow. A sign announced 'Seven percent grade next two miles' and I tried to visualize how steep that was. Is this a really bad one? I suddenly wished I would have paid more attention in my high school geometry (or was it trigonometry?) classes. All I could remember was that if $x=2y$, then the cosine is connected to the tangent bone or something like that. We were at the bottom of the hill and ready to take on another before I could come up with an answer. Next time, I'm paying attention in class.

We topped another rise and ahead of us was a picturesque scene of cows on a steep hillside. I tried telling Susie the old story about their legs being longer on one side so they could stand on the hill like that. Her being a city girl and all, I thought maybe she'd believe it but Susie is not that gullible.

Oh sure, she steadfastly clings to the notion that pulling a person's finger will produce an explosion of a gaseous nature but she wasn't buying any of this story.

"I suppose they'd have to back up all the way home, if that were the case." She told me.

"Who would have to back up?"

"The cows."

"Do what?"

"Well, if they turned around, their short legs would be on the downhill side and they'd tip over so the only way they could go home would be to back up."

"Uhhh, right. I hadn't thought of that."

I was busy trying to figure out how the cows did get home when Susie saw an interesting item in the AAA tour guide. We were near Blackwater Falls State Park in the heart of the West Virginia ski resort country and she wanted to go check it out. It ended up being about a forty mile detour and there was a time I wouldn't have taken it but I'm trying to mellow out and smell the roses in my old age. The scenery in the park was pretty but it wasn't any prettier than our own McCormick's Creek or Turkey Run state parks. There's probably a moral in that conclusion if I were eloquent enough to yank it out.

We returned to Highway fifty just about worn-out from all the mountain driving and I was suddenly counting the miles till we could get to an Interstate highway and be able to leisurely finish the drive to Harper's Ferry, our destination for the night. We climbed another mountain (Mount Storm, I think) and when we reached the top, the flashing sign said nine percent grade next five miles. Hah, that's only two percent more that the last one, I thought. How bad can that be? Bad would be an understatement in this case. We shot down that hill like Little Abner being chased by Daisy Mae. I know enough not to ride the brakes down mountain grades but at times the fifteen mph switchbacks had me pumping furiously on the brake pedal. A turnout showed up about halfway down the mountain and this looked like a good time to pull over and take a break. The smoke poured off the front wheels of our truck as we came to a stop. I assumed it was a normal reaction so we let the brakes cool for a while and went on down the mountain and sixty or so miles later, we turned on to Interstate 81 and headed north.

I later found out that the trailer brakes had been damaged and weren't working. Had I known that… But I didn't and it turned out to be a great trip. I have finally exorcised the demon that Leonard planted in my head when I was thirteen years old. I probably burnt up the brakes on my truck, shook loose everything not tied down in the camper, and scared the wits out of Susie and myself a couple of times but we made it. Now if I could go back and take my rightful place at that long ago truckers table, life would be complete.

"You talking Grandma gear, Leonard? Let me tell you, when I started down that Storm Mountain with ten thousand pounds of trailer in tow….."

My God Susie, Put some socks on.

When we travel, we try to camp in State or National parks to save money and we definitely needed to save some money while camping in the Washington, D.C. area. Prices on the two private campgrounds we checked were way out of our budget. Fees ranged between thirty six and fifty-two dollars per night. Of course, you get amenities with this price that you don't get in the state and federal parks in the area. Water and electric hookups, cable television and swimming pools are nice but if you're on a tight budget and are seasoned camping veterans who can rough it, National park campgrounds work real well. We don't need much since our only real camping requirement is finding a place somewhere in the park where Susie can plug in her curling iron.

I found a park on the NPS.gov web site in Greenbelt, Maryland, a suburb of Washington that had camping facilities. It was, strangely enough, called Greenbelt National Park. We have a Golden Age pass for the National parks so the camping fee was seven dollars a night, half of the regular price. There were no hookups for the camper but there were modern restrooms with hot showers and an electric plug for doing Susie's hair. Our camper is self contained which means that it is equipped with a battery that will operate lights, the radio and a pump that allows us to use the water in our holding tank. We don't have a television to watch when we don't have hookups but it's surprising how little you miss without having that thing flickering all the time.

The microwave and coffee pot won't work on battery, either. We have an Inverter in our truck that converts battery power to 120 volts. It will run our laptop computer and charge the batteries in our camera. Susie has tried her curling iron with this thing but it quickly yells 'Uncle' and quits. We do have a propane furnace that runs on the camper battery but it doesn't take long to suck all the power out of it so we very seldom use it. The secret to staying warm while camping is staying out of places where it gets cold.

We took a chance going to Washington, D.C. in November but we reasoned that it's sort of located in the south so maybe we'd get lucky. For the most part we did, but we had a couple of nights where the temperature got below freezing. On those nights, we stayed late in D.C. and then ran the furnace in the camper long enough to warm up the place enough to jump in bed and climb under the covers. This works fairly well as long as you're not married to someone who because of some freak of nature, has extremities whose temperature ranges border on zero degrees Celsius. Susie falls into that category. One of the entries I'm going to put in the marriage proposal questionnaire I'm putting together goes like this. "On a scale of one to five, how cold would you say your feet are?" Susie is a five and probably should leave those feet to science. I made her wear her socks to bed to alleviate some of the shock.

The cold mornings were warmed with coffee made on our propane stove and a hot bowl of chili. Susie drew the line at the chili and made do with instant oatmeal, fortifying her for the trip to the city. Our previous visits to Washington never provided enough time to take advantage of everything the city has to offer so this time we decided to stay until we saw all the sights we could handle.

The city of Greenbelt has a Metro station that we used on a daily basis. If you have been to Washington, you know that driving in the city is not for the faint hearted. The morning rush hour lasts until around eleven thirty and then they break for lunch before resuming the afternoon rush hour around one p.m.. Parking in downtown Washington is also impossible so public transportation is the best way to get there. We used this for the five days we were there before we decided we had seen enough of the city for this trip.

We had been to the Presidential memorials along the mall before so we did not spend any time in them. We did note that all of them are protected by concrete barriers, courtesy of the nine-eleven fanatics. The Smithsonian was our first stop and we spent two full days in the various Museums and could have spent another three or four but we stopped before we overdosed on History.

We also spent a day and a half in the U.S. Holocaust museum and what we saw there will not go away. We left there with enough questions about the frailties of the human race to fill a lifetime. On both occasions when we left the building for the day, I had to comfort Susie to stop her crying.

Also, A place that is like a magnet to me is the Vietnam Memorial. We have been to the Wall several times and I always feel humbled by the fifty-nine thousand names that represent fallen members of my generation. There is always a crowd there and it especially seems to be a Mecca for Vietnam Veterans. They're not hard to pick out because they're usually wearing something from his or her past. Nothing flaunted, maybe just a battle ribbon or some vestige of their uniform. When I saw a group of them, talking together, walking to a particular name or names on the wall, I felt somehow ashamed. I was not in Vietnam and I knew instinctively that I've not earned the right to walk around a sacred place like this with them. I always go away feeling inadequate.

Another memorial that left an impression on us was the Korean War monument. Several statues capture the image of cold and wet soldiers on patrol. They are so life like, it seems as if you could almost knock the water off their poncho's. They are positioned in a tree lined, garden like setting. I knew several Korean war veterans including two who never made it back so the visit to this place left me a little morose.

A fence around the unfinished but almost complete World war two memorial prevented us from visiting there. My father was in this war and even though he has been dead over fifty years, I wanted to see what the designers of this monument had come up with to pay homage to the 'greatest generation.' It will give us an excuse to go back when the memorial is opened.

Walk or get the hell out of the way.

Our visit to Washington, D.C required only about ten minutes to find out that our truck was useless in this city. The traffic is horrific at all hours and there is nowhere to park. We found the best way to get around is by using the Metro. This combination of surface and subterranean trains serve the Capital city and the suburban area in Virginia and Maryland. The park ranger in the campground where we are staying told us about it.

We arrived at the Metro terminal about nine o'clock in the morning and the parking lot was a sea of cars and SUV's. What seemed like thousands of them almost as far as the eye can see.

"Do all of these people work in Washington? What could they all possibly do?" I asked Susie.

Susie, who has heard my ultra conservative, and to her, distorted views of government largesse before, says nothing but just gives me a warning look that says 'Don't start it, Buster. I don't want to listen to you bitching about too much government.'

A helpful station manager explained the myriad of ticket combinations available. Rush hour, Non rush hour, no transfer, transfer, point to point. We settled on a six dollar all day pass that allows us access to all the routes at any time. We ascended the stairs to the elevated tracks and settle in for our twenty minute ride downtown. The acceleration of the train is surprising; it doesn't exactly push you back against your seat but the passengers standing in the aisle brace themselves and lean into the direction the train is going. Five minutes into the ride, we dive underground and the lights in the tunnel walls go by in a blur accentuating the sensation of speed.

I looked at my map of the system and the station names seem to be right out of American History. Arlington Cemetery, Farragut North, National Archives, Smithsonian, Capitol South. We get off the Green line train at L'enfant plaza to transfer to the Blue line. We found ourselves in an enormous area filled with people and quickly discovered that we have no sense of direction underground. We are dependent on the directional signs and a sense of panic starts to overwhelm me but we follow the signs like lambs being guided by a sheep dog. We need to go up an escalator and Susie steps on and I move next to her. A hand taps me on the shoulder and a man glares at me as I move aside and allow him to move on up the steps. A lady also passes me and pauses long enough to say in a very polite way "stay to the right if you're not going to walk up." I move in behind Susie, chastened by my escalator riding ignorance.

The station is well lit but I can't figure out where the light is coming from. I know I'm from the country and all that but I've seen recessed lighting before and I don't see it here. I don't see any bulbs or fluorescent tubes either. I finally gave up trying to determine where it's coming from. We moved onto the platform for our next ride even though we had no idea from which of the four tunnels the train will emerge. A small glimmer of light shows in one of the darkened tunnels and I wonder if the light is playing tricks with my eyes. The light grows brighter and brighter until I know it's either the train or a man with an awfully big flashlight. Suddenly the round lights recessed into the floor begin to blink on and off.

So that's why they're in the floor, I think as I subconsciously grab Susie's arm and move us back from the edge of the platform. An electronic overhead sign lights up. 'Blue line Vienna Fairfax six car train approaching.'

I tried to make an educated guess as to where we should stand so that we'll be in position when the doors open. Susie is unconcerned about this problem. The train seems to have more than six cars as it hisses by and I don't see how it can get stopped before it shoots out the other end of the station. The cars are all filled with people and I wonder if we'll find a place to sit. The train somehow stops, the doors silently slide open and bodies of all sizes are shot from the exits. People with their nose buried in a book or the newspaper barely glance up as they exit. Other people doing the same thing enter the cars and take their place.

My poor selection of a place to stand on the platform causes us to end up standing and the acceleration of the train throws us backward into a man in a suit.

"Sorry." I say and he nods his head.

A young man at my shoulder talks animatedly to two of his friends. He is loudly peppering his speech with the mother and granddaddy of all curse words. I look around and no one is paying any attention so I try to ignore him while I pray that the nuns who taught me years ago to watch my mouth are not now watching me remain silent.

A heavy set lady in the seat next to where we stand suddenly buries her head in her hands, quietly sobbing over some sadness that we know nothing about. A lady behind her pats her on the shoulder but no one else reacts. I don't either.

A boy of about nine or ten wears his headphones while his mother talks incessantly to him. He doesn't hear a word of what she is saying as his head bobs back and forth to the rhythm that only he hears. She shakes him by the shoulder and he pulls up one ear of the headset and she says something to him. He nods his head in the affirmative and repositions the earpiece on his bushy head and goes back to his blank look while she continues talking. What is he listening to, I wonder? A small boy, let me think. Disney, Mother Goose? Nah. More likely Insync or… or who? I suddenly realize I don't even have the foggiest notion who is entertaining pre-teens. As far as that goes, I don't have the slightest idea who the current king or queen of teen age music is. I've got to quit listening to the golden oldies and get out more.

A detached voice from the ceiling mounted speakers announces the next station. Is that a recording or a real person? It must be the latter because on some trains, the voice speaks clearly and with some enthusiasm but on this train, I had no idea what the voice was saying. The words were mumbled and they ran together like perhaps the person has said them ten thousand times and is bored out of his mind.

We arrive at our destination and exit the system into the sunlight and find ourselves on the lawn in the middle of the Smithsonian museums. We spend the day in the Jewish Holocaust museum and leave the place aghast at man's inhumanity to man. How could this possibly have happened? How could the German people, the regular people, have ignored it? We certainly would not have. Would we?

Travels With Susie

We re-entered the transportation system in the evening along with all the workers leaving the imposing government buildings. The escalator ride down into the bowels of the system is done in the proper manner. We're quick learners, hugging the right side of the railing as people flew by us, taking the steps two at a time. What's their hurry, I wonder, but since I've retired, I wonder that a lot.

Standing in the Smithsonian subway station at five thirty in the afternoon with thousands of people preparing to scatter in every direction is exciting for a while but the people hurrying about and ignoring all that is going on around them begins to wear on me. I suddenly feel a world away from Mooresville, Indiana and I find myself wanting to be in my car waiting for the stoplight at Main and Indiana streets to turn green.

"Maybe we'd better go home." I said to Susie.

"Are you crazy? This is exciting." she said.

"Okay, but tonight, you're wearing socks to bed." I told her as we walked into the fading late afternoon sunlight.

Pass me the peanuts, please.

It all began innocently enough and now as I look back on it, the circumstances that lined up like so many planets in the heavens was eerie. I think the whole sordid mess must have been predestined and I should have seen it coming, but I'm getting ahead of myself. We were preparing to leave Mooresville for our tour of the historical east coast and on our way out of town, I stopped at the pharmacy to pick up a prescription. While I was in the store, I bumped into a display of roasted peanuts on sale; the giant sixteen ounce jar.

"Those would be good to munch on while we're on the road." I told Susie and she agreed. We finished the jar shortly after we crossed the Virginia state Line.

Our plan was to spend several days touring Washington, D.C, buying our lunch each day but prices were a little high in the city. After paying twelve dollars for one chicken sandwich and an order of potato salad, we decided we'd pack our lunch for the rest of the tour. Peanut butter and jelly sandwiches made the most sense because they didn't require refrigeration. We found peanut butter on sale in a Greenbelt, Maryland market and I bought six jars of the extra crunchy kind. Four days of peanut butter sandwiches wiped out one of the jars.

We spent a couple of more days touring the civil war battlefields of Antietam and Bull Run before leaving the D.C. area. Driving around battlefields and reading memorial plaques makes a person hungry so we went into Manassas and bought a package of peanut butter cookies and another jar of peanuts, the honey roasted variety this time.

Our next destination was the Historical triangle area around Williamsburg, Virginia. We decided to eat at one of the authentic colonial taverns in the village on our first evening in Williamsburg. The tavern was authentic right down to the ale mugs. All the help was in colonial dress as were several of the customers. Unfortunately, the colonial atmosphere did not apply to the dinner prices and the amount of present day money it took to buy a cup of Brunswick stew would have sufficed to support Washington's troops through the terrible winter at Valley Forge. We elected to just have a drink and then eat when we got back to the camper.

Bowls of peanuts still in the shell sat on all the tables and we munched on those. Susie, who loves games, was soon in a lively revolutionary war era dice game called buck-buck with several different characters in period regalia. There was a woman who claimed to be the wife of Daniel Boone, a couple of officers in the Continental Army and an Indian, complete with loincloth, who had come into town to trade some skins. I wanted to tell Mr. Boone's wife that she was in the wrong time period but was unsure of my footing on that observation.

Dan'ls wife and the officers were drinking ale and Susie had a colonial era drink called the Rummer that was mostly rum. The Indian, who also had a small clay pipe poking through his earlobe, was into hot buttered rum which made me a little nervous. I had these mental pictures of what can happen when a loincloth wearing individual has too much to drink and none of the pictures were very pretty. I hoped he had some jockeys on under there.

I also decided I might be better off just observing this little bit of history so I declined their offer to play. The dice and the peanut shells were soon flying and the bonnet wearing maid kept bringing more peanuts and more drinks as the competition heated up. The game finally broke up and we bid the other players adieu.

"That was fun but I don't want any dinner now. I ate one too many peanuts." Susie said as we walked towards the truck.

The next day we toured the other two towns in the historic triangle. The first of these was Yorktown where the British Army surrendered to Washington's troops. We walked around the battlefield and visited a Colonial army encampment where the Company cook gave us boiled peanuts fresh out of a hearth dug into the hillside. We then toured a working eighteenth century farm where, as part of a demonstration, Susie dug up peanuts with the farmer. We ate only one of the freshly dug legumes because a peanut in its raw, natural state is not very tasty.

Leaving the peanut shell behind, we went on to our second stop; the Jamestown settlement; the first permanent settlement in the new world. Much of the exhibit was closed because of damage done by Hurricane Isabel but the tour guide did tell us of a wonderful restaurant reached by a ferry ride across the James River.

Having eaten nothing but a few peanuts since breakfast, We left Jamestown and drove to the pier. We arrived at the ferry just as it started to load cars and fifteen minutes later, we drove off the ferry and down the road into a little town where a sign on the side of the road announced that we were in the heart of Virginia peanut country.

The restaurant was only a short drive from there in the town of Surry. Our AAA book said we would find the help dressed in 1700's garb but that was no longer true, if it ever was. Still, it was a nice place and very crowded so I knew the food must be good. Many of the evenings specials revolved around peanuts. I figured this was because of the peanut country claim. Susie had the special which included a peanut soup appetizer, ham croquettes with a raisin-peanut sauce and peanut pie for dessert.

The soup had crumbled peanuts in it and was so creamy and rich, it was like eating melted peanut butter. Susie picked at her Ham croquettes and when the dessert came, she took one bite and pushed it away.

"Eat your pie." I told her.

"I don't think I can even look at that pie, much less eat it."

"One more bite."

"Huh-uh."

I looked up and Susie was suddenly very pale. Her face had a pasty white hue that made her look almost transparent. She appeared as if she might gag at any moment so I paid the bill and half carried her out into the cool misty night air where the color came back into her face.

On the ride back, the mist changed to a steady rain and the rhythmic swish of the windshield wipers soon had Susie asleep. She remained that way as the ferry carried us back across the river. We reached the shoreline and I drove slowly up the ferry ramp trying not to wake her. The truck made it's way up the dark, narrow road towards Williamsburg. The falling leaves, heavy with moisture, scattered as they were blown across the roadway by the wind. The lights of the truck pierced the blackness as Susie began to stir.

"Aaaagh" she suddenly screamed, sitting up and waving her arms at the wet leaves clinging to the windshield.

"Get him away. Get him away."

The truck swerved as I slammed on the brakes and skidded to a stop on the side of the road.

"Who? Get who away?" I said, grabbing her arms.

"It was trying to eat me. Oh God. It was horrible."

"What was trying to eat you?"

"A peanut. A giant peanut. He had on a top hat and a monocle. He shook his cane at me and opened his mouth and….. and…. he had terrible jagged fangs. It was terrifying. He reached for me and…. "

She let out a tiny gasp, getting her breath. "And….. And…"

"And what??"

"I don't know. I woke up."

"Well, you just scared the peanut butter out of me." I told her.

"It's your fault. I told you I couldn't eat that pie. No more peanuts. If I never eat another peanut, it will be too soon. Don't ever let me eat another peanut."

It's been a few days now and Susie is steering clear of peanuts. I put the five remaining jars of peanut butter in the storage area of the camper out of Susie's sight. I guess I'll eat them myself when we get home.

Note from Susie: G2 took more than a few liberties with his literary license in putting together this story.

I didn't push nothing.

You'll be glad to hear that my better half is talking to me again. You probably weren't aware of it but Susie has been silent for a while because of an accident that happened recently. We were on our way from the Virginia coast to Georgia for the Thanksgiving holidays when we happened upon a Pottery Festival in Seagrove, North Carolina, a small town of a few hundred people with fully one third of them in the pottery business. It was a beautiful day and we decided to stop.

There were probably a hundred potters exhibiting their wares in a huge tent. It was warm for mid November and Susie drank a bottle of water while we walked around and it wasn't long before nature was tapping her on the shoulder. There were no public restrooms available, only the portable kind that were lined up along the back of the tent. Susie hates those things and would not normally consider using one but Mother Nature was knocking pretty hard so she made me promise to stand outside and not let anybody come near.

"Are you still out there?" she said a few seconds after getting inside.

"Yep, I'm still here." I told her.

"Don't leave."

"I'm not going anywhere." I assured her.

Then in one of those mysteries of life that leaves a person forever wondering what happened, I accidentally leaned against the back of the apparatus and it tipped forward. My Goodness, it was surprising how easily it tipped. It was a complete accident. I don't know why she got so mad. I didn't know it was going to do that. And it's not like it turned over or anything. It just tipped a little bit, although I guess now that I think about it, it might have been more than just a little but it was an accident so I was surprised when she got angry. Well, maybe she got a little more than angry.

The worst part was the scream. Well, it was actually more than a scream. It was more like a shriek from a hoot owl who had wandered into the corn field and found the marijuana plants but even with that, maybe it wasn't really the worst part. I suppose that was when she came flying out of that porta-potty door yelling something unprintable and grabbed me by my sweater.

"Are you crazy? What kind of stunt was that? If that thing would have turned over, I could have died a horrible death."

Her yelling embarrassed me in front of maybe a thousand North Carolina pottery lovers but I didn't get mad at her. No-o-o-o-oh, sir. I just kind of grinned weakly.

"Well, first of all," I said, "it wasn't going to turn over and secondly, it was an accident. I just sort of leaned up against it and it just sort of tipped. How was I supposed to know it was going to tip? Do I look like some sort of Privy engineer?"

"I'll make you an engineer, Buster. If you ever so much as think about doing that again, I'll ….. I'lll …… Oh god, can you imagine how horrible that would have been?"

"I know it, Susie." I sympathized with her. "Maybe we ought to sue somebody for mental anguish, letting wobbly, dangerous stuff like that sit around. ."

"Oh. Right, just what I want for Christmas. A story about me and this wobbly porta-potty in the paper." She turned around and pushed on the side of the structure. It didn't budge. She pushed a little harder. It still didn't move.

"This thing is not wobbly." She said.

"I… I.. don't understand. "I told her. "I just barely pushe…."

"Pushed is right. I'm not talking to you." With that, she turned around and walked back towards the pottery tent.

I followed her, protesting my innocence, but to no avail. I can't imagine why she would think I did that on purpose. She did agree to walk with me but she remained silent so I had to do all the talking. We stopped and watched as an old gentleman stood at a potter's wheel making a graceful vase. Susie, who is quite talented with crafts and makes stuff look easy, asked some questions of the potter. It was very interesting and it only took a minute before I thought 'I can do that.'

I should have stopped right there. I have not yet learned that I am a klutz when it comes to making home made things. Every time Susie drags me to some art or craft show, I come away with a new hobby. Take me to an art show and I'm going to be the next Grandma Moses.

I've walked away from craft shows making plans to build wooden lawn furniture or cute, lovable, hobby horses a hundred times. I once was going to string up melodic, symphony class, wind chimes by the score. Last year, I made plans to weave beautiful, decorative, not to mention, functional baskets from dried Pine needles. Not just any old pine needles, either. We were going to put on our flannel shirts, gather the needles in the mountains of Eastern Tennessee and lovingly dry them by hand using a wood fired ceramic oven. It always sounds good but I never actually get around to doing any of this.

But pottery now. Pottery was different because luckily, I have a nephew in Georgia who makes pottery. He has studied under some of the better known folk art potters in the south and I was sure he could show me how to make pottery.

I expected that with a couple of lessons after dinner, I would be ready to go. I would start with a beautiful, one of a kind set of mixing bowls for my daughter. Just in time for Christmas and an instant heirloom that can be passed down from generation to generation.

For my granddaughter, it would be a tea set. An Elegant, yet tastefully simple, piece that she would cherish into her old age. Good Lord, I could probably even sell this stuff. I should have thought of this years ago.

When we arrived in Georgia, my nephew was more than happy to give me lessons after our Thanksgiving celebration. I spent most of a day working on the wheel but making pottery turned out to be just a little bit harder than I thought.

I doubt that I'm going to get to the heirloom quality mixing bowls this year. I'm also abandoning the tea set idea for now. Instead, I've made what can best be described as a combination ash tray and cereal bowl that my daughter and granddaughter will share. Neither of them smoke so they'll probably just use it for cereal. If you're interested in purchasing one of these, I'll be taking orders after Christmas.

The line forms on the right.

PART SIX
The Lone Star State.

You ain't nothing but a hound dog.

We decided to be winter Texans for our third winter of retirement but we didn't want to spend the entire winter in one place. We wanted to try the Gulf Coast, the Rio Grande Valley, the Big Bend National Park area and the Hill Country around Austin. The Gulf Coast was our first stop so we made a reservation for a month at a campground in Rockport, Texas. We had met a couple in California a couple of years earlier and they had told us how nice it was.

We planned a route from Indiana taking us through Memphis, Little Rock, Texarkana, and Houston to get to our destination. The driving distance is only about a hundred miles more than the trip to Fort Myers, Florida but there's a lot of westerly driving in those miles. We weren't going to be as far south and the weather would not be as warm but still it would be better than an Indiana winter.

We left in early afternoon on New Years Eve, a day before we had planned. We stayed in Indiana after Christmas to go to a New Years Eve dance but got antsy and got on the road a few hours before the party started.

We slept for a few hours in a rest area on Interstate 57 near the junction of the Ohio and Mississippi rivers; a swampy, sparsely populated area. New Madrid, Missouri, the site of the country's most powerful earthquake, was a few miles down the road. This quake occurred in the mid nineteenth century, rerouting the Mississippi river and forming Reelfoot Lake in the aftermath. That bit of history was in the back of my mind as we tried to sleep but the anticipation of being on the road heading for new places kept me awake. The possibility that another big tremor could toss us into the middle of that muck also occurred to me. Having been a Boy Scout, I early on adopted that 'Be prepared' motto. I put my shoes on in case we had to forage our way out of the swamp.

I also considered waking Susie and expressing my concern but years of experience have taught me that she would only scoff at the possibility my concern. The comforting feel of the shoes tied round my feet soon had me drifting off to sleep.

We were on the road early and it wasn't long before we passed through West Memphis, Tennessee. This put us pretty close to Graceland, the home and burial site of Elvis Presley. There was no way I was going to get within twenty miles of that shrine and not visit. My mid teenage years were spent emulating the king even though I couldn't play the guitar nor could I sing although I didn't know that at the time. I thought I sounded a lot like him and I knew I could do that Elvis lip sneer maybe even better than he could. No one could ever say I was a quart low on hair oil either. I had a ducktail cut that kept me broke buying Brylcreem. My theory was that if a little dab would do you, a handful would do even more. There was so much of that stuff in my hair that I had to wear a turtleneck sweater to keep my head erect.

That hair allowed me multiple personalities. When I wasn't being Elvis, I thought I was James Dean personified. I've tried to tell Susie how good I looked but she doesn't believe me. For some reason, the few pictures that remain from those days make me look misshapen. Of course, you have to remember that my Brownie Hawkeye cameras couldn't really do me justice. I only weighed a hundred and twenty five pounds and forty of that was oil coated hair. My head was so out of proportion with the rest of my body that I looked like I belonged on a Star Trek movie set.

Fifty years and a dried up head later, we walked through the mansion admiring the tacky decorating that just fit the image of Elvis. Outside, Susie was certain she saw the ghost of Elvis watching as adoring fans put flowers on his grave. It was a great visit but I did come away a little surprised about the size of the place. It was pretty big but there's probably fifty homes in my home county in Indiana that are bigger and every city we pass through has a plethora of oversize monuments to American excess that put the Graceland mansion to shame.

I put my square footage concerns to rest and we completed our pilgrimage. We left the Memphis area clutching a handful of Graceland post cards which we planned to mail to our friends and neighbors to make them jealous. A year later, they' were still somewhere in the truck.

We had about six hours of daylight to drive the two hundred and seventy five miles but driving though Arkansas turned out to be a task that took most of that time. Interstate forty is not real scenic and the highway surface has cracks in the surface every few feet that resulted in a constant thump-thump-thump from the tires. It drove me crazy.

We did find a great place to stay in a Corps of Engineers campground at Wright-Patman lake a few miles south of Texarkana, Texas. The lake covers about 1500 acres and the Corps maintains three campgrounds around the shoreline. The campsites were about as large as any we've ever seen and shaded by Pine and sweet gum trees. The camping fee was twelve dollars a night but with our Golden Age passport, we only had to pay half that amount. That explained the fifty or so senior citizen campers who spend the winter in this campground. We talked to several who had tried places further south but did not like the crowds in the warmer spots. We heard a lot of "Oh, it gets a little chilly here but it isn't ever going to be as cold as Minnesota (or Wisconsin or North Dakota.) and besides that, the fishing is great."

We walked by a tranquil campfire scene with three older gentlemen sitting around looking as if they were ready to roast hot dogs. They waved at us and Susie, who loves conversing with strangers, stuck her foot in her mouth.

"You got your wieners out?" She asked. Before she could ask about marshmallows, one of the old gentlemen spoke up in a serious voice.

"No mamm, this ain't that kind of campground."

I wanted to stop and chat with 'em but I couldn't get a red faced Susie to even slow down.

We left Texarkana headed for Houston via Highway Fifty-Nine. It's not an interstate highway but there are a lot of signs that proclaim this route as the future Interstate sixty-nine so I guess Texas, like Indiana, has made up it's mind about the location of the proposed Canada to Mexico freeway. We arrived in Houston, the country's fourth largest city, about eight in the evening.

I will never again complain about city traffic. It wasn't the two mile an hour gridlock found on the northeast side of Indianapolis because nothing slowed down enough to get gridlocked. White knuckle driving on eight lanes of interstate with nine thousand pounds of camper on your tail and at speeds up to eighty miles an hour left me physically drained. Never again.

We stopped for the night in El Campo, Texas about a hundred miles from our destination where I could drink a beer and recuperate a little.

Pulling into a Truck stop or an interstate rest area is our first choice when all we need to do is sleep but there was neither available around El Campo. There was also no state or federal campground nearby and since it was about nine o'clock, we pulled into a Wal-mart parking lot. We only stay at Wal-mart if all we're going to do is sleep. Our budget won't let us pay twenty five or thirty dollars to a private campground for a place to sit for a few hours.

There is a lot of debate in the RV community about the practice of overnight parking in a Wal-Mart lot and private campground owners can get downright livid about the subject. I think Wal-mart stays out of the discussion although I have seen 'No overnight Parking' signs in their parking lots in areas where there are a lot of tourists. Interestingly enough, it's only Wal-mart where the subject comes up. I don't hear about K-Mart or Mall parking lots. Maybe it's because Wal-mart is open all the time.

There is one thing worthy of note while we're on the subject. It seemed like almost half the towns we went through along the way contained an abandoned big box store of one brand or another. I expect before it's over, practically every town will have an abandoned building or two as the country decides on one gargantuan home improvement chain and one discount department store chain for everything else. I wish I was smart enough to come up with a use for these eyesores. Maybe they could be turned into a ten dollar a night place where weary Rv'ers can stop for a few hours and maybe get a hot shower.

Too bad I never follow through with these ideas. I could get rich.

After a few hours rest, we were up early and arrived at our destination before breakfast. We took almost four days to drive the thirteen hundred miles to our destination. We pulled into the Rockport RV campground and they provided us with a big site and lots of live oak trees for shade. The town was small so our initial exploration didn't take a long time. We found the church, a grocery and several interesting looking restaurants and then drove to the gulf, about a quarter mile from our camp site.

We did not yet feel like winter Texans as we looked out on the water and we didn't know yet if we had even made a wise choice in the location we chose. One indicator that was heartening: we heard a lot of Willie Nelson on the radio. It looked as if we were off to a good start.

Free popcorn?? Where do I sign up?

We see a few other people from the Hoosier state in Rockport but most of the license plates in this part of the country are from States west of the Mississippi. This being our third winter on the road, I figure that's long enough to allow me to make a few unscientific observations about the migration patterns of retired folks.

As a general rule, Florida is overwhelmed in the winter by snowbirds living east of the Mississippi while Residents of the northwest and the mountain states who want to escape the cold tend to spend the winter months in Southern Arizona. Winter Texans, at least in Rockport, are composed primarily of people living in the Plains states; Iowa, Missouri, Minnesota, Kansas and the Dakotas. There are also a lot of Michiganders here but then again, there are a lot of Michiganders everywhere. The travel habits of Michigan retirees are pretty unpredictable. No matter where we go in this country, the place is overrun with Michigan license plates. The state must be empty in the winter.

Rockport is one of the fishing towns on the gulf coast. On the trip down, We went through the town of Palacios farther up the coast to visit friends. The horizon near that town seemed to be dotted with tall structures that at first glance seemed to be oil derricks but they were so close together, that didn't seem to be possible. It turns out they were the masts of the shrimp boat fleet. Our friends were staying in a campground and they eat a lot of shrimp because their campsite is right on the shoreline where they watch the coming and goings of the fishing fleet. Their campground fee in the winter of 2003-2004 was two hundred and ten dollars a month and while it didn't have a lot of amenities, a comparable site on the water in southwest Florida, if one even existed, would be five or six times that amount.

The sign at the edge of Rockport says there are about eight thousand residents but the available shopping doesn't make it feel that big. There is only one good size grocery store in town although there is a Wal-Mart under construction. Fresh seafood can be found at reasonable prices on the docks and you can always drive thirty miles to Corpus Christi for all the shopping you want.

There is also only one movie theatre in town but it has five screens playing first run movies. It also had a unique feature the year we were there; free popcorn on Tuesday nights if you bring your own bowl. We took advantage of that twice but then had to stop. I found that I react to free popcorn the way I do with 'all you can eat' buffets. I eat way too much and going to bed with five pounds of popcorn in my stomach is a dumb idea. My first bout of heartburn occurred as a 30 year old after a movie session which included two large boxes of popcorn. I should have known better when I went to the free popcorn movie but I didn't. I ended up in the middle of the night rummaging through our tiny medicine cabinet looking for antacids.

The town has a friendly atmosphere and I never came across that feeling of just being tolerated that I got in Florida. The merchants I dealt with in Rockport didn't try to gouge their visitors. One example of this was propane. I filled up one of the camper tanks and paid about half of what I'd paid the previous year in Florida.

The traffic in Rockport also is not nightmarish like it is in Southwest Florida. It took me a while to realize that, unlike Fort Myers, Florida, you can actually visit stores on the opposite side of the road. I would never attempt that in Florida because it takes to long to make a left turn. Also, in Florida, the natives wouldn't understand the question about the chicken crossing the road because there is no crossing the road. There is never enough of a break in the traffic.

Rockport is not perfect. It is not a manicured place like cities in southwest Florida. There are some decaying parts of town here and maybe there are in Naples or Punta Gorda, Florida as well, but they must do a good job of hiding them. Any weather comparisons would favor southwest Florida. The temperatures are comfortable here but there have been many days that were cool and overcast. To be fair, people who had been coming here for a lot of years told me this is unusual.

There's also a little notoriety in the region. Some years ago, there was a mother who put out a murder contract so that her daughter could make the cheerleading squad. This occurred up the coast from Rockport and I think Rockport must also be very big on cheerleading because the library periodical section here features a magazine called American Cheerleader. I didn't even know such a magazine existed but I found it mildly interesting because of my high school cheerleading experiences. Maybe you didn't know I was a cheer captain and modesty forbids me to speak of it but perhaps I'll tell you about it sometime.

Fishing is big. A former bridge across Copano bay north of town is now a two mile long State Park fishing pier with a section in the middle removed to allow boat traffic to pass through. You can fish to your heart's content for two dollars. We walk the pier for exercise and have seen a lot of fish landed. We did not come prepared to fish but did invest in a pole to try our luck. There must be more to fishing than putting a squirming shrimp on a hook and throwing it in the water because we didn't catch anything.

No matter. A great number of local restaurants serve very good fresh seafood at reasonable prices. The restaurant chains, other than McDonalds and Sonic Burger, have not found Rockport yet.

What I consider a kiss of death blow has been given to Rockport, however. A popular 'places to retire' magazine featured the town on its cover. This same thing happened to the sleepy little towns of Port Charlotte and Punta Gorda, Florida back in the nineteen-nineties. Money Magazine named these two towns to be among the best places to live in the country and since that time, people have flocked there. The horrific devastation of Hurricane Charley seemed to accelerate the growth and now, traffic is terrible and you need to be a former Enron executive to afford the opulent housing being built. It will be interesting and sad to see if this same thing happens to Rockport.

The horror of it all.

A day after our arrival in Rockport, the people parked next to us invited us to come along to a pitch in dinner. They had been coming to the same campground for five years and were the unofficial welcoming committee. They knew almost everyone and introduced us around. We spent the evening learning the ropes on being winter Texans. One of the things talked about was a yearly trip to Matamoros, Mexico across the Rio Grande from Brownsville, Texas. Susie was ready to visit Matamoros fve minutes after the conversation started.

It was roughly 175 miles to Brownsville but I think I said earlier that a trip of that distance is nothing to westerners. The west is so big, you just have to get used to driving miles and miles if you want to go anywhere. There was not much to see on our trip to Brownsville; The King Ranch, an armadillo or two and lots of cows. A trip of this sort is perfect for listening to books on tape. It was a very unassuming drive considering what would take place once we arrived.

The first thing we did when we hit town was to have lunch at a crowded Mexican restaurant. We wandered through some of the shops around the border crossing and that was enough for me. Susie and a couple who had made the trip with us went across the bridge into Matamoros but I decided to beg off. It was warm and after that big lunch, I needed a nap. I wandered over to a little park on the riverbank where an inviting park bench sat under a tree.

I sat down and the first thing I saw was a huge warehouse looming in the background across the river on the Mexican side. Through the live oak trees,

I could make out a large pair of applauding hands painted on the side of this monstrous building. Around the hands were painted a huge red circle with a diagonal line, perhaps fifty feet in length, crossing the circle and passing through the hands. Beneath it, in twenty foot tall letters, were the words 'No Ablaudas'. Something shiny on the front of the building was reflecting the sunlight so I got out my binoculars. A small brass embossed plaque, visible only within five feet of the building had raised letters spelling out the words 'The Clapper Corporation.' ™

"Good Lord," I said to myself. "So this is where they go." Like many other people, I've often wondered what happens to the inventory of Clappers after the holidays. They're everywhere at Christmas and then they just seem to drop off the map. In case you've forgotten, Clappers are the electronic devices that allow you to turn your lights on or off just by clapping your hands. That explained the 'No Ablaudas' on the side of the building.

'There must be a million of those things in there', I thought. 'Can you imagine what would happen if somebody clapped around that building?

I was just about to go find Susie to tell her of my discovery when a small group of English speaking children came into the park to play. We were on the American side of the river and they paid no attention to the giant warehouse some hundred feet away across the water. Two little girls twirled a jump rope around and watched as their brother, Bobby, slowly jumped through the arc made by the rope. It was a little eerie because Bobby looked remarkably like the kid in the movie who sees dead people. You know, the one with Bruce whats-his-name.

The rope arced and the kids chanted: "Bobby and Sarah, sitting in a tree, k——-i———-s———-s————i————n————G". On the G, they clapped their hands and in the background, I was astounded to see the roof of the giant clapper warehouse bounce a little.

"Kids!!!" I yelled, pointing at the 'NO Ablaudas' sign. They apparently knew no Spanish because they paid no attention. Other children standing by joined in.

K—-I—-S—-S—-I—-N—-G. The kids clapped again and the roof jumped a little higher as an untold number of clappers turned on or, or off as it were, in unison and their little individual mechanical 'click' was magnified millions of times.

Suddenly, people wearing what appeared to be huge mittens on their hands ran out the doorway of the Clapper warehouse. They waved their mitten clad arms, searching the horizon as they looked for the source of the Clapper activation.

K—I—S—S—I—N—G. The kids were yelling quickly as the jump rope went faster and faster. Bobby's little feet were flying up and down like a pogo stick on steroids. The children were applauding in unison and the warehouse roof across the river took on the gyrations of a Chubby Checker dance routine.

All of a sudden, people started baling out of every opening of the building. Two men in uniform ran outside and spied the kids. They ran with guns drawn, splashing across the almost dried up Rio Grande and reached with their outstretched arms towards the little rope jumpers……

I was already on my feet. I yelled 'RUN!!' and the kids scattered. I looked back at the ruined warehouse as I took off. The roof was sitting cockeyed on the collapsed walls and I knew as I ran that no one would believe this story.

I have been unable to convince anyone it happened, maybe because no one died although I'm sure several hundred thousand Clappers had to have been destroyed. There was no way their little clapper innards could have handled the strain.

Oh God, just let me die.

When we decided to winter in Texas, Susie and I vowed that this trip would make fishermen out of us. I have never possessed the patience it takes for fishing but Susie was fond of the sport. She just wasn't crazy about the peripheral functions required. Whether it was handling the bait or taking the fish off the hook; neither of those set very well with her.

My father, who was a devout outdoorsman, died when I was very young and I never had the opportunity to avail myself of his fishing knowledge. I always felt like that same outdoorsman was buried deep inside my psyche somewhere and I needed to bring it out now that I had some time to spare. I also felt that I could help Susie with her fear of worms. We were practically starting a new life in Texas so why not become fishermen in the process? We decided that we needed expert help so we signed up for a deep sea fishing expedition on a large party boat. We could just bypass catching the non-keepers and start right out by catching a few of the big guys. Another couple from the campground who were also friends from back in Indiana, volunteered to go along on the fishing trip and help us out. Danny is a big man, a retired plumber and a hunter; what you'd call a man's man. His wife, Mary Ann, is a genteel lady and not the sort whom you could picture baiting hooks with a squirming worm but looks are deceiving. Both of them were anglers of the first order.

As the day for the trip approached, I began to have second thoughts. In truth, I am uncomfortable in any water deeper than I am tall and the Gulf of

Mexico certainly was that and more. I was a little reluctant to be boarding a not very big boat and sailing out into what amounted to an ocean. After being the fool who talked us all into this, however, I couldn't very well back out.

We stopped for breakfast before boarding. Susie was to excited to eat but she did have a glass of tomato juice. I didn't even do that. I didn't think my stomach could handle food. Danny, who likes his food, had a healthy breakfast of Ham and eggs with biscuits and gravy on the side. He also finished off the remainder of Mary Ann's waffle while we waited on the boat's departure.

The boat was bigger than I had thought. There were about seventy people on it in addition to the crew. Just before we got underway, I became somewhat agitated when I noticed that the crew's first mate looked amazingly like Bob Denver of Gilligan's Island. I know. It was only a television show but still, an omen is an omen. I decided that if the Skipper turned out to be a rotund, jolly fellow, we were getting off the boat. Before I had a chance to check out the Captain's credentials, however, he came on the loudspeaker.

"This is your Captain. Welcome aboard. We've got some good news to deliver. We have a report that they're hitting like crazy today." He paused as the crowd murmured it's appreciation. I elbowed Susie in the ribs.

"You hear that? Today's our day." I told her. "I hope we can carry everything we catch."

The Captain jumped back in. "We'll be going out thirty miles or so. Be ready to catch fish in a couple of hours."

Thirty miles! I mentally began to calculate if I could swim that far should the need arise. I doubted that I could so once again I considered getting off but decided to cast my fate with the boat because of that need to put a little adventure in my life. Besides, Susie loves fishing adventures and I couldn't have pried her off that boat with a crowbar.

The morning sun was peeking over the horizon as we left. The wind was blowing but it didn't bother me. All it meant was setting my baseball cap on my head a little tighter. None of us had any idea what effect this wind would have on stirring up the waters of the Gulf of Mexico. On the open water, the wind turned out to be a gale and the resulting waves tossed the boat around like a dog shaking a rag doll. We sat inside the cabin out of the wind as the boat made its way out to sea. We braced ourselves as the cabin rocked and rolled like a cheap roller coaster.

We were seated next to the concession stand where an otherwise skinny man with the biggest stomach I've ever seen held court behind the counter. He wore a yellowish white tee shirt with the sleeves cut out. The remaining material in the shirt was stretched across his gargantuan stomach in a failed attempt to cover up his belly. An unlit portion of a cigar jutted from his lips. I studied him and the chalkboard menu while the boat tossed this way and that.

"They've got cheese fries here." I said to no one in particular.

"Please don't mention food." Susie said. I looked at her and noticed that her normally pink complexion had taken on the pallor normally associated with processed flour. The boat suddenly pitched sideways and Susie stood up.

"Air. I need air."

"Need to get your sea legs, eh?" Danny said as she pushed past us toward the door. I followed close behind. When she opened the door, I noticed a lady near the back of the boat leaning over the railing as we went out. 'Seasick?' I thought. How is that possible? We had been on the boat less than a hour and besides, I didn't feel a thing. If anyone should be seasick, it would be me. We went down into a white capped trough as we walked outside and then back up on an enormous wave where the boat hung balanced before plunging over the other side of the wave and down into the next foamy area. Without warning, people all around me, a very pale green Susie among them, were leaning far out over the railing calling for someone named Ralph. The bright red tomato juice leaving Susie's mouth scared me momentarily but after talking to her, realized she was okay; shaken and sick, but okay.

Danny had taken a seat on a bench watching the action. He looked over from where he was sitting and winked at me.

"I guess they don't have the stomach for this stuff."

He had no more than finished when the lady sitting next to him moaned. Up came her breakfast and maybe last night's dinner, splashing down the side of his leg and over his right shoe.

"Don't come any closer." He told Mary Ann as she turned from the rail to see what was causing the noise. I was trying to help Susie sit down when the lady in distress turned to me, apparently thinking I was in some position of authority.

I was taken aback at her eyes. I've seen more life in the eyes of road kill than she had in hers. Her face was a study in shades of gray.

"Please, Sir." She said, grabbing my arm with the grip of a longshoreman. She gasped as she attempted to take in great gulps of air, "Get me off of this boat. I'll give you anything you want if you can make them turn around."

"I don't know..." I started to tell her.

"Five hundred dollars. I'll give you five hundred dollars. Just stop this damn boat."

"Try to concentrate on the horizon." I said in my best doctor voice while trying to sound as if I knew what I was talking about.

"There is no horizon, you fool." She said, moaning. "Oh God, please make them stop." A man I took to be her husband returned with wet paper towels and I moved away before she could grab me again.

Two hours into the trip, the boat finally stopped but the waves didn't. I looked around at the open water, seeing nothing but mammoth oil drilling platforms in the distance. They would appear and then disappear as we rolled with the waves. The deck hands started bringing out the cut up squid we were to use for bait. One look at those slimy tentacles sent Susie scrambling for her second trip to the railing. I found her a place to sit after she stopped her agonizing retching.

"Please take me home." She whimpered.

"I don't think I can. I'm not in charge."

I could do nothing but pat her hand and wonder why I wasn't affected. She finally stopped her retching and I found her a place to sit among a group of people huddled on a bench. I tried to fish but it was nearly impossible to even stand up. I guess it was good that half the crowd was sick because the other half mobbed the railing trying to put out a line.

It was hopeless. I hung up my pole and waited for the scurrying deck hands to untangle the six or seven lines that had become entangled with mine.

I noticed Danny putting down his fishing pole while moving away from the railing. The waves, the squid guts, his vomit soaked pants leg, combined with the squishy sound his shoe made with each step had finally gotten to him. He perched on the edge of a bench making guttural sounds which I can best describe as primeval. I thought of the breakfast he had eaten and became concerned that if a man his size continued to let that pressure build, it could be catastrophic when it let loose. I moved a feeble Susie upwind of him and made her comfortable.

"Don't ever let me eat chunky peanut butter again." she said to me in a voice as pitiful as any I've ever heard. I looked again at Danny. I knew he would feel better getting it over with but he did not want to admit that the sea had gotten the best of him.

"Let it go, man." I told him.

'No!" he said through gritted teeth, shaking his head so violently I was afraid his cheeks might fly off. He needed to upchuck in the worst way but I had no idea how to convince him of that..

The concession attendant came by with the now lit cigar still dangling from his lips. He was walking as if he was in Central Park. The too short tee-shirt had given up on covering the man's stomach and contented itself with displaying the splatters of foodstuffs from his morning's endeavors. The aroma of nasty cigar smoke was blowing in the wind as he announced:

"Anybody out here need anything?"

A light bulb went off in my head. 'Let's give Mother Nature a little push.' I thought.

I turned to the concession guy, trying to avoid looking at his enormous gut.

"I'll have a couple of those chili cheese dogs you've been bragging about." Danny raised his sagging head and gave me a look of despair. The corners of his mouth were turned up in a macabre imitation of a man trying to swallow a mouthful of nightcrawlers.

Susie, whom I forgotten about, murmured, "Oh please don't…." I couldn't catch the rest of what she said as her voice tailed off.

"Y'all want some chopped up onion on those?"

"Yeah, and some relish. Throw on a little mustard if you got any but not the stuff that looks like baby poop. I don't like that kind." I said in my best hillbilly voice. Being around southerners causes me to affect that twang every time. It normally drives Susie nuts but not on this day. She had nothing to say because at the mention of relish, she had made her third dash for the railing.

I was busy watching Danny and had no time to help her. At the request of a chili and cheese topping for my hotdog, his stomach began to behave like he had been taking belly dancing lessons. It rose and fell as if it had a life of its own. I made sure Susie was out of harm's way as Danny began to turn towards the rail.

"Are you oka......." The attendant started to ask but he never finished. Danny just made it to the windward side of the rail before he let go with an eruption that was about a three on the Richter scale.

I later spent the entire evening trying to calculate the velocity involved when a big boned individual like that with a good sized breakfast churning around in his stomach throws up into a twenty mile an hour headwind. I'm certain there is some sort of mathematical formula but I couldn't nail it down. He was leaning over the bow and he managed, with the help of the wind, to reach the stern of the boat with his breakfast. Just in case I haven't told you, this was no small boat.

Many of the fisherman lined up along the rail never knew what hit them. They were packed in so tightly that they couldn't have gotten away even had they known what was coming. It didn't cause so much as a ripple among the people trying to land fish. Some of the others though, wiping bits of Danny's breakfast off their person, joined him in leaning over the rail and peering down into the white capped, deep blue water.

The Captain mercifully decided we'd had enough and headed for home. We all survived the trip and Mary Ann, who had remained quiet during the whole episode caught the only edible fish. I caught something that was immediately cut up for bait by the deck hand and I also snagged one gentleman's ball cap.

In time, Susie and Danny regained their equilibrium and we're all planning our next fishing trip. We're going out on the pier where hopefully everything will hold still.

Randolph Scott was no scaredy cat.

Rockport turned out to be a great place for seafood but we got our fill and we were quickly learning that we get itchy feet easily and a month in one place is enough. We looked at our road Atlas for places that might be scenic or historically significant and decided to go to Big Bend National park in Southwestern Texas. The AAA book tells us that it has world class scenery and is surrounded by old west history. The only problem with it is that it's not a place you just happen to drive by.

The park is in the middle of the Chihuhuan desert on the Mexican border. It's also about a six hundred and fifty mile trip from Rockport to Big Bend and there was a time when I would have done that many miles in a day and tacked on a couple of hundred more. Those days are over. First of all, we're not in a hurry. Secondly, the old spinal column seizes up after about six hours of jostling around causing me to walk around bent over like a furniture mover with a couch on his back. I would need Quasimodo's picture on my drivers license if I tried to do a six hundred and fifty mile day now.

Two hundred and fifty miles is enough. It happened that we talked to a fisherman who told us of a great state park and campground about that distance in southwest Texas between Rio Grande City and Zapata, Texas, both of which are on the Mexican border. The campground was in Falcon State park, part of which contained Falcon Lake, ninety eight thousand acres of dammed up Rio Grande river.

The lake is administered by both Mexico and the United States. It is also on the northern end of the 'Valley' where thousands of winter Texans congregate.

We paid for a week's camping and were given a huge campsite on the edge of the brush. We were camped next to a couple named Bill and Louise. Bill wore a cowboy hat and looked a lot like Randolph Scott, one of my boyhood heroes.

I wandered over to chat with him after we got the camper set up.

"We spend our winter here but I still do a little ranching and some oil drilling on a small spread up by Abilene." He told me. He started throwing handfuls of deer corn to a herd of Javelinas who wandered up out of the brush as we talked. Javelinas look a lot like wild pigs but they're not. Animal Husbandry is not my strong suit but I understand they're related to the antelope family. They looked a little bit menacing but I resisted the urge to climb up on the picnic table because Bill seemed unconcerned. I also knew Randolph Scott would never climb up on anything to get away from a little wild animal.

Bill reached down and pulled a blade of buffalo grass and stuck it in his mouth. He chewed on it as he continued.

"You goin' across the border?"

"Yessir, I think we will. I'm a little leery but… "

"Don't be taking any firearms over there." He warned. They'll throw you in the hoosegow if they find so much as a bullet on you." He shook his head in disgust.

"Twenty years ago, you could ride in there with a gun belt and a forty four in the holster and they wouldn't say anything. Now it's downright dangerous for Americans to venture into the interior of the country and you can't pack even so much as a hand gun to protect yourself from the pistoleros and the bandidos." I assured him we didn't even own a b-b gun.

"You'll be alright but when you get over there but you'll see the Federales everywhere. You don't want to fool around with them. They look like sixteen year old kids with automatic weapons but them ol' boys would just as soon shoot you as look at you."

I felt like I was sitting in Lonesome Dove discussing Mexican affairs with Augustus McRae. I reached over and pulled a blade of that Buffalo grass and stuck it between my teeth. My God. A terrible taste flooded my taste buds. I spit it out, hacking and gagging.

"Gotcha' a ripe piece, did ya?" he says.

"Yessir." A hack-hack noise came from my throat. "What exactly is ripe?"

"I was just funnin' with you. Ya probably got one with a little javelina stink on it." He said. "Them ol' boys like to mark their territory."

I tried wiping the taste out of my mouth with my fingertips, scraping my tongue at around five hundred RPM, all the while trying not to envision what materials Javelinas might use to set up their boundaries.

After I stopped spitting, I told him of our plans to travel to Big Bend while hoping he hadn't noticed my spitting frenzy.

"Me and the wife have been there but it's right smart of a ways." He said.

"The wife." The term rolled off this gentleman's tongue like melted butter. His cowboy hat was perched back on his head exposing his leathery face to the afternoon sun. He sat fiddling with his 'git along, little dogie' rope while he spoke of 'the wife'. He obviously was a cowboy and I wanted to be one. I also thought mentioning the little woman in this manner sounded very manly. I thanked him for the information and went back to our camper.

"Susie" I said in my best Randolph Scott voice. "I think maybe I'll be referring to you as 'the wife' from now on.

"If I hear you say 'the wife' even one time, you'll be calling me the ex-wife." She said, in that cute little way she has of letting me know her feelings on a subject.

I forgot 'the wife' idea immediately. Randolph Scott probably isn't allowed to call his mate something like that either.

I like my steaks medium rare.

A day or so after we had settled in to our campsite at Falcon Lake, we went to a cookout at the campground recreation center. A couple named Ed and Rosalie were the cooks and they, like Bill and Louise, spend the winter in this campground. Ed gave Susie and I T-Bone steak fresh off the grill.

He was very familiar with the area and told us about some T-bone steaks he bought in Nuevo Guerrero across the Dam in Mexico.

"They're only a dollar apiece." He said.

"Let's go." Susie said.

"I don't think I should be driving in Mexico, Susie." I said. I was a little reluctant to go because of a conversation I had with another camper who had warned me of the Federales.

"I'm fixin' to go tomorrow. Y'all can go with me." Ed volunteered. "It's only a mile or so across the dam." I was stuck. I had to go or admit to this man that I was scared of the Federales. "I'll pick y'all up at nine." He said.

The next day, just before nine o'clock, Susie decided to go with a group of birdwatchers to Salineno, a small town outside the park well known for it's birds.

"Wait a minute!" I said. "What about Nuevo Guerrero?"

"You can go by yourself. You're a big boy. Get some eggs and some Crisco while you're over there."

"But Susie, what about the Federales?" The thought of spending the rest of my days in a Mexican jail already had me on the edge of panic and I was having trouble keeping my voice down.

"Oh right. The Federales." She said. "I did want to see them. Would you take their picture?"

"Their picture? I'm not taking their picture, for God's sake. Why would I want to irritate the Federales!"

"What are you talking about?" she said.

"Have you never listened to Willie Nelson?"

"Willie Nelson? She said.

"Yes, Willie Nelson. Pancho and Lefty. Mexico. You know."

I cleared my throat and strummed my air guitar.

"All the Federales say, they could have had 'em anyday." I sang in my best Willie imitation, lacking only a red bandanna to complete the act.

"Those Federales." I said, my voice breaking. "The ones in Willie's song is what I'm talking about. If those ol' boys can handle Pancho and Lefty, I imagine they can make mincemeat out of me."

"Pancho and Lefty?"

"Yes. Pancho and Lefty. They only let 'em slip away. Out of kindness, I suppose."

"You need to have your head examined." She said, climbing into the car filled with women clutching their bird books.

When Ed arrived, he made sure I wasn't packing any heat. We would definitely go to jail if we had firearms or even a bullet in his truck. The border crossing was uneventful and Ed dropped me off in front of a little building with 'Mercado' painted above the door.

"I'm going up to the Farmacio to see about Rosalie's medicine. I'll pick you up here."

"But I don't know any Spanish. I don't think I...."

"Just tell 'em T-bone. "They'll know what you want."

"But..." was all I got out before he drove on up the street. I went up to the door and noticed a placard taped to the window. The word ' Desperado' in big black letters was spread across the top of it. A photograph obviously taken by a telephoto lens was in the center of the poster. The picture was of an American tourist caught in mid stride and running for all he was worth. It reminded me of Wiley Coyote chasing the roadrunner, but yet, at the same time, the running figure seemed to be familiar. The desperado wore Bermuda shorts and knee high white tube socks with a red stripe around the top. "That looks like my favorite socks." I said to myself. I walked up to the front of the building to get a closer look. "Holy Smokes, that's me. That's my I.U. hat." I said, looking around to see if anyone noticed the picture. I didn't understand any of the Spanish verbiage except for the words 'Clapper' and 'recompensa — cinco pesos.' My God, these people think I had something to do with that Clapper warehouse collapse. The poster was a result of an incident I witnessed a few weeks back after a bunch of kids were jumping rope and clapping in a park on the border where I happened to be sitting on a park bench. The activity set off a massive Clapper clicking frenzy that destroyed the warehouse. I was an innocent bystander but somehow the authorities must have thought I was involved since they took my picture. I had taken off because I thought the guards from the warehouse were the dreaded Federales and now they're offering a reward of Cinco pesos.

Cinco? Six pesos? That all I'm worth? I snatched the poster off the window and shoved it in the back pocket of my shorts. I rolled my socks down so the red stripe didn't show and said a quiet prayer that these posters weren't hanging all over town.

I walked into the tiny Mercado, no bigger than the greeting card section at Kroger.

"T-bone." I told the smiling young man behind the counter. I held up six fingers to let him know how many. "Cinco." I said, feeling very proud of my bilingual efforts.

The young man looked at me quizzically but I wasn't sure why so I just smiled at him. He smiled back and got a slab of meat out of the small cooler.

"Tres Quattro?" He said, holding up his thumb and forefinger about three quarters of an inch apart.

I got it. He obviously wanted to know where I was from. "United States." I said, pointing at the American flag on my tee-shirt.

"Een-de-anna." I spoke very slowly and gestured to my IU hat and then towards El Norte, the north.

He tilted his head sideways and held up his hand again with the two fingers spread.

"Tres Quattro?" he said once again.

"Lairr-rey Bir-rdd." I said, even more slowly, shooting an imaginary basketball at the back wall.

He shook his head and turned on his band saw. When he finished, I took the package to the counter in the front of the store. Then I remembered the eggs and the Crisco. I looked around and didn't see either.

"Eggs?" I said to the girl behind the counter. She shook her head.

"No habla ingles."

Drat. Now what do I do? I was about to forget it when suddenly I had an idea. I began to whistle the tune to the chicken dance reasoning that surely the Mexican people were acquainted with this song. Maybe I could make the connection that way but the girl just backed up a step and looked at me. I whistled a little louder and tucked my hands up into my armpits. I flapped my arms in the international gesture of the chicken dancing. No good. She backed up another step. I reached behind me as if to pull an egg out of my backside and this only served to unnerve her even more.

"Loco." She said to the meat cutter. "Loco."

He came out from behind the meat case carrying his meat cleaver and just then, Ed walked in.

"Ed," I said. "Thank God you're here. I need to get some eggs and they don't know what I'm talking about."

He turned to the girl. "Huevos".

'Ahhhhh." She said and reached under the counter. She pulled out a plastic bag filled with the biggest eggs I'd ever seen.

"Not refrigerated?" I said.

The girl backed away another step.

"I expect they're fresh although I've never bought eggs over here." Ed said.

I'm wasn't sure if my American trained stomach would handle room temperature eggs but I just wanted to get out of there so I took the bag.

"What about Crisco?" I said to Ed but before he could answer, the girl jumped up, said 'Ahhhhhh' once again and disappeared around the corner. She returned with about a twelve inch square block of white stuff wrapped in wax paper.

"What is that?" I said to the girl.

"It looks like lard to me." Ed said.

"Lard? I didn't even know lard existed anymore."

The girl was grinning from ear to ear, obviously proud of herself and I didn't think I should say anything else. I had no idea what we were going to do with a chunk of lard the size of the blarney stone but I reached for my wallet, wanting to get this over with so we could get back across the border.

'The border?" I suddenly thought. "My God, would they have that Clapper poster at the border? I could be in a Mexican jail before dark."

Ed interrupted my thoughts. "I forgot to tell you about the billy goat ribs they got back there." He said, gesturing toward the rear. "There ain't a lot of meat on 'em but them 'ol boys make for some tasty eatin'."

"Billy Goats?"

'Billy goats. Sure. They just butchered yesterday. " He gestured toward the side window where I could see several goats prancing around in the empty lot next door.

"You messin' with me, Ed?" I said, handing the girl money. She had shown me a calculator with 9.60 on the display.

"No sir. I expect if you was to walk around back there, you'd find a fresh goatskin or two."

"I think I'll pass, Ed. Have you ever heard anything about mad goat disease?"

He grinned and opened the door. "Sometimes, I think maybe that's what the wife's got."

I waved at the girl behind the counter as I walked out the door.

"Sayonara." I said.

We walked outside and there sat the Federales. An American made Humvee was in the middle of the road with a uniformed young man leaning against the back. He appeared to be about fourteen years old and was loosely holding a very menacing looking machine gun across his chest. Three other uniformed men were walking out of a storefront across the street.

My heart dropped into my socks. 'I'm done for.' I thought. 'I love you Susie, but if I could get my hands on you right now....'

I eased back against the wall. If we can just get to the truck before they notice us....

"Ola. Como Estas." Ed waved at them and they waved back. I tentatively raised an arm and watched as The Federales climbed into the humvee, waved again and drove away.

Willie Nelson, I could wring your neck.

Give my compliments to Mr. Tchaikovsky.

Big Bend National Park is named for the bend in the Rio Grande where the river changes its southeasterly direction to head northeast. The park is immense and at 800,000 acres, I figured it must be one of biggest in the National Park system but it's not even close. That honor, at 13 million acres, goes to Wrangell-St Elias National Park in Alaska.

It's not an easy place to get to, being some 80 miles from Alpine, Texas, the nearest city of any size. Even with that, Big Bend is not a place to be missed.

We camped near the western entrance of the park in the small town of Terlingua, Texas. According to the lady who assigned us a campsite, The name Terlingua is butchered Spanish for 'three languages' in recognition of the English, Spanish and Commanche spoken in the area.

When I heard 'Commanche', I was immediately on the alert because I had battled the Commanches as well as the Apaches and occasionally the Blackfeet every Saturday afternoon at the Ritz theatre when I was a kid. In those days, I had my broomstick horse, Black Diamond, my Lash Larue model six shooter and my Red Ryder B-B gun. Now, even though I was smack in the middle of their territory, it did little good to be on the alert because I had none of those tools to help. If we came under attack today, the best I could do was point my Microsoft Mouse at them.

Gordon Grindstaff

Those cowboy and Indian movies were a big part of my growing up. I spent many a Saturday afternoon crouched behind the boulders with Roy Rogers and Gabby Hayes waiting on the bad guys to come over the hill. I also spent time behind other boulders with the whip wielding Lash Larue and singing Gene Autry as well as Rocky Lane and his stallion Blackjack. The hero I was riding with depended on what movie was playing at the Ritz that afternoon. I never missed a Saturday at that theatre except during those forty days of Lent when the Catholic kids had to forego attending movies. It was just assumed in Loogootee, Indiana that Lent and its rite of sacrifice included giving up movies. It was good for my soul but I suspect many a cowboy suffered because of some Indian fighting trick I failed to learn during those long, dark days leading up to Easter Sunday.

Terlingua, with a population of only two hundred (including commanches), has a quirky little radio station that plays every conceivable kind of music. Bluegrass, twangy country, Rock and roll and Classical rolled over those airwaves . If it could be played with a musical instrument, it was on that station. There were no advertisements and no talking, just music playing throughout the park. The variety of music went well with the scenery of Big Bend. Craggy mountains, wide open valleys that went on for miles and incredible canyons with soaring rock walls overwhelmed our senses.

The isolation of Big Bend also contributed to a problem we had not considered when we headed out for the road. We received news while we were there that one of my favorite cousins, a lady named Milma, had died after a long illness. Bad news does not just arrive when you're at home and it becomes harder to deal with when you're on the road because you don't have anyone to commiserate with. Missing Funerals is something we will need to learn to live with, I guess.

I was still coming to grips with Milma's passing when we set out to do some exploring. We stopped at one of the Rio Grande River overlooks and just as we started to get out of the truck, that little 200 watt radio station in Terlingua finished up a Flatt and Scruggs tune and then began playing the 1812 overture, of all things. This is one of my favorite pieces of music and when they use the military cannons in place of cymbals, it stirs my soul in such a way that I cannot pass up any chance to listen to it. The music made it's way out over the airwaves and I hesitated.

"Go ahead, Susie. I'll catch up." I told her. It had been cold earlier in the morning and now, the sun coming through the windows was hot and the combination of the heat and the music made me drowsy. I sat there thinking of my cousin and her recent passing as well as my Saturday afternoon movies. I pictured myself as that long ago young boy who played Cowboys and Indians after spending an afternoon at the movie. The distant canyon where Susie now stood peering into it could have been the setting for anyone of those movies. I pondered the scenery as I wondered when the innocence of my youth had been replaced by my current curmudgeonly cynicism.

It occurred to me that my generation, with my cousin's passing, had already started to join the countless other generations who had to move over and give the next generation their turn. Pretty heavy stuff, I know, but being around death and such magnificent scenery does that to a person.

The overture slowly wound its way to the moment when the cannon fire joins with the music, producing an incredibly intense feeling that only the most callous of people could ignore. I looked out into the river valley where an abandoned ranch house stood. Some pioneer family had most likely used up their allotted time on this earth trying, and failing, to tame this rugged piece of our land. Any little kids who lived here then didn't have to play cowboys and Indians. They, along with their parents, got to live it.

All of a sudden, I was thinking of my own father and mother. Even though I was barely six years old when my father died, I had been told enough about his love of nature to be certain he and my mother would have loved this place. It occurred to me that neither of them ever got the chance to do the things Susie and I were experiencing. That's just wrong and unfair. I shook my head, trying to get such maudlin thoughts out of my head.

I reached over to turn the music up as the boom of the Cannons and the music's crescendo reverberated through the truck. The melody coursed through my veins, carrying the song from the top of my head to the tip of my toes. The grandeur of Big Bend surrounding us coupled with the grandeur of the music sent a chill scurrying up my back and before I knew what was happening, my eyes were flooded with tears. The music crashed around me as I tried to get the tears to stop. I was a 63 year old man and I wasn't supposed to cry. But I couldn't stop. I cried for Milma, I cried for my mom and dad, I cried for that little boy who missed those Lenten cowboy movies and then I cried for me and for everyone else who can't stay young forever.

The music ended just as Susie came walking up the path towards me and I hurriedly put on my sunglasses and turned the radio down. I wasn't ashamed of the tears but I could not have explained why I had been crying because I didn't know why. I knew it had something to do with the realization that life and everything about it is precious.

The good experiences I've had as well as the bad ones are what made me who I am and that fifteen minutes sitting in my truck parked at a scenic overlook made me appreciate having the chance to experience all of them.

It was quite a revelation and I wouldn't trade any of it for anything except maybe the chance to go back and sneak into one of those Lenten cowboy movies.

The answer is blowin' in the wind.

Last Fall, we talked at length with a couple from Maine about volunteering at National parks around the country. We met these folks while we were visiting the National park in Harper's Ferry, West Virginia. The two of them were working in the park and they spoke of the chance to learn more about our country's history as well as see some of the country. They also mentioned free campsites. It sounded like a good deal and we decided to follow up on it.

At the same time, we were talking about spending the early spring in the Hill Country of Texas north of San Antonio. This came about because we had talked to some other folks in Louisiana who told us about the Hill Country wildflowers.

We put the two conversations together and decided we'd need several weeks to explore the whole central Texas area so we found a National park in the Hill Country area and volunteered to work there.

The park was the President Lyndon B. Johnson National Park. LBJ and his wife Lady Bird donated the Texas White House and 640 acres of the LBJ ranch to create this park. The park service built a visitors center, acquired his boyhood home and the original Johnson Ancestors settlement in Johnson City, Texas. Together, this complex made up the park. Susie worked in the Library at the Visitors center and in the flower gardens at the Texas White House. A year or so earlier, I had gotten a commercial drivers license that allowed me to drive a bus so this provided me with an opportunity to conduct interpretative tours of the Ranch while guiding the guests around in a National Park Bus. In exchange for our service. the Park Service provided us with a campsite and the opportunity to meet new friends who were also volunteering.

Volunteering in National Parks is a great way to see the country and help out with your campground expenses at the same time. It pays to do a little homework, though. The first night after we settled in Johnson City, we had a good rain before we went to bed and then we had a king size thunderstorm. As the storm raged all around us, I remembered that while we were in Big Bend National Park, some people in our campground went on a hike and had to spend the night in the wilderness. A dry arroyo had flooded and prevented their getting back to the campground. There had not been any rain, in fact, not a cloud was in the sky all day but it turned out the cause was a real gully washer about eighty miles north of the park. It left quite an impression on me when they finally were rescued and came back to tell us of their harrowing adventure.

I had also watched a program one evening a few months back on the weather channel called Storm Stories. (— I know. I know. We lead a real fascinating life.—) The program was about a cloudburst flooding a campground. It was a terrible sight. The raging floodwaters picked up the campers and flung them about like toothpicks.

The trapped campers in Big Bend, the gully washer and the toothpick like campers came to the forefront when I realized I had no notion of the topography of where we were. We could be parked in the middle of a flood plain. We were set up in a field behind the visitor center and I tried to recall if we had crossed a stream going back to the campsite.

Good Lord, I think we had. I lay awake most of the night as the storm carried on outside the camper, picturing the stranded hikers and those travel trailers bobbing down the river right along with trees ripped out by the roots. Luckily, Texas thunderstorms seem to be a lot like their politicians (and ours as well). There was a lot of thunder and lightning but nothing much of any consequence happened. We came through the storm unscathed.

Conducting tours was quite an interesting job. I had to immerse myself in LBJ history and it was pretty fascinating. Susie and I had a couple of young children during the LBJ presidency and I worked a lot of hours at my job trying to get ahead. Consequently, I really didn't pay a lot of attention to the national scene.

The Vietnam war, however, was another matter. It was not to be ignored. The war was on TV every night and almost tore the country apart. In the end, it forced LBJ out of office. I had forgotten a lot of that but it all came rushing back at me as I watched tapes of LBJ and the nineteen sixties. He was such a complex, larger than life person and the more I read about him, the more I found myself alternately admiring him or despising him and occasionally feeling sorry for him but never, ever liking him.

He was a braggart who was crude, gruff, arrogant and rode roughshod over anyone who got in his way. He was also generous and loyal to a fault and cared deeply about the plight of the underprivileged. I've met several people who knew the man and all of them either hated him or loved him. There was no neutrality.

Those of you who are too young to remember LBJ's time in office might not realize his effect. In my opinion, we live in a very different country today than we did before LBJ took office. He authored an immense number of social programs. The Head Start program, Public Safety, Medicare, Medicaid, the Civil Rights Act, National Public Radio and sixty different laws dealing with the promotion of education all came from LBJ. Of course, no one remembers him for those things. His legacy is Vietnam and the fifty eight thousand plus people who died there so I guess we'll have to wait for fifty years or so and let History decide if he did more good than harm. In the meantime, I just drove my bus and told people what I knew about him.

Ich Bin Luckenbach? Ya, Ya, Ya.

Fredericksburg, Texas is just down the road from the Lyndon Johnson National Park and we spent a lot of our spare time there while volunteering at LBJ. Johnson City, where we were camping, had a population of about 900 and was a little light on shopping. Susie has been honing her shopping skills for forty odd years and it was sad to watch her grow rusty. Fredericksburg provided the venues Susie needed to stay sharp in the competitive field of shopping so we made the trip as often as possible.

This town of about twenty thousand was established by German immigrants and the influence of those early settlers is found throughout the city. There are a couple of German bakeries as well as several German restaurants and we found ourselves eating sauerkraut, Opa's sausage, spaetzle and red cabbage about every other day. All except for the sauerkraut, that is. I ate it only once and it had a startling effect on my digestive system. That stuff made the thirty miles back to our camper a harrowing trip through the hill country.

Being surrounded by all this German tradition has also had another effect on me. After visiting about the sixth German restaurant, I enrolled in a yodeling class, went shopping for lederhosen and found myself planning on buying a Volkswagen when we got home. I also took to calling Susie 'Frau' but she didn't appreciate it and threatened to take away my lederhosen if I didn't stop it.

Fredericksburg has a famous neighbor, the town of Luckenbach, Texas, just a ten minute drive to the south east. We had no more than settled into our campsite when I picked up my air guitar, turned to Susie and said;

"Let's go to Luckenbach, Texas with Waylon and Willie and the boys. I was hoping to meet up with Willie Nelson and ask him how Pancho and Lefty had managed to elude the Federales for so long. Unfortunately, he wasn't around.

Luckenbach wasn't anything like I expected. It consisted of a combination General Store, Post office and beer joint. There was also a dance hall and a couple of homes. One gentleman whose name I forget, bought the whole town and turned it into a famous watering hole. I don't know why I never think of doing things like that.

Susie went to the General Store to browse and I wandered over under the Live Oak trees where several guys in cowboy hats and jeans were congregated. They were drinking long neck Lone Stars and playing a game called washers. The game looked very similar to horseshoes except they were throwing two inch diameter washers at a similar sized hole in the ground.

I went into the bar, ordered a Lone Star beer and walked back outside to watch. Guitar Music wafted out from the bar as the washer players looked me over. Thank God I hadn't worn my lederhosen but I sort of wished I hadn't worn my Bermuda shorts and my red striped white tube socks. The cowboys looked me over real close and it made me a little nervous.

"You boys know any bluegrass?" I said. I figured this might be common ground and even though I knew nothing at all about Bluegrass, I had driven by the Bill Monroe bluegrass festival site in Brown County, Indiana. If nothing else, I'd just tell 'em that.

A tall, skinny cowboy looked me over, fingered his washer and said "A little, I reckon." He reached in the back pocket of his jeans and extended a plug of tobacco.

"Need a chaw, tenrrrrrrfdft?" His voice tailed off, but I'm pretty sure he called me 'tenderfoot'. He spit a stream of tobacco juice expertly into the dirt.

"A little, I reckon." I said in my best John Wayne voice, resisting the urge to call him pilgrim.

I figured I could handle that chewing tobacco since I had chewed on occasion forty five years ago when I was working in the furniture factory. Chewing tobacco then had been a defense mechanism to keep the sawdust out of my mouth and nose but it was a little different this time. This Texas tobacco burnt my tongue and made my saliva glands work overtime.

The cowboys threw the washers as I desperately fought the river of saliva that was trying to drool down the corners of my mouth. I needed to spit but knew instinctively I'd get it all over me so I took my leave.

"I better go check on the wife. Don't want her gettin' lost." I said, spilling only a little tobacco juice. This was the second time since we got to Texas that I ended up with stuff in my mouth that didn't agree with me. I ducked behind a Live Oak tree, bent over and spit that stuff all over my tennis shoes, fighting back the urge to gag. Satisfied that I didn't have it all over my shirt, I went to find Susie. I didn't return to the washer pit.

Another interesting thing about Fredericksburg is that Admiral Chester Nimitz was born there and since he was Commander of the Pacific fleet during World War Two, the National museum of the Pacific war is here. We spent a day looking at the exhibits and I found a project they are doing that interested me. The museum is gathering oral accounts of military men and women who served in the Pacific during World War Two.

There was only one name on the sign up sheet so I decided that when I got home, I would tell all my WWII friends and relatives about the request. I went through a mental list of everyone I knew who might have served in the Pacific. I thought of several people but they were all dead. I couldn't even envision anyone alive that served in WWII, period. Holy Smoke. I couldn't believe it.

I lay awake all night going through names; Uncle Albert and Uncle Bud. Dead. Cousin Lester. Dead. Cousin Bob. Gone. My God, how is this possible? When did all these people die?

They were just here yesterday. I think.

Really? I look that good? Honest?

You wouldn't think Del Rio, Texas would be high on our list of places to visit and it wasn't but during our winter in the hill Country, We ended up staying in Del Rio overnight on three different occasions. We had not really intended to spend any time there but we learned that if you're in southwest Texas, you just about have to go through there.

The first time we stayed was accidental since we needed a place to stop for the night on our way to Big Bend. The other two times we were there on purpose. Del Rio is a handy place to cross the border into Mexico to visit Ciudad Acuna, a Mexican border town with a couple of good restaurants and great shopping. I've made great strides in conquering my fear of leaving the country to go to Mexico. My impressions of Mexico as a place filled with bandidos and Federales lurking on every corner were formed fifty years ago at the Saturday afternoon movies and it's taken some time to get over that. But I'm getting there.

The only hard part about going to Ciudad Acuna is the walk across the bridge. It's about a mile from the border station into the town. We decided not to drive because finding a place to park is almost impossible. It's also a little unnerving to know you can go to jail over a minor scrape. A Cab will take you for across for twenty dollars each way but since 9/11, there can be as much as an hour's wait when coming back to the U.S. by motor vehicle. Pedestrians fare much better so we decided to walk across.

The first trip was made with some Volunteer friends of ours from LBJ National Park. They make an annual trip to get a year's worth of all their prescription medicines in Ciudad Acuna. The money that they save is well worth the five hour drive and the mile long walk across the bridge. It doesn't seem to be hurting them any, either. They're in their mid seventies and still walk a mile to their volunteer jobs. I considered buying a year's supply of the one prescription I really need but I couldn't do it. I could have saved seven or eight hundred dollars but I've been a Hoosier much to long to trust those little bottles with the Spanish labels. The fine print was in Spanish as well and while I never read the English version of the fine print on my own prescriptions, I wanted to know exactly what the Spanish version said before I even considered buying anything.

I did get a terrific buy on a Cowboy hat. I had wanted one since the day we crossed the Arkansas border and drove into Texarkana, Texas. Susie was not particularly enamored of the idea so I had to pester her until she relented. We stopped in a Cowboy boot shop on one of the side streets in Ciudad Acuna and on the back wall hung a tan hat with a leather band. It looked like me. I walked back to the wall and put it on. A lovely young Hispanic girl came out of a back room and speaking in broken English, said "Can I help you, Senor?"

"Yes, how much for the hat?"

"Twunty fav dollah." She smiled one of the more beautiful smiles I have ever seen.

Susie joined in: "That's too much for something you'll never wear."

"Yes, I will." I said.

"When and where would you wear it?"

"I don't know; church maybe."

"You will not. Why don't you wait? We might find a cheaper one." She said, walking with some finality out of the shop and down the street.

I took the hat off to hang it back up and young clerk took me by the arm, stopping the hat in mid-air.

"Senor, I must tell you that the hat looks better on you than on any man I have ever seen."

Well-l-ll-ll, what was I supposed to do then? I hesitated. Better than any man? Do you suppose she really meant it? She certainly sounded genuine.

"Because you look so-ooo-ooo handsome in this hat, I will let you have it for twunty dolllah," she told me, smiling that toothpaste commercial smile.

How could I pass that up? I couldn't. I pulled out a twenty dollar bill, already trying to think of something to tell Susie. I left the shop with my hat in a bag because I was a little nervous wearing it around all these caballeros. By the time I caught up with Susie, I had decided telling her the truth was my best bet.

"She said I looked better in that hat than any man she had ever seen." I told her.

"Better than any man? "

"Yep." I told her proudly.

"And you believed her?"

"Of course, I did. Why wouldn't I?"

"Then why aren't you wearing the hat?"

"Susie, there's a lot of real cowboys here, not to mention the Federales. I'm gonna wait until we get back to Johnson City."

"You are a piece of work." She said, moving on down the street.

We had such a good time on that trip, we decided to go back a few weeks later. Susie had seen several beautiful ceramic flower pots on the first trip and they sold for a fraction of the U.S. cost She wanted one to bring back to Indiana and picked one that weighed about fifty pounds.

"Uhhh, Susie," I said. "How are we gonna get that thing back to the truck? Don't forget, we have to walk at least a mile." The guy trying to sell the planter, a young Mexican man dressed in hip-hop attire said 'Ees not heavy, Senor. See." He picked the planter up and held it over his head like it was made of paper.

"I'll help you carry it." Susie said, seeming to me like she was admiring the young man's bulging forearms. I wasn't about to let some young whippersnapper show me up so I agreed.

Big Mistake. It was all I could do to wrap my arms around that thing. We headed for the border with Susie lugging a little dress that we bought for our granddaughter. It might have weighed half a pound. Me? I was half carrying, half dragging that fifty pound planter. I can safely say that the next hour was sixty of the most miserable minutes I have spent on God's green earth. I initially made maybe a hundred yards before having to stop and rest but as we slowly approached the U.S. border station I was down to about fifteen feet between rest stops.

I had lost all the feeling in my right arm and my left hip bone felt as if it had somehow gotten out of the socket it was supposed to be resting in. My spinal column had assumed a semi permanent curve not unlike the St Louis arch. The sweat was pouring off my brow when we finally reached the border station. I felt like Rocky Balboa must have felt upon reaching the top of the steps at the Philadelphia museum and was it my imagination or were these hundreds of people gathered around me all cheering?

"Anything to declare?" The bored man in the U.S. Border Patrol hat said to me.

"Just the Pot." I told him, still stuck in my best Quasimodo pose. That was the wrong answer. His head snapped up and I realized what I had said.

"Planter. I mean planter. Not Pot, planter." I stammered, trying and failing, to lift the beautiful Ceramic pot up on to the table. He looked at the planter and then at me.

"You carry that thing over here?" he said. I nodded my head.

"You must work out." he said with what I perceived to be a smirk on his face.

"Not really." I answered nonchalantly. The wise guy motioned us through the gate and I noticed as I tried to walk that my knuckles were dragging the concrete floor.

I wrestled the planter into the back of the truck as Susie watched.

"You know something?" she said.

"What?" the movement of my lips almost caused me to cry out in pain.

"A pair of these planters would look a lot better on our porch." She said, helping me into the truck "Can we come back next Week?"

It tastes like sweat? I'll have a bowl.

One of the reasons we like traveling is because we can dine on foods from different cultures as well as different regions of the country. We try to bypass the chain restaurants although you can usually depend on them for a decent meal. The food we love to eat can best be found in small out of the way places that serve regional specialties. We loved the Seafood along the Texas coast. The shrimp, oysters and fish right off the boat were wonderful.

When we got to the Hill country of Texas, we were looking forward to it's own regional specialties. Barbeque can be found on almost every corner but the word is that you can't be a real Hill country Texan until you've eaten Chicken fried steak smothered in white gravy. It's a very popular dish and my waistline will attest to the number of times I have tried it. I have eaten chicken fried steak in at least ten places from Austin to Johnson City to San Antonio to Fredericksburg. There is a restaurant in Johnson City that advertises in very large letters on the front of their building that they make the world's best chicken fried steak. Underneath that claim, in slightly smaller letters, it says 'nearly three dozen served.'

I figured they must know what they were doing with that kind of experience so I had an order for lunch and while it was good, I think they're stretching the truth with that 'world's greatest' claim.

The best chicken fried steak I had was in a place called the Plateau Café in Fredericksburg. The steak was probably a foot in diameter, pounded to a tenderness where it took only slight pressure on my fork to slice through it. The breading was a crispy golden brown and the gravy; my gawd, the gravy. What can I say about it? Milk white and creamy with just the right amount of pepper. It was served with an order of real mashed potatoes made with red 'skins on' spuds. My mouth is watering just writing about this and if I lived within ten miles of that place, I would probably weigh four hundred pounds.

Of course, steak isn't everything. You can't be in Texas and not eat Mexican food. We've had Tex-Mex in San Antonio and we've also eaten regular Mexican meals in Old Mexico. One thing I have learned from our south of the border experiences. I now know enough Spanish never to order anything when the word 'Diablo' is part of the name. An example of this would be 'enchiladas diablo'. There is not enough bottled water in Mexico to put out the fire when you order that stuff.

In the old Mexico restaurants, we usually stick to the things we recognize like Enchiladas, tacos and burritos. You can also find baby goat on menus across the border. I have yet to get up the nerve to try it and don't hold your breath waiting on Susie to try this baby goat stuff. She'd sooner eat worms.

Our meanderings on the dining circuit are slowly taking us north, which means we are also working our way out of what I call the Menudo zone. Every grocery store we have been in since we got to southern Texas has a whitish substance called Tripe in their meat cases. This tripe substance is made from the stomach lining of a cow and is used for making Menudo, a traditional Mexican dish that apparently one either loves or hates. We have not found anyone who is neutral about it.

The first opinion we received a couple of years ago was negative, very negative. We had a tire blow out along interstate 10 and after mounting the spare, we stopped to get a new tire in Blythe, California. A small Mexican restaurant across the street had a whitewashed sign on the window advertising Menudo. We had never heard of it.

"What is Menudo?" I asked the man fixing our tire.

"A terrible soup. It tastes like the sweat of a horse" he said.

"Ah, maybe so, but it is very good for a hangover." said his partner who was in charge of the air hose. "Too much Dos Equis on Saturday can be cured by eating Menudo on Sunday." He grinned widely and winked at me.

That little conversation around the tire changer made us reluctant to try it. As a matter of fact, after hearing the 'sweat' comment, Susie would not have eaten it if she'd been offered a thousand dollars.

Menudo is hard to make so you don't always find it. Most restaurants only serve it on the weekends. In fact, one place we were in, a Mexican restaurant in Alpine, Texas, only served it on Sundays. "How do you feel about Menudo?" I asked our waitress.

"I love it." She said.

"Really?"

"Yes senor. If I had a big bowl here right now, I would eat it all up."

"Well, you can have some tomorrow."

"Tomorrow? We are not open on Sundays, Senor."

"But it says right here that you serve Menudo on Sundays."

She laughed. "That is why we have so much Menudo left on Monday."

"Wait a minute. That doesn't make sense." I said.

"The owner is the cook. He loves the Menudo and works all day Saturday making it. He doesn't want to sell any so that is why we only serve it on Sunday."

"Right." I said, my head suddenly hurting.

Pass me another crawdad, please.

By the time the bluebonnets were popping out along the roadside, we decided it was time to leave the Hill country and head north. It had been a great winter in Texas. We made some new friends, did a lot of sight seeing, learned to be comfortable in Mexico and got a whole new picture of LBJ, the man.

We also immersed ourselves in some spectacular scenery. The drive from Terlingua outside of Big Bend National Park to Presidio, Texas has been rated by one of those companies that do such things as one of the top five scenic drives in the United states. I don't know what the other four are but this was a good one. Ten years ago I would not have made that trip because of my fear of high places. That fear was so bad that I used to get nosebleeds sleeping in the upper half of a bunk bed. I decided when we retired and planned to travel that I would have to get over this fear if we wanted to see anything. I convinced myself that even if we drove off the side of a mountain, I still had probably lived most of my life so I didn't really have that much to lose. I tried explaining this to Susie but she failed to see the rationale in this reasoning.

The first few high places we tackled found me petrified but then gradually, the fear went away. I guess I had to get old to get rid of it but then I've also picked up age spots and a back that won't let me straighten up until ten-thirty in the morning so I'm not a hundred percent sure it is worth it.

This past winter was also spent trying out different cuisine, including things that I wouldn't have touched before I retired but like conquering the fear of heights, I dove right in using the same 'getting old' argument. One such cuisine sampling occurred on our way home. We wanted to spend some time in the Cajun country and decided to drive along the Louisiana coast to take in the view of the Gulf of Mexico.

While not the world's most scenic drive, we did manage to see some water amidst the oil derricks poking out of the horizon. The road from Port Arthur, Texas to New Iberia, Louisiana is also not the most crowded place in the world and as it got later in the day, we decided we had better find a place to stop for the night.

We found a little campground in Holly Beach, a town of a couple hundred people. This turned out to be one of the smarter things we have ever done in our life. We had not even finished setting up when we were invited to a party celebrating the installation of a new septic tank in the campground. The couple next to us explained that the campground owners were a fun loving couple and would find something to celebrate practically every weekend. That's not to imply that a new septic tank is not cause for celebration.

The festivities were already under way when we walked out onto the sandy beach. A wheelbarrow full of crabs stood next to a pot of boiling water and a gentleman wearing a Harley Davidson shirt was manning a huge charcoal grill filled with nuggets of alligator meat wrapped in bacon, catfish fillets, Cajun sausage and something gray called boudain.

Another wheelbarrow contained what had to be several thousand crayfish boiled in some sort of hot sauce with potatoes and corn on the cob. Cajun music was coming from a pickup pulled up on the beach as a very nice lady showed Susie and I how to eat the crayfish.

"You just pull on the hind end and eat the meat that comes out." she said, while yanking on one of the unfortunate creatures' nether regions. "What's that yellow stuff that squirted out of there?" Susie asked the lady.

"Ah, just wipe that off. You don't need to eat that."

This would normally have had Susie turning around and heading for the camper but not today. Throwing caution to the wind, we joined three other people at a long picnic table working on a pile of these little critters. I kept looking around, thinking maybe we had stumbled into the middle of filming a Budweiser beer commercial and it could have been, except that all the people in attendance were old.

I don't know how the people who owned that campground made any money. We paid fifteen dollars to camp and probably ate fifty dollars worth of sea food. I'll take that deal anytime.

G2 note.

In September of 2005, Holly Beach took a direct hit from Hurricane Rita. As I watched the coverage of the disaster, I wondered how the town and the campground fared. Most of the news was still focused on New Orleans and on other towns bigger than Holly Beach. Perhaps part of the town survived but with all that water, it's possible that the Campground septic system didn't. My gosh, they may even need another new one. That could mean another party.

A month after the hurricane, I happened to be watching the morning news when a team of reporters visited Holly Beach. I watched in horror as the camera panned the area. Nothing was left standing, the whole place was just a barren patch of sand with the occasional clump of sea oats breaking the dullness of the flat horizon.

If what they showed me was Holly Beach, then all the seaside homes were gone. The church where we stopped to attend mass was gone. The beautiful live oaks, their branches filled with clinging Spanish Moss were gone.

And the campground….. Well, even if I had known where it had stood before, there was no evidence there ever was a campground. Under the sand, maybe, that new septic system was still in place but somehow, I doubt it.

Ten dollars? Not a problem.

We were somewhere in Mississippi and we stopped to buy fuel. I say somewhere because fuel stops tend to run together in your mind after a while and sometimes Susie and I will argue about places we have stopped.

"When we stopped back there in Lafayette,,....." she will say.

"We didn't stop in Lafayette." I have to remind her. "It was Baton Rouge."

"No, it wasn't."

"I believe it was, Susie dear."

"No, Gordon dear, it wasn't."

This goes on for a while until we forget why we even brought it up in the first place. I know, I know. Why don't we write it down? We're going to start doing that on our next trip. I'm planning on signing up for a 'get your life organized' seminar that some old-people group is offering as soon as I remember where I put the brochure.

Getting back to the reason I started this tale. We stopped for fuel and as I was standing there by the diesel pump, I was approached by a clean cut young man who had a very plausible story to tell.

"I live in Monroe, Louisiana." He started out telling me. "I've been at a business conference in Memphis and I'm on my way home. When I loaded up my car this morning at the hotel, stupid me, I must have set my briefcase on the top of the car when I opened the door. I know I had it when I walked out to the car. It was stupid of me. Everything I had was in that case. My wallet, extra cash. Everything."

"Why, that's terrible." I sympathized. "But don't be so hard on yourself. I did something like that once only it was my cell phone."

He nodded his head. "I just realized what I did when I stopped here to get gas. I've been on the phone cancelling my credit cards and trying to call my wife but she must be at the club. I even called my Pastor but he's out visiting with the sick folks in our congregation, one of whom is my mother."

I shook my head in understanding. Poor man.

"My problem is I don't have enough gas to get home." He continued, looking at me. "You look like a good Christian man. If you can lend me ten dollars and give me your name and address, I'll send you a check as soon as I get back to Louisiana." He handed me a piece of paper with his name, address and phone number written on it.

'This is where I live. If you don't hear from me in a week, call me and remind me."

I hesitated because I pride myself on being one of those old folks who's not going to be fooled by driveway paving gypsies or any of those other scam artist schemes you read about. I have a keen instinct about people and I can tell when a person's lying a mile away and this guy wasn't lying. 'He's okay.' I told myself. 'He's goes to church and he's got a sick mother. My Gosh, he and his wife even belong to a club. Scam artists don't belong to clubs and they're not churchgoers. And he gave me his address. Do crooks give you their address? He's alright.'

"Okay." I said, handing him a ten spot and a card with our address on it. "Just send the check here."

"I will. I will." He said, already moving away.

He climbed in a Ford Explorer and drove away.

"That's strange." I said to Susie. "He didn't buy any gas." As he pulled out into traffic, I noticed that his SUV had Mississippi license plates.

"Where did that guy say he was from?"

"Somewhere in Louisiana." Susie said. "Why?"

"His car has Mississippi plates." I said, looking at the piece of paper he's given me. 'Monroe, Louisiana.' I told her.

"I think you can kiss that ten dollars good-bye." Susie said

"Nahhh. He wasn't that kind of guy. My instincts have never failed me. I know a crook when I see one. He probably just moved to Louisiana and hasn't had time to get his plates changed."

It's been almost a month now and I haven't heard from him. Maybe he lost the card I gave him. I tried calling the number he gave me but some girl working in a tanning bed place answered the phone. She'd never heard of the guy. He must have gotten the numbers mixed up somehow.

I wish I could remember exactly where it was we ran into this guy. I think it was Jackson, and Susie thinks it was Meridian, Mississippi. Do me a favor, would you? If you're ever in either of those places and you run into a church going guy named Steve Sparkman who has a sick mother and who lives in Monroe, Louisiana, tell him I'm still waiting on my ten dollars.

PART SEVEN
The great Northwest

Imitating Daniel Boone never hurt anybody.

Susie and I were beginning to become pretty savvy travelers amongst the RV set. We had been at this living off the land business for over two years when we began talking about the camping trip that all RV'ers hope to make in their lifetime. The Mecca that beckons most of us who live the RV lifestyle is Alaska and we were in the talking stages of making that trip but were hesitating. Pulling Fionna, our fifth wheel, ten thousand miles or more didin't seem too appealing because of the rising fuel prices. Still, I wouldn't be satisfied until we got up there.

"What about an Alaskan cruise?" Susie said.

I didn't really want to do a cruise. They go by so fast, other people control what you see and I eat too much.

"Too expensive and you can't get out and see the real Alaska." I told her, trying to sound like I knew what I was talking about. "I've got an even better idea." Why don't we drive like we planned but we'll camp along the way."

"I thought you didn't want to take Fionna." Susie said, referring to the pet name we gave the fifth wheel.

"I'm not talking about taking Fionna." I told her. "None of that sissy resort stuff. I mean really camp. You know, a tent and a camp stove. Maybe even sleeping under the stars. Chopping our own wood. A couple of months of real Daniel Boone stuff." I whipped out my coonskin hat as we talked but I didn't need to do that. Susie, who loves the great outdoors, readily agreed.

After I said this however, I began to have second thoughts. I had heard about the mosquitoes the size of cantaloupes. I also wasn't sure my back would handle sleeping on the ground one night, much less thirty or forty nights. No point in overdoing it so I did a little backpedaling and tried to come up with a reason to buy one of those campers that slide in the bed of the truck. I quickly forgot that idea when I saw what they cost. That idea was way too extravagant for one trip.

"You know, Susie" I told her. "All we really need is a place to sleep."

"Yeah, so what?"

"We could just buy a cheap truck cap for the bed of our truck and put a mattress back there."

"Cheap? What's cheap?"

"I don't know." I said. "It couldn't be more than a few hundred dollars and we really could use one anyway."

"Okay." She agreed "But I think we ought to try it out before we go driving ten thousand miles." Susie said.

We weren't really prepared to be leaving for the summer anyway. Our granddaughter was growing by leaps and bounds as were the plants in my vegetable garden. What we needed was a three or four week trip to give the whole idea a good test and to make sure we could function in that environment.

A good excuse came up when my brother bought a home on the Oregon coast and began pestering us to come see it. We decided to do that and kill two birds with one stone at the same time by driving on up the coast to Seattle where our son lives. By the time we got done, I figured we'd have about five thousand miles of testing, a little more than we'd considered and then after we looked at how far it was, we considered flying but I couldn't bring myself to do that. We would be flying over a lot of beautiful country between here and there and I hated the idea of not seeing it.

So we took the plunge. It turned out to be six hundred dollars for an Aluminum truck cap with racks to carry our Kayaks. I built a platform in the truck bed and laid the mattress off our hide-a-bed in there. It was very cozy looking but it was also a bit dicey crawling in and laying down but, with some wriggling and a bump or two on the head, we managed.

We were ready.

"You get some clothes together and I'll get the camping gear and we'll be on our way." I told Susie. I busied myself with my chores and when I turned around, Susie had piled a mound of stuff behind the truck that wouldn't have fit in a semi-trailer. You would think that a little camping trip of a few thousand miles wouldn't require taking along the contents of an average sized three bedroom bungalow but apparently, in her mind, it did. "We can't take all this stuff." I said, going through a suitcase that had every shirt I owned crammed in there along with an equal number of hers.

"I don't need all these. Let's see, we'll be gone about five or six weeks. If I wear one shirt a week and we make one trip to the laundry, I figure I'll need three shirts."

"I'm not riding in a truck with you in a shirt you've had on for a week." She said.

"Two belts? Why do I need two belts?" I pleaded.

"You'll need 'em, believe me." She said, ending the discussion. I seldom even wear a belt because as I've gotten older, I've found I look better in these 'relaxed fit' clothes that use elastic around the waist to hold your pants up. 'Sansabelt', I believe they call it in all the high fashion places. I think that's French for 'No belt required.'

In the end, it turned out to be easier to take everything than it was to argue with her. I raised the platform in the back of the truck to get more stuff under our bed. I got it all in there but it created a problem when we climbed into the bed. There was not a lot of head room to begin with and when I was finished raising the platform, there was even less. It was a little claustrophobic; hell, it was a whole lot claustrophobic. We had to crawl like snakes to inch our way into the tiny space. Then, when we wanted to get out, we had to scoot along on our keister like one of the three stooges whose hind-end is on fire.

Were we crazy? After some consideration, I decided probably so. But we were going. Our daughter, Julie, gave us a book titled 'One thousand things to do before you die." Some we had already done and others we probably never would do because they were intended for people with more money than we have. But I came up with other things that were not in the book and managed to come up with a thousand things we want to do before I die. I hope to whittle down the list on this trip. I've already eaten in the original Cracker Barrel restaurant so I only have 999 left. I should get several more on this trip.

Air. I need air.

I like to get up early and be on the road in time to greet the early morning daylight. It sort of makes me feel like one of the hardy pioneers heading west to Oregon because I'm sure they were up early every morning while making their way to a new life.

I was also wondering if pioneers had the same sorts of travel problems we have when we're preparing to get on the road. Interestingly enough, I discovered that, at least, husbands did. I happened to come across the diary of a Brigham Jones, an early settler and traveler on the Oregon Trail. He recorded an early morning conversation he was having with his wife, Rachel, as they prepared to hit the trail.

"We're going to have to hurry a little, Rachel, sweetheart." He said gently, sticking his head in the covered wagon. "You know the wagon master said we needed to get an early start in case we're attacked by Indians later today."

"I'm not setting one foot on that Oregon trail, Brigham, with my hair looking like this."

"But Rachel darling…"

"Don't Rachel darling me, Brigham Jones. Have you fed the oxen?" She says, sticking her head out of the wagon.

"Yes dear." He replies, resignedly.

"You could also be sweeping out this filthy wagon instead of just standing there telling me to hurry up." she reminded him.

"But Susie, er, ah, I mean, Rachel, we're burning daylight."

Travels With Susie

The diary ended there and I never was able to find out if Brigham and Rachel made it to Oregon or if they just decided to chuck it and return to Cleveland.

Our own early start, thanks to last minute hair appointments and such, ended up being about five in the evening. We left Mooresville and headed for Denver and the Rocky mountains. We spent the first night in a Flying J parking lot west of Saint Louis. For those of you wondering how it was sleeping in the truck bed, it was a little awkward climbing in and out but it was tolerable. Accomplishing that once a night is enough however so I suspect I'll have to quit taking my diuretic for the remainder of the trip.

After a breakfast of orange juice and a boiled egg, we headed for Independence, Missouri. My list of 999 things to do before I die was the reason. I accomplished two of them when we got there.

A visit to the home of President Harry Truman was one of the items. He was the first president I really remember and I always had a soft spot in my heart for him. For many years after he left office, calling anyone else President sounded foreign to me. Even after 8 years of doing it, calling General Eisenhower, 'President', had a foreign ring to it.

The second item on the list was a two-parter, the first part of which I had already accomplished a couple of years ago. That's when I stood right in the middle of the spot that marked the end of the Santa Fe trail in Santa Fe, New Mexico. The beginning of the original Santa Fe trail is in Independence and when I walked there and planted my feet, I had done both ends and crossed that off my list. I know it's not exactly climbing Mount Everest but hey, legally I'm a senior citizen. I get my adventure where I can.

Leaving Missouri behind, we quickly determined that no sleeping was going to get done in the back of the truck on our second night out. The temperature had reached 101 degrees in western Kansas so we found an American owned motel in Russell, the hometown of Bob Dole, and cooled off there.

I awoke early and tuned to the weather channel to see how far we'd have to go to leave the heat behind. I don't watch the weather channel very often but it seemed to me it didn't take very much in the way of weather to get the forecasters pretty excited. In fact, after listening to them, I got the impression we were in for a rough trip. Armageddon apparently lay in every direction. Floods here, wildfires there and pestilence right in the middle.

We left Russell with more than a little trepidation, not knowing what we might encounter weather wise but we hit the highway keeping an eye out for one of those famous Kansas tornadoes. Susie, as is her habit, was thumbing through the Triple A tour book. She turned to me and said,

"How close are we to Cawker City?"

"Cawker City what?" I asked.

"Kansas."

Uh oh, I thought. Susie loves little, out of the way stuff and her tone of voice indicated she'd found something.

"Why is that, Susie, dear?" I said cautiously.

"They actually do have the world's largest ball of twine there." She told me. We have been making fun of that since we heard it mentioned in a movie some years back. I don't remember the movie but a huge ball of twine was not on my list of things to see. We had already visited what was purported to be the world's second largest a couple of years back, an event that could be described as less than memorable.

"I think Cawker City is a couple of hundred miles back." I told her. "Just as well, it doesn't sound very interesting, anyway." She answered.

I breathed a sigh of relief and kept heading west. Despite the warnings of the weather channel, the day's driving was uneventful. We left the heat wave behind as we got nearer the Rocky Mountains. We watched our onboard thermometer as the temperature dropped into the low fifties while we spent our third night on the road west of Denver. Our original plan had been to go north from Denver on Interstate 25 but after looking at the Atlas, it seemed to be only a few hundred miles out of the way to go west to Arches National Park in Utah. We took only a minute to decide to go that way. It was a good decision.

We got out our campground book and found a place to stay the night near Black Hawk, Colorado. It was unintentional but I added an entry to my list of beautiful highways. Driving U.S. Route Six from Golden, Colorado to Black Hawk was about a forty mile drive and it was breathtaking, even in the rain that had started to fall as we left Denver.

We spent the night in that rain at an elevation of 9200 feet. I knew it was that high because a sign on the campground office door said '9200 feet elevation. Walk. Don't run." The rain was cold so I ran the hundred yards back to the truck after registering and found I didn't have the strength to open the door.

"Open the door." I gasped to Susie.

"Do what?"

I didn't have enough wind to repeat myself so I just pointed at the door. Susie, seeing the look on my face, opened the door for me and I climbed slowly into the truck.

"Pay attention to the signs." I told her after I had gotten enough oxygen to take a breath.

Several casinos were tucked up in the mountains around Black Hawk and we found a great prime rib dinner for 3.99 at one of them. It was called Diamond Lil's or Mustang Sally's or something similar.

We also encountered one of my pet peeves when we got back to the campground. The people next to us ran their gasoline powered generator all night, the better to watch television, I suppose. I assumed it was a television because they also had their satellite set up out front.

While I like the little extras in life as much as the next guy, I have never understood why someone has to pollute the air in a campground with a noisy, smelly generator. If a person needs all the modern conveniences, get a motel room or stay home, for God's sake.

I considered knocking on the door of the Motor Home and complaining but I had seen the guy earlier and knew I could end up with a broken nose or something if I said anything so we suffered in silence.

We awoke early, albeit half frozen in the forty degree temperature and were greeted by a beautiful rising sun. Now this is what life's really all about.

Next stop was Arches National Park.

How much fat will ten inches of Spandex hold?

We traveled Interstate Seventy through the Rocky Mountains, a drive at one time I thought I'd never make. I had a fear of heights that went all the way back to be carried high in the womb and I had only recently started to overcome it. We went through the Eisenhower Memorial tunnel at an elevation of eleven thousand feet and when we emerged, what seemed to be the whole state was spread out before us. I was expecting that fear of heights to flare up but the road was so beautiful I forgot to be scared. We passed through or near several of the Colorado ski areas; Aspen, Breckenridge, Arapahoe Basin, Steamboat Springs. Neither of us had ever been skiing but the names conjured up visions of adventure and romance.

We drove through Vail with it's quaint buildings. The view and the chalets hanging on the side of the mountains was spectacular. I could see myself plunging down the mountainside on my new skis, side by side with all the Hollywood stars; Brad, Matt, Cameron.

"Let's go skiing here next winter, Susie." I asked.

"If you got the money, honey, I got the time."

The subtle reminder that we are not a part of the Jet set stopped my musings. We drove on, my dreams of rubbing elbows around the ski lift with the great and the near great shattered by fiscal reality.

Another fifty miles down the road found us in an area called Glenwood canyon. I've been wanting to drive this portion of the interstate since I read about it twenty years ago and as a matter of fact, it was on my list of 999 things to do.

The engineering feats required to put the road through the canyon were staggering and as we got in the middle of it, I could see why. The canyon was unbelievably beautiful. Sheer rock cliffs, hundreds of feet high with the Colorado river flowing through the steep walls of the canyon. The river here is just getting up a full head of steam before plunging through the Grand Canyon. a couple of hundred miles farther down river.

The highway clings to the edge of the canyon, gracefully sweeping out over the river. It appears as natural as the surrounding landscape. We stopped at a huge rest area at a bend in the river where pathways wound their way for a mile or more along the river bank. We eventually found our way to the visitor center where we read about the planning that went into the highway. The whole effect needs to be seen because I cannot do it justice writing about it.

We stopped to talk to a couple straddling their sleek bicycles, as they stood taking in the scenery. We told them of our RV lifestyle and our experiences on this trip.

"You guys need to try bicycling the canyon." The man said. "You can rent bikes at the resort in Glenwood Springs. Good ones. K-2's. Shimano gears." He pointed at the back of his bike. He might as well have been talking Greek but I nodded my head as if I was a distant cousin to Lance Armstrong.

I looked at their slim, maybe thirty year old bodies, tucked into form fitting spandex shorts. A shudder went through me as I pictured my body stuffed into a pair of those things. Spandex is not designed to hide anything and I was not ready to put my 'anythings' on display. A little late, I thought, about twenty years and at least that same number of pounds. It made me sad to think of that and I vowed to do something about it when we got home, even though I knew that I probably wouldn't.

We left the canyon behind and Susie got on the cell phone to find us a campsite at Arches National Park, our destination for the evening. We quickly found that traveling without planning ahead is going the way of the dinosaur. All Federal and State campground reservations are contracted out to private concerns and you need four days advance notice to reserve anything. Also, everything is prepaid and effectively, no money will be returned should you fail to get to your destination. The days of calling the campground and asking them to hold you a spot are over. It's progress, I suppose, but it drives me crazy.

We arrived at Moab, Utah in time to find a very nice private campground outside the park. I also added another highway to my most beautiful list while getting there. Utah Highway 128 travels from the middle of the Utah desert where it follows the Colorado river through incredibly red rock canyons for forty or so miles until it reaches Moab. We stopped so many times to take pictures that it took us about three hours to traverse the distance.

We spent two days touring Arches National park and once again, my words can't do it justice. The beauty of the place needs to be seen. One drawback to being here in July was that the heat was stifling and even though it was a dry heat, hiking through the park was pretty hard on my six decade old lungs. We climbed a hillside to get a look at a particularly photogenic arch and I thought I would pass out before I got a picture.

When I did get the arch focused in the lens, the picture turned out fuzzy because I was also busy checking my pulse and feeling my left arm to see if it was going numb. I really didn't have any symptoms but hey, you can never be too careful.

I was worn out though by the time we got back to the truck. I thought I had felt old talking to the flat stomached bicyclists but I really felt old after struggling up that hillside. I should have done this twenty five years ago.

We left Moab early enough that we decided to try reaching Nevada for our next night's stay. We left Interstate Seventy behind and proceeded north on U.S. Highway Six. It did not make my list of beautiful highways, but were I not such a discriminating person, it would have. If you're in this neighborhood, it's a great shortcut to Salt Lake City. We stopped in that city long enough to get a picture of the Mormon Tabernacle, not because we're Mormon, but because we like their choir.

We didn't spend much time exploring the city because Susie was frantic to see the Great Salt Lake. I was interested as well but not adamant about getting there. I wanted to look around the place and maybe visit the Mormon Genealogy library because I didn't know that we'd ever get back there. I dabbled in tracing my ancestry a few years back and thought maybe I could bag another great- grandparent or two in Salt Lake City but Susie was adamant.

"Let's get to the lake."

"What's your hurry?"

"It's gonna get dark if we don't get out there."

"It's only two o'clock." I told her.

"I don't care. Let's get going."

Knowing better than to continue this argument, I turned the truck to the west and left the city behind.

The lake was on my list of things to see but it was sort of a disappointment. At the time we were there, the water had receded from the docks by a couple of hundred yards and left former waterfront property high and dry. I didn't know if that was a temporary situation or not and never did find out. The place also smelled. It reeked of fishy smell and I knew, what with Susie's olfactory sensitivities, that we wouldn't be there long. And we weren't. We approached the water where Susie stood holding her nose, ankle deep in the brine and collected a bottle of water that she stored in the back of the truck.

We drove across the Great Salt desert just about sundown and another item on my list was crossed off. I got another of the 999 when a sign announcing that we were on the Bonneville Salt Flats loomed up out of the darkness. I was suddenly tempted to find out just what this old truck could do. The speedometer needle was hovering at ninety, had another thirty to go and the truck had not even broken a sweat but I had. That was about all I could handle. I'm not an immortal nineteen year old anymore.

A bright glow ahead of us on the horizon had both of us wondering what it could be. Wendover, Nevada, according to the map, was the next town down the road but it didn't seem big enough to merit lighting up the night sky like a roman candle. The instant we crossed the Nevada State Line, we knew what it was. Casinos. A dozen or more in the middle of the desert crowded with people on a Sunday night. Where did they all come from? There were no cities within a hundred miles. This was a puzzle we never did figure out.

This night was the second on our still young trip where there was no sleeping in the truck. The Red Garter Hotel and Casino had rooms that were cheaper than the local KOA and we got a ninety-nine cent breakfast on top of that. We did risk a dollar each in the nickel slots but no good fortune was forthcoming.

My internal clock still being on Indiana time, I was up before sunrise and went downstairs to find coffee. The casino was pretty sparsely populated but a disheveled looking lady in her fifties was perched on a stool feeding quarters into a slot machine. A cigarette hung from the corner of her lips and she had to squint through the smoke to see the spinning symbols. I didn't know if she'd been there all night or had just arrived but I wanted to sit down beside her and ask her to tell me her life's story. That's the great part of traveling, meeting people and hearing what they have to say on life and it's little pleasures, not to mention it's trials and tribulations.

I stood beside the lady for a while and watched her feed quarters into that machine like she was spooning out food to her cat. She never looked up nor did she even seem aware of my existence so I decided this lady's life would have to go unreported.

I went back upstairs to hurry Susie along. I had decided that with a little bit of hard driving and a shortcut or two, We could make Crater Lake, Oregon before nightfall. I don't know why I was in such a hurry but a lifetime of hurrying was a hard habit to break. When we're on a trip, I keep forgetting that the journey is just as interesting as the destination but I'm trying to become more patient. Maybe by the time I'm seventy.

Sweet Jesus, Get me to the bottom.

We left the Red Garter Hotel and casino behind, getting out of there before we could be tempted to part with any more of our money. I was beginning to have second thoughts about reaching Crater Lake before evening but still, I couldn't ignore the challenge.

I had been trying to find a good way to get up there from where we were in Nevada. When we planned the trip, the Triple A people suggested I drive Interstate Eighty to Interstate five in California and go North to my destination. That seemed to be out of the way and besides, I'd been warned by more than one fellow traveler to stay out of California because of the fuel prices.

I looked at the road Atlas and decided it would be much closer to drive as far as Winnemuca, Nevada and then turn northwest on U.S. ninety five and Nevada highway 140. My brother, who has lived in the west for many years, cautioned me over the phone about that because of the many mountain ranges in the area. He knew about the fear of heights I used to have and was unaware that I had banished that fear from my psyche.

That particular flaw in my character was legendary in our family. My mother first noticed it when as a young boy, my nose began to bleed after I was assigned the top bunk at my Uncle's farmhouse. Things only went down hill from there. I went through a good part of my life avoiding anything much higher than a threshold but no more. It's a simple equation of mind over matter. I was not going to be afraid.

I told my brother about my new resolve but he persisted. "Some of those side roads can get a bit scary. Especially those with the little dots." The 'little dots' on a map signified a scenic highway and we have always enjoyed those in the eastern part of the country but little dot highways in the west are different. They can scare the water out of a normal God-fearing person but with my new-found bravery, there was nothing to worry about. Besides, this was not a little dot highway.

Another standard part of mountain driving are the 'chains required' signs and the accompanying 'chain-up area' sign which point out parking areas where chains can be put on a vehicle. We had passed through several of these places in Colorado and Utah. Even though there was no snow, the signs still meant that there was an ascent or descent in the next few miles, usually one of the very high up variety. These roads produced a bit of excitement but I handled them quite well. After I saw a few of the signs and the resulting roadways they were warning about, however, the signs began to produce a Pavlonian response in my behavior. I wouldn't exactly slobber like one of Comrade Pavlov's dogs but my breathing would quicken a bit and my limbs would take on what could best be described as a twitchy motion. It tended to unnerve Susie.

"Will you quit that"

"Quit what?"

"That shaking like a dog trying to pass a peach seed."

We left the Interstate system behind and headed up highway Ninety Five, a relatively flat piece of landscape although it was lined on both sides by craggy, brown mountains. We turned on to Highway 140 and looked at a mountain range off in the distance to the west. Between where we were and the mountains was the biggest valley I'd ever seen. The roadway went straight across it. Not a ripple in it. It seemed to stretch forever.

"My God." I told Susie. "I'll bet it's twenty five miles across that valley.' A sign next to the highway read 'No services on highway 140.' The next town on my map was 146 miles away so I would see no service stations at least that far.

As it turned out, not only did we not see a service station, we didn't see anything. Not a tree. Not a cow. Not anything. Just desert cut by a ribbon of narrow, lonely two lane blacktop that got lonelier by the mile. It turned out to be over fifty miles across that valley, fifty miles where I barely had to move the steering wheel.

Travels With Susie

We entered the mountains on the west side of the valley, passing several 'chains required' roads which got the by now, predictable response. We crossed the Oregon border and found ourselves in what the Triple A guide called high desert. It was pretty flat and we were making good time. I made a mental note to call my brother and brag. Another 'chain up area' sign appeared and I was mystified, There were no mountains around, just that high desert the guidebook talked about. I didn't believe it for about three seconds and then we rounded a curve and the landscape changed dramatically, Suddenly, we now had a better idea of what the 'high' in 'high desert' meant. We had been driving on a mesa, a five thousand foot high mesa and had come to the end of it. In front of us, just over the hood of the truck, was what I perceived to be the whole of North America laid out at our feet. The Horizon was miles away in the distance and looking down required all the courage I could muster. It wasn't even a mountain with switchbacks that would get us to the bottom. The narrow road just went down, clinging to the edge of the cliff. No guardrail, no shoulder. One false move and it was Goodbye, Mr. Spalding.

My newly found courage dissolved instantly into abject fear. I was now just a sniveling coward clutching the steering wheel so hard I thought it might break. (I did loosen my grip slightly when I realized that). I inched down the roadway to a spot where the asphalt dissolved into a rough piece of patchwork where it appeared that a rockslide had taken the roadbed on over the edge and down to Glory. It had been patched with gravel but slanted precipitously toward the edge.

"Sweet Jesus." I prayed, "Just let me get to the bottom of this and I'll be so good the rest of my life that it will positively make you sick." We made it across the gravelly patch but the effort had me within seconds of hyperventilation. I looked over at Susie, certain that she was grateful my superior driving skills were rescuing us from certain death. She had not even noticed and was in fact, leaning out the window taking pictures. Here we were, inches from the grim reaper and she was snapping photos.

While that initially terrified me even more, it also brought me to my senses. Susie was completely unconcerned and I was so scared, I couldn't breathe. Her relaxed demeanor convinced me that we weren't in any real danger. It was just my fear of heights. I calmed myself by debating whether this highway deserved to be on my list of beautiful drives. The hours of boredom coupled with the few minutes of terror dictated that, no, it did not. I took a deep breath and prayed again.

"Sweet Jesus, get me down off here and I'll be good for at least the next two and half months."

I don't know if he heard me or not but before I knew it, we were at the bottom. I took a very deep breath and blew it out.

"That wasn't so bad." I told Susie.

"What wasn't so bad?" She replied.

I'm moving to Oregon.

We arrived in the Crater Lake, Oregon area late in the afternoon after having added another entry to the list of beautiful highways on my list. This highway bordered Upper Klamath Lake north of Klamath Falls, Oregon. It is another of those 'little dot' highways we navigated on our way to Crater Lake. The lake is inside a volcano that had its guts blown out some 7000 years ago, similar to the explosion on Mount St. Helen which is just up the road, geologically speaking.

We spent the night in a campground south of the park where the lady in the next camp site told me that the ride around the rim of the Crater was the most terrifying thing she had ever done. She was wasting her breath with that information if she was trying to scare me. She was unaware that I had recently buried deep down in my psyche a fear of heights and the information she so readily provided bothered me not. Oh, naturally, I didn't sleep very well that night but I'm certain it was all that fresh high altitude air. Even had she scared me, which, of course, she didn't, we had come this far and seeing Crater Lake was near the top of the 999 list.

I wasn't about to miss it. We started up the mountain and a roadside sign told us that one of the roads in the park was closed because of snow drifts. This information did nothing for my peace of mind but we plunged ahead. It's good we did. The scenery at the top is overwhelming. The sheer walls of the crater are a thousand feet high and the incredibly blue water is almost two thousand feet deep. The crater is about six miles in diameter but none of those figures do it justice. It needs to be seen to be believed. Also, like the Grand Canyon, there is nothing to keep one from falling over the side. We walked along the edge and Susie spent much of her time peering over taking pictures. I wanted to yell at her to get back but I kept quiet, closing my eyes only occasionally.

I finally talked her into getting back in the truck and we drove around the rim of the crater. The highway is considered quite an engineering feat and driving it provides some spectacular views. Admittedly, a couple of areas had me wanting to close my eyes again but the splendor of the landscape was too much too miss.

We spent the day in the park and then set sail for the Oregon coast. (We didn't really set sail because we were in our truck. I was just introducing a nautical theme to this piece as a metaphor to give you a sense of the romance involved in traveling near the ocean.) Highway 101 along the coast immediately went to the top of my list of most beautiful highways but the list is getting so long, I may have to stop collecting new entries. We were heading for Newport, Oregon where my brother has a home on the beach.

When we arrived, I immediately encountered another challenge to my still developing bravery. His home, while beautiful, lies within the Tsunami warning area for that region of the coast. Normally, my new quotient on the bravery scale would make Rambo envious but the thought of being tossed into the Pacific Ocean by some hundred foot tall wave bothered me some.

(G2 note: This visit took place a few months before the terrible Christmas Tsunami in the far east. Had we been there after that, I doubt I would have stayed.)

I expressed my concern to my brother but he reassured me.

"We have the Tsunami warning system." He said, pointing to a little smoke alarm like thing. "There's nothing to worry about."

"Warning system?"

"Yep, it's connected to NOAA and uses GPS and the earthquake center and a bunch of other stuff. When the signal goes off, we just proceed in an orderly fashion to the Airport. It's high enough there that we'll be safe."

"We? Who's we?" I asked.

"The town of Newport, I guess." He answered. "A few thousand people."

'Right.' I thought. Orderly? In a pig's eye. If that Tsunami siren goes off, it will be every man for himself. I'd seen the movie 'Titanic' a couple of times.

I knew what would happen. Pandemonium city, that's what. I slept with one foot on the floor so that any approaching water might wake me and give us a fighting chance. A week went by and nothing happened. I had been worried for nothing. I couldn't even find anyone that had ever heard of a Tsunami striking the Oregon coast until I went to the fish market.

"How often do you have these Tsunamis?" I asked the man behind the counter.

"There was a big one around the year seventeen hundred.' He replied.

"That's over three hundred years ago." I said, the relief in my voice almost visible.

"Yep, but we're about due." He said.

"Are you serious, Clark?" I said, for Clark was the man's name. "Yessir," He said. "The experts predict one about every three hundred and four years." He laughed heartily as my face went pale. Ten thousand comedians out of work and I have to run into one of them.

We enjoyed our stay in Oregon. Fresh off the boat fish is one reason. By the time we left, I had become an expert on where to get the best Fish and Chips. Another reason we enjoyed it is because the state has no sales tax. That actually took some getting used to. You buy something for five dollars and ninety cents and that's what you owe. Five dollars and ninety cents. It seemed un-American somehow.

I would like to know how the government of Oregon manages, though. Maybe we could find out their secret and institute it in Indiana...... I know. I know, ten thousand comedians....

Our last stop in the state was at Fort Clatsop outside of Astoria, where Lewis and Clark spent the winter of 1805-1806. Susie had been enamored of Meriweather Lewis since third grade so any chance we get to visit a L & C historical site, we take it. Leaving the fort, we crossed the four mile long bridge over the Columbia river (A bridge I would not have attempted a few years ago) and went to Cape Disappointment, a park in the state of Washington on the mouth of the Columbia. This is where Lewis and Clark first observed the Pacific Ocean from the top of a hill and the first thing we did was trek up that hill in their footsteps. All the doubts I have about the lifestyle we've adopted (and there are many) were erased when that ocean came into view. It makes one thankful to be alive and a part of this country.

Don't talk with your mouth full.

We ran into some campground availability problems as we moved up the coast of Washington State. It was a Saturday and thirty or so miles inland, the temperature in both Oregon and Washington was approaching 100 degrees. We were at a comfortable seventy degrees alongside the ocean so all the parks anywhere near the water were full. After several phone calls, we finally found a spot at a place called Mike's Resort out on the Olympic Peninsula. It meant we had to alter our traveling plans a little but we're glad we did.

The campground was located on a body of water called the Hood Canal. I don't know where the canal name came from because it's actually a leg of Puget Sound running down the east side of the Peninsula for fifty miles or so. The narrow, two lane highway parallels the water for much of the way and if I were still making a list of beautiful roads, it would definitely be on it. I gave up on the list because I had picked up so many entries on this trip that the list became meaningless.

We arrived at Mike's resort and had no more than gotten the tablecloth on the picnic table when the people camped across the way wandered over to talk about the Sonics, the Seattle basketball team. We have an Indiana Pacers plate mounted on the front of our truck and this has initiated several conversations with basketball fans around the country. This being the off-season, there wasn't much to talk about so the conversation soon turned to regional food, another of our favorite subjects. It doesn't take a rocket scientist to see that I could stand to lose a little weight but still, Susie and I must have some sort of starved look about us because for the third or fourth time in our travels, we were invited to eat with fellow campers.

The two picnic tables on their sites were loaded with a plethora of seafood. One of our hosts wore a bandanna and had tattoos covering both arms. He looked like the sort of fellow I usually avoid whenever possible but he was a very nice, articulate person. I have to learn to quit forming opinions on those first impressions. I watched as he loaded a charcoal grill with oysters still in the shell. He pulled them out of a thirty gallon trash can sitting beside the grill.

"Where'd you get those?" I asked.

He gestured toward the water. "Out in the Sound." Before I could ask exactly where, several of the shells on the hot coals opened up as if they had received some sort of signal. He picked one out of the group.

"There's a lot of ways to fix these babies but here's how I like 'em."

He sprinkled hot sauce on the oyster meat from an open bottle and then handed me a Rainier beer, a fork and the shell. I dug the meat out of the hot shell and shoved it in my mouth. The combination of the hot oyster and the hotter sauce created a wonderful taste. My eyes must have lit up because he handed me another.

While I was stuffing myself with oysters, Susie was busy with our hostess digging meat out of a large pot full of Dungeness crabs. All this food turned out to be no accident. Our new friends explained to us that they camped here a couple of times a month because the campground's location on Puget Sound meant that Oysters and Clams were available on the property and campers were free to find them when the tide went out. I could just barely contain Susie, who loves new adventures, when she heard this. She would not have eaten an oyster or a clam if her life depended on it but she was so excited about the prospect of finding these things that we went directly to the campground office after dinner. The tide would not be out until the following morning but she (and I as well) wanted to be ready. No equipment was needed to pick up oysters out of the beds and all we needed to dig clams was a five gallon bucket and a shovel which the young man behind the counter handed us.

"How do we catch crabs?" she asked the young man at the counter. He grinned at her.

"Why, the old fashioned way."

"Now just a minute, young man." I started to say, thinking that this guy was about to redden the cheeks of my lovely bride. Little did I know. He turned around and lifted a crab trap up on to the counter.

"You're going to need a boat and a license to set the traps." He told us. Not having either, we passed on the crabbing. Our dinner hosts, who were leaving early the next day, had given us six huge crabs on ice so we were not too disappointed.

We got back to the campsite and our Pacer plate brought another neighboring camper over. Her name was Lisa and she was a Portland Trailblazer fan. She also knew a lot about clamming and offered to help us with our upcoming adventure. It was a good thing she did because we had no idea what we were doing.

Early Sunday morning found us standing in the sand as the tide went out. Lisa took us to the Oyster beds and gave us a lesson on selecting Oysters. The shells were laying everywhere and we picked them up like we were discovering gold. I love oysters; raw, grilled, cooked in stuffing or served Rockefeller style. Susie, on the other hand, wouldn't eat one if she found it in the Fountain of Youth. Still, she rummaged through the shells as if she ate oysters every day. My six pack cooler was full when I yelled "enough."

We moved over to the water's edge where Lisa showed us how to figure out where the clams were.

"Find the Tiny holes in the sand." She said, pointing to an infinitesimally small black speck in the brown sand.

My first couple of tries were dry holes but Susie was a natural. She seemed to have a built in radar for identifying the little blow holes in the terrain where the little guys had dug in. She was running here and there exclaiming, "Here's one." And "Here's another." I was following her with my shovel, full of excitement as I turned over a shovel full of sand to find two or three clams. In no time at all, we had our limit. But what to do with them?

The first 23 years of my life were spent in the meat and potatoes protection of small town Southern Indiana. I thought fried chicken on Sunday was a state law. So one of the first new culinary experiences I enjoyed after leaving the nest was a bowl of New England clam chowder I sat down with on a cool fall evening in Indianapolis. I fell in love; first with Susie and then with the chowder or was it the other way around? I had found my life's calling, gastronomically speaking. I went in search of the perfect bowl of chowder, quickly ruling out the canned version as chaff.

Over the years, I have sampled chowder in every seaport in which I have set foot, including several in New England. I have argued with other chowder lovers on the merits of Manhattan style versus New England but no matter. I found delectable chowder all over the place but perfect? I didn't know, having no benchmark. Now, however, with a cooler full of clams, I was determined to create one.

We left the campground the next morning, my truck bed laden with iced down seafood. Our destination was Seattle and the abode of our son, Joe, where we planned, God willing, to make the best clam chowder ever.

How does one identify an organic cow?

Our son, Joe, lived on Vashon Island across the Puget Sound from Seattle. He had given us this information when he first moved to the northwest but being a Midwestern landlubber, I really did not have a good feel for what that meant. After our twenty minute ride on the Ferry system to get there, I knew. It was wonderful. Unlike my continuing quest for finding the perfect chowder, I had found without even looking what I considered the perfect place to live.

The island was a hippie refuge back in the sixties and a lot of the lifestyle is inherited from that legacy. The inhabitants of both sexes sport a lot of long hair. Sandals seem to be the most popular footwear although rubber boots (galoshes, we used to call them) for the rainy season run a close second.

There are two or three natural medicine offices and more than one midwifery advertised on the side of the road. Flowers abound everywhere as do espresso shops. There are several second hand shops, a couple of antique stores and an art store of some sort or other every few hundred yards. Another attractive feature to the island is that as of this writing, anyway, there are no big box mega stores.

Dogs are another favorite of the island residents. It seems as if everyone has a dog and most of the shops on the island have food and water bowls for dogs by the front door. There is an outdoor espresso shop down the street where we have stopped while walking Joe's dog, Abbie. It is quite pleasant to pull up an Adirondack chair and discuss current events or the latest book with a diverse group of people who are in no hurry while drinking coffee that would easily remove facial hair.

There are also shops that cater to organic gardeners. Organic stuff is a big thing on this island. I stopped to get milk at the market and not paying any attention, grabbed a gallon of low fat milk and went to the checkout. The register rang up 6.69 for the milk. The price shocked me but I knew stuff on the island is expensive. When I got to Joe's house and told Susie about it, she looked at the label.

"You bought organic milk, dummy." She said.

Organic milk!!! What the hell was that? I was under the impression that all the milk I drank was organic. How much more organic can you get than something coming from a cow, for God's sake? Where do they think non-organic milk comes from? An oil refinery?

Other evidence of the sixties lies in the 'live and let live' attitude and the laid back pace on the island. This is evidenced by yard work. It seems to be given only a minimum of attention. Lawns are left as natural as possible. Nothing seems to be trimmed. I doubt that there is a single gas fired trimmer on the whole island.

I suppose the natural look is part of the environmentalism that is an integral part of the island. Recycling is taken very seriously. We went to a huge recycling station in the middle of the island where we joined a quarter mile long line of residents in cars and trucks waiting to drop off their glass and paper products. Susie, who is the consummate recycler, was quite impressed.

Homes on the island are incredibly expensive. There aren't any McMansions, though, just a lot of cottage style places. This eclectic collection of homes lends a certain charm to the island. A realtor told me that it's not unusual to find a million dollar two bedroom bungalow next to a run down hundred thousand dollar house trailer.

I have no idea where people get the money to buy these homes. I met a man on the ferry driving a rusted out volkswagen bus. He appeared to be returning from a Grateful Dead concert and he told me that he owns a place on the waterfront where he carves authentic Indian masks and does a little massage therapy on the side. How he lives in a million dollar property is beyond me. Massages must pay well.

Bicycles and guitars are another common commodity on the island. The bikes are great for riding the ferries because you don't need to get in line like the folks in automobiles do. Many commuters, including Joe, leave their cars at home and ride bicycles to work. It saves several dollars a day on the ferry ride and there is no long wait during the evening rush hour. The guitars are used to occupy some of the spare time available to the people not mowing grass or trimming around trees. All in all, the island is quite a nice place to be although the laidback lifestyle would take some getting used to.

This attitude of working to live instead of living to work has me lying awake at night wondering what our son is doing spending an hour a day on a ferry with his nose in a book, riding his bike up and down the hills of Seattle and playing the guitar when he could be manicuring his lawn or getting in a little overtime.

Where did we go wrong? He should be here in Indiana with his contemporaries in one of the new neighborhoods springing up on a seemingly endless basis. He could have a mortgage payment, a wife and a four wheel drive SUV. More importantly, He could be raising some grandbabies for us. He's not a chip off the old block. He doesn't even have high blood pressure. What is this world coming to?

Move it, pilgrim.

Of all the places in the country that our retirement adventures took us to, none impressed me more than Vashon Island. I was also amazed by the mundane attitude that the ferry riders take about the twenty minute trip across the water to the mainland. The island is reachable only by a ferry ride which our son Joe, as well as the other people who live on the island and work in Seattle, uses on a daily basis. It's as much a part of their day as is breakfast or dinner.

If you want to live on this island, The ferry is the first thing you need to get used to. Timing it just right, the wait in line and the ride across is maybe thirty to forty minutes. If you don't time it right, it might be an hour. It's definitely not for the type A personality. You can honk your horn till it melts, cuss up a storm or shake your fist till your fingers turn blue but it doesn't hurry the ferry at all. Consequently, people seem to be relaxed and resigned to the wait so they have found a myriad of things to do either on the ride across or while sitting in their cars waiting to get on the ferry.

In the morning, just like in Indianapolis, you see the laptops open, the cell phones going and a lot of makeup being applied via rear view mirrors. The difference on the ferry is that the cars are not moving.

In the evening you see a lot of people sleeping. There seems to be as many comfortable sleeping positions as there are people. Some are in the passenger cabin on the upper deck stretched out in the booths that run along the windows. Others have the driver's seat in reclining position and one lady even had her feet out the drivers side window.

Other people who are not busy with either work, sleep or makeup use the morning and evening blocks of time to accomplish things that there is never time to do elsewhere. A couple of people are waxing their vehicles, some are sunning themselves on the car hood and one man seems to be practicing yoga while sitting cross legged in the bed of his pickup truck. More than a few people are hunkered down in their seat with a nice fat book.

All of these people seem very relaxed so it surprised me how quickly they moved when the time came to actually put the vehicles on the ship. Most seem to know exactly when they need to be behind the wheel with the engine running.

I hadn't a clue about this so the process of parking the truck got to be kind of nerve wracking for a neurotic mid westerner. Humbling is probably a better word. Some of the ferry people (that sounds stupid, I know, but I don't know what else to call them.) who motion for you to move and who point you into your slot on the ship are probably related to Seinfeld's "soup nazi." There's not a lot of time to waste when they're loading the ferry. It goes very quick so you need to be prepared to get your vehicle in the right lane and in the spot where they want you or you'll get a dirty look and maybe even get a finger pointing at you for all the world to see. When all this scurrying around started, for some inane reason, I had a panicky thought that my truck might not start and I would hold up the whole thing so I said a little prayer before I turned the ignition key. The engine fired right up. Thank you, Lord.

The ferry ride is expensive but it is also spectacular. You don't have to stay in your vehicle so as soon as we got the truck parked, we headed to the upper deck to check out the scenery. Before we even left the dock, we saw the Olympic mountains, jutting up out of the land mass to the west. They are white with snow even in mid June and hidden partially behind the haze that always seems to be around mountain ranges. They own the horizon from south to North. I immediately began planning to be on this ferry sometime when the sun sets over this indescribable splendor.

After we left the dock and got out into the water a few hundred yards, we could see in the southeast, Mount Rainier looming over the water and dominating the landscape in that direction. We were very fortunate because this sight isn't always available. The weather has to be good and the sky needs to be clear. Even then, the mountain can be covered with clouds but on our first trip across, the mountain was "out".

When we first saw it from the deck of the ferry, it really didn't seem real. It looked more like one of those garish mountain scenes that are painted on the wall (above the aquarium with the two huge goldfish) at the seven ninety-five Chinese buffet.

Then you realize that it's not a cheap painting. It's real and though your flatlander mind has trouble adjusting to it, the mass of it overwhelms your senses. Some people on the deck look at the mountain but it's old hat to most of them so it goes unnoticed by this group.

The trip across went by very quickly. We tried standing on deck in the front of the ship but the wind and the cool air soon drove us back inside.

We also had a special treat on our first trip. A baby Orca whale was hanging out in the waters around the island. She had somehow gotten separated from her pod. She had some sort of skin problem which had the marine biologists worried and she was also very friendly and approachable so people were concerned that she might be hit by a ship . There was much discussion in the media about what to do with her. When we neared the landing on the island, we saw her just off the to the left of the ship. She raced back and forth and once jumped completely out of the water. An unbelievable event for a land locked Hoosier.

The baby Orca was captured in a net a few days later while television camera crews surrounded the rescue operation. She was placed in a large holding tank aboard a barge and was treated for her various ills and transported to British Columbia where she rejoined her pod.

Where's Babe, the blue ox?

A good part of the reason for our being in the Northwestern part of the country was to visit with our son Joe in Seattle for a few days. We added plans for a camping trip in British Columbia with Joe and two of his friends, Mike and Jeff. This was their annual salmon fishing trip but the trip was jeopardized when Mike's truck went on the fritz. Salmon fishing was not on our list of things to do but it sounded good so I volunteered to pull his boat to the fishing camp. It wasn't like we were in any hurry to get home.

Susie and I headed North in the truck while the other three traveled by car. We crossed the border into British Columbia and the city of Vancouver where we got in line for a ferry to Vancouver Island. A couple hundred cars, thirty or so semi trucks loaded with everything imaginable, campers, motor homes, pickups with boat trailers attached, bicyclists and pedestrians were in line with us. I didn't see how everyone would fit but we did. The fee for the crossing was a hundred and seventy dollars for the five of us and our vehicles.

Two hours later, we rolled off the ferry into the city of Nainamo, B.C. Our next destination was Telegraph Cove some two hundred and fifty miles distant near the northernmost tip of the Island. The camp was tucked in a cove on the shore of the Queen Charlotte strait. This water is also the home of several Orca whale pods and the prospect of seeing them had been another reason for making the trip.

The surroundings became more remote and the mountains and trees got bigger with each passing mile. We reached the turnoff for the camp about sunset and drove ten or so miles on a dusty, rut filled road built by logging companies and used primarily by trucks hauling the logs out of those hills. The headlights of the truck picked up a mountain lion sitting on the edge of the road in total darkness enjoying a snack of God knows what and I knew then we were pretty isolated. We set up camp in that same dark and I kept a keen ear at the ready in case that mountain lion wanted another snack. I was pretty sure we were safe in our little nest in the back of the truck but I wasn't sure if the other tents the three young men were in would survive an attack.

The temperature was in the high forties when we arose early the following morning. This was about 30 degrees cooler than we had experienced since the previous winter and while it was invigorating, I didn't care for it. Joe and his friends had left before dawn to get on the water and Susie had headed for the heated bathrooms the minute we climbed out of the truck. I stood shivering in my sweatshirt and my Bermuda shorts wondering why I didn't bring long pants. It was so cold my goosebumps were poking through my tube socks. The early risers had made a pot of that strong coffee they drink in the northwest and I poured myself a cup, clutching it to get warm.

I watched as an Amazon of a lady stoked a fire in the next campsite. Her husband (I assume), a man who appeared to be Paul Bunyan's great grandson, stuck his head out of their tent. Well over six feet tall, blond headed and blue eyed, he stood there flexing incredible muscles wearing only shorts and a yellow tank top undershirt. You would have thought it was eighty degrees.

'Good morning.' The lady said.

I sucked in my stomach and wandered over to their campsite, hoping to get close to their fire. Not seeing a coffeepot, I offered them a cup of our coffee.

"It's a little strong for me." I laughed "but I've found that if you take an antacid tablet with it, it won't completely destroy your insides."

Mr. Bunyan declined and picked up a sack of Starbucks coffee beans from the picnic table. He poured out a handful of the beans and tossed them in his mouth. "Better just to chew 'em." He Said. "None of that sissy stuff watering down the flavor."

My stomach leaped. "I'll have to try that sometime." I said, shivering again.

"Care for a cup now? " He said, grinning and offered the sack to me. It was my turn to decline. "I've had enough today." I said and then added "Does Juan Valdez know you do that?"

The words came out in a very deep baritone since I was still sucking in my stomach. He laughed heartily in a real baritone as Susie returned to our campsite and I excused myself before I was offered raw meat for breakfast.

When the sun shine finally made its way through the trees, The temperature warmed up and the day was beautiful. The three fishermen returned for an early lunch and then Mike took Susie and I out in the boat. We headed for one of their favorite fishing spots and I imagined myself preparing my tackle and getting ready to take my place as one of the world's great salmon fishermen by reeling in a thirty pounder even though I have never in my life caught a fish more than four inches long. We left the cove and went out into open water where we hoped to catch sight of an Orca or two. We stopped to take a picture of the distant mountains reflected in the deep, blue water. When it comes to water depths, the stuff that's not over my head is my preference so I asked Mike how deep the water was. He got a chart out and studied it for a minute.

"Four hundred and forty three meters at the mouth of the Cove." He said. My heart leaped into my mouth and I resisted the urge to curl up in the fetal position in the bottom of the boat. But we were on an adventure so I tightened up my pucker string and comforted myself with the knowledge that we were in a big, sturdy boat. I also did a little mental arithmetic, remembering that metric conversions had something to do with dividing by four.

"Over a hundred feet" I said quietly, expelling a breath of air at the same time.

"No." Mike said, drawing the word out slowly while looking at a small dial on the boat's dash. "It's more like fifteen hundred feet."

My math was a little rusty. 'Not division; multiplication.' I thought as I watched that sturdy nineteen foot boat suddenly take on the dimensions of a leaky inner tube. Our little porch in Indiana never looked as good as it did at this moment. I have been making some headway overcoming a fear of heights and now, to my dismay, I discover that I'm pretty apprehensive about depths as well.

Mike noticed that all the blood had left my face. "It's only about three hundred feet where we fish." He said reassuringly.

I said nothing but I instinctively knew my Walter Mitty-esque adventure was over. I needed the security of a big steel sided ship in whale infested waters. I sat back and started a deep breathing technique that the man who taught it to me assured me it was supposed to bring on an inner peace. It didn't exactly do that but it slowed my heart rate down into the triple digits and I managed to remain upright until we reached the dock. I climbed out of the boat nonchalantly and never returned to it. Now that I look back on it from the safety of my desk chair, it actually turned out to be a beautiful boat ride.

The land of the free and the home of the arrogant.

I decided to err on the side of caution when I found out how deep the water was and stayed pretty much on dry land. The fishermen in our crowd, including Susie, brought in halibut and Salmon and we ate fresh fish almost every evening of the six days we were there. There's something to be said about lazy days where your only objective is to determine how the fish is to be cooked. I wasn't without things to do though. Susie and I spent one day exploring the northern tip of Vancouver Island where we ended up on an Indian reservation outside of the town of Port Hardy talking to the residents.

We met an older lady who told us of a forced resettlement of this tribe in the nineteen sixties. I don't know any of the details of why it was done but I vowed to find out more when we got home. I should have been a history teacher, I guess. I love hearing about that old stuff. Too bad I didn't recognize that in high school.

We also watched as some Indian authority, the tribal council perhaps, distributed Sockeye salmon to the members of the tribe. Giant, gleaming and still squirming fish were handed off a huge tanker truck and taken by the residents where they were cleaned and the meat was canned for the long winter. Susie was itching to help them but I wouldn't let her.

Another excursion had us spending a half day on a boat big enough that the deep water didn't bother me. Our objective was to see the whales that inhabit the waters of the Queen Charlotte straits. It didn't take me long to get my sea legs as we sailed out into the endless and very deep waters of the straits. Two thirds of the fifty passengers were European or Asian; only a handful of us were American. Our guide on the trip was a Canadian naturalist who was one of those dedicated individuals spending her life in a worthwhile endeavor, in this case, watching out for the whales.

She spent the first half hour of the trip appealing to us to do what we could to protect the oceans of the world so that the huge mammals we were seeing could have a chance to thrive. British Columbia has set aside several square miles of water in the area that served as habitat for the whales. This area is off limits to any boating traffic. The Orcas venture out of this reserve to feed and this provides the opportunity to see them. We joined a half dozen other boats in the strait and the Captain shut down the engine while we lined the rails hoping to catch a glimpse of one of these leviathans. Suddenly, there they were; majestic creatures, moving gracefully through the water. The guide was explaining the habits of the different pods and how they are a harbinger of conditions in the world's oceans when a yacht that dwarfed our boat came on the scene. It was flying the United States flag and was heading for the reserve area, a mile or so away.

The guide, a normally soft spoken lady, said something like "Arrogant bastard" very loudly. She explained to all the passengers, in German, French and English, that the captain of that yacht had allegedly been warned twice to stay out of the Orca's habitat but pretty much thumbed his nose at them. "Our captain will call it in." she said disgustedly and I zipped up my jacket in an effort to cover up my tee shirt with 'Indiana' printed across the front. I fervently hoped that the mostly non-American crowd understood that we're not all like that and that they would not go back home talking about "The Arrogant American bastards."

When we left Canada, Our trip back across the border was also an instant reminder of the war on terror. We sat in a very long line for close to an hour before getting our turn to cross. Having been born and raised in Southern Indiana, I was naive enough to assume that the border patrol should know just by looking that we're Americans and that we belong in the states. I also personally doubted that any self respecting terrorist would disguise himself as me but the border guards did not feel that way.

I was looking for a 'Welcome Back" from the guy in the booth but it was nothing like that. He didn't crack a smile as he told me to shut the engine off and hand him the keys

Better safe than sorry, I suppose. Susie's activity didn't help. As we had neared the border she located a friendly cell phone tower and was quickly connected to our daughter in Indiana. Neither the phone nor the sunglasses she had on sat well with the uniformed man at the booth. He told Susie to put down the phone and remove her sunglasses.

"The phone could be a bomb." He explained without cracking a smile. "And the sunglasses could be part of a disguise." He examined our passports and then did a thorough search of our truck and I understood why there was such a long wait in line. I would get on my soapbox about this treatment except for the fact that it's a necessary evil today.

While I waited on him to look in, over and under the truck, I reflected on a very busy year of 2004. We have been across both our Northern and Southern borders in the past six months and the contrast is remarkable. The area where we sat waiting to cross was beautiful. A marble arch dedicated to Peace is shared by both countries. The waters of the pacific were visible on our right. Flowers were everywhere and the grass was as green as any I've ever seen.

Contrast this with any one of the half dozen Mexican borders that we crossed in the past year. The crossings down south are blacktop on blacktop and dusty gravel is the norm. There are no flowers. The bridge across the river in Del Rio, Texas is decorated with hundreds of blue plastic Wal-mart bags caught in the barbed wire fencing lining the bridge. The banks of the Rio Grande are covered with trash.

Why such a big difference? I don't know. I wish I had the ability to see a big picture of why this is the way it is.

When we finally passed inspection and were safely ensconced on Interstate five heading south for Seattle, I thought of the search at the border, the Indians in British Columbia, the whales, the 'Ugly American' yacht owner and the sea of blue plastic bags in Del Rio, flapping in the wind in an effort to free themselves from the barbed wire.

These things, along with countless others, make our world today a very complicated place to be. Our eventual return to Morgan County, Indiana and our uncomplicated life there suddenly became a very appealing prospect.

How did Oysters get to the Rocky Mountains?

All the beautiful scenery of Washington State and new adventures not withstanding, we decided it was time to go home and see our granddaughter. The fishing trip had just about done me in and besides, our neighbors in Indiana reported that our garden was overflowing with vegetables and the thought of some juicy Indiana tomatoes had us packing the truck.

We checked our travel software and the consensus of the computer was that the quickest way home was across the top of the country on Interstates ninety and ninety four through Minneapolis. I thought maybe a central route through Nebraska and Iowa would be quicker but who can argue with a computer?

We left Seattle during the morning rush hour traffic, having said our goodbyes to Joe early as he left for work. In what seemed like no time at all, we were out of the city and on our way east. The changes in the landscape crossing the State of Washington were startling. We left the water and Seattle behind, crossing the Cascades Mountains thru Snoqualmie Pass. Cool air and lush greenery were also left behind and we entered a flat arid land that bordered on being desert. The temperature went up about twenty five degrees to the mid nineties and stayed there. Midway through the state, we crossed the Columbia River Gorge This huge canyon carved out of the mostly flat terrain is one of the more spectacular things we saw on this trip so of course, we stopped to take more pictures. We have crossed this gorge four times now and we have stopped to take the same pictures each time.

We continued through the dry, desert like terrain until we reached the Rocky Mountains east of Spokane. The trip across Idaho took an hour or so but the scenery made it seem like just a few minutes. The temperature was still hovering in the mid nineties and the prospect of spending a night in the hot truck bed had us thinking we should find a nice, air conditioned motel room.

We spent the night in Missoula, the home of the University of Montana. There was some sort of function at the University so I could not find any cheap hotel rooms. I am just miserly enough to think that anything over fifty bucks for a bed to sleep in is too much but much to my chagrin, we ended up paying much more than that.

I spent the evening studying our Road Atlas and finally concluded that maybe we could reach North Dakota with an early start and a little hard driving. Unfortunately, I kept thinking about all the money I'd spent on that Motel room and spent much of the night tossing and turning. That meant that the early start was History. It was more like eleven when we left and the first order of business was to get something to eat. We had not driven far when we saw a billboard advertising a restaurant whose specialty was rocky mountain oysters. Seeing as how we were in the Rockies and also seeing as how Susie loves to sample local fare, I suggested we try it. I pulled in to the parking lot and got out of the truck. Above the entrance to the place was a painting of a bull with his legs crossed and a very scared look on his face. Susie wanted to know what that was all about and I had to explain the origin of "Rocky Mountain Oysters" to her.

"You think I'm eating that?" she said. "In a pig's eye, Buster."

"But Susie, you eat steak, why wouldn't you eat.. ."

"Aaaaaagghh. Are you crazy?" She said, interrupting me. "Steak is one thing but it comes from the more public parts of the cow. If it comes from the private parts, I'm not eating it."

I didn't get to try the oysters but I did learn the limits of her sense of adventure when it comes to dining.

We were a few miles outside Bozeman, Montana and I was beginning to realize I might have been a little optimistic in thinking we could make it to the North Dakota border that day. Making your way across Montana isn't exactly like driving to Terre Haute, even with an early start. We weren't going to get home as quick as I thought. But then again, I had to remind myself, what's the hurry?

Road signs in this area were all pointing south to Yellowstone National Park. This was on list of places to see some day but there were no plans to visit on this trip. I looked at Susie and she looked at me.

"Let's go." She said. I'm still uncomfortable deviating from a travel plan but I'm learning that it's okay. I grabbed the road atlas and steering with my knee, decided we could find our way back to Indiana even by going through the Park. We left the Interstate at Belgrade, Montana and headed south on Highway 191 to West Yellowstone and the western entrance of the park .

In the back of mind were all the things I'd read about the height of the mountains in the area but I had also been wanting to visit Yellowstone since I was in grade school. I decided I could handle anything in our way and if it got too bad, I'd just hold my breath.

The park contains so many geologic oddities you could spend a month visiting all of them. We decided we had a couple of days to spare and that would do the highlights but we didn't even begin to see everything. We used our Golden Age pass and got a campsite with no hookups for nine dollars.

If you've not been there, Yellowstone is a big place. You get some idea of how big when the ranger at the entrance gate tells us that Norris Campground, where we were headed, is forty miles away. Normally, I like to go to the campground and get set up before anything else but not this trip. That forty mile drive plus a few more took us to places almost unimaginable. The Upper and Lower Falls, the Grand Canyon, the paint pots, assorted geysers, buffalo herds; It was almost inconceivable that so many different things could be in one spot.

It was almost dark when we got to our campsite. A hot shower was the first thing on my mind after an exhausting day of exploring but my good deal on the camping price went away when we had to pay three dollars apiece to take a shower. We tried to sell the lady guarding the showers on letting us take one together but she was having none of that. Perhaps she was a prude or more likely, she was there to make money for the company who managed the showers.

Our campsite was beautiful but the whole area was plastered with signs about Yellowstone's bears. 'Please place anything that contains the smell of food in a hard sided structure.' The signs informed me. Wait a minute, I thought. Even with my three dollar shower, I suspected that I still smelled like bear food and I had no idea if the camper shell on the back of our truck qualified as a hard sided structure. This fact, along with the pitch black darkness and a myriad of strange noises, made for a restless night.

We broke camp early, planning to move to the Grant's Village campground where we could take in the sights in that area. There was lots of beautiful country to see and of course, we didn't want to leave until we saw at least one herd of Buffalo. We also knew we would have to make the trip to see 'Old Faithful'. The storm clouds were rolling in from all directions as we worked our way past Yellowstone lake and through one of the Buffalo herds. We considered bypassing "Old Faithful" because of the rain but you can't go to Yellowstone and not see the world's most famous geyser.

We parked a quarter mile from a crowd of people, guessing that was the site of the geyser. As we got closer, a sign near the crowd told us that the geyser would go off at 3:02 p.m. The rain and the wind picked up as we stood with probably a thousand other people waiting on Old Faithful to do its thing. The hail was next and I was checking my watch. 3:02 came and went and the geyser just sort of sat there. Maybe it's on some other time zone, I thought as I stood there shivering but we stood our ground. A couple of minutes later, the geyser sputtered and sprang to life. It was a weak eruption; "not normal" someone in the crowd said, but no matter. We had bagged another entry on our list of 999 things to see.

The temperature had dropped to forty five degrees and we were soaked to the skin as we ran the quarter mile back to the truck. The rain went from torrent to full blown gully washer as we drove to our campground on Yellowstone Lake. We struggled out of our wet clothes while sitting in the truck and managed to get dry things on without throwing our back out. It was just turning dark when we climbed into our little nest in the back of the truck. It was a pretty miserable evening. The dark was impenetrable and the combination of rain and cold had condensation from the aluminum of our truck cap dripping on my forehead.

Suddenly, even with being surrounded by ten thousand foot mountain peaks and camped on the largest fresh water lake above 7000 feet in North America, Mooresville, Indiana looked pretty inviting.

We still planned to get up early and head for Jackson Hole, Wyoming, a refuge of the jet set at the base of the Grand Teton mountains. We hoped to do a little hobnobbing with the greats and the near greats of our country who hang out in Jackson Hole. The rain was still coming down when we awoke and added to that was pea soup thick fog. We decided to skip the hobnobbing and head east.

Somewhere in Wyoming, I noticed we could use some fuel. When you're driving a truck with a diesel engine, you can't always find fuel, so I tended to keep the tank close to full. I decided to get some diesel fuel at the truck stop up ahead. I pulled into the covered island and couldn't find any diesel pumps. I went in and asked where the diesel fuel was. The gum chewing lady behind the counter pointed to an island out where all the semi-trucks were parked

"Pickups on Number five." she said. I thought this to be peculiar putting a pickup truck pump station in with the big boys and I didn't particularly want to do that but we needed fuel.

I pulled the truck around to number five and found myself with semi trucks on both sides of me. The engines of these leviathans were throbbing with that low rattle that puts the macho, cocky strut in many a five foot, six inch truck driver. The truck cabs loomed over us dwarfing my little three quarter ton pickup with the dorky Camper shell on the bed,

Suddenly I felt very inadequate and naked. The feeling was much like one I experienced on the first day of freshman gym class almost fifty years ago. Without so much as a backward glance, I was transported from that diesel fuel pump to the boys locker room and shower at St. John High. I was discovering that some of my classmates, unlike myself, had hair in some very private places. Those who did were quick to point out that I didn't and that was the beginning of feeling inadequate for much of my life. It was very traumatic at the time but just as quickly as I'd left, I was back, standing at the diesel fuel station with the pump handle in my hand, feeling hairless once again.

Pumping diesel fuel as fast as I could and wanting only to get out of there, I turned when the driver on my left climbed down from his cab and said something that sounded like "what ya haulin there, son?" He might as well have asked me why I had no hair on my body. I was dumbstruck.

He was probably twenty years younger than me so I don't know why he was calling me "son". I also might have misunderstood what he had asked. He could have said something about the weather but the feelings of inadequacy prompted by these giant trucks wouldn't let me think rationally.

I mumbled something about personal belongings but I don't really think he was interested in what was in my truck. I hung the pump handle back in its cradle, climbed into my little truck and resolved never to do that again. I think we might be about traveled out.

Idiot? Your mother thinks I'm an idiot?

Two months after leaving Indiana, we returned home a little poorer, a little wiser and with 7200 more miles on our truck. The trip was an experiment as to whether we could comfortably camp in the back of our Pickup with only a truck cap as shelter. Had we been successful, we had hoped to spend next summer in Alaska in these accommodations.

We wanted to leave Fionna, our fifth wheel, at home on a trip to our Northern most state because we have found the best usage for her is when we stop for weeks at a time and we plan to be on the move a lot up there. Also, pulling her ten or twelve thousand miles does not seem like a good thing to do, especially now with the price of fuel.

We left Indiana in July paying a dollar fifty six for diesel fuel. The farther west we went, the more expensive it got until it was over two dollars a gallon on the other side of the Rockies. We paid even more than that in Canada but I couldn't tell you how much. Up there, the pumps register what is being dispensed in liters instead of gallons. I guess I should have paid more attention in Trigonometry class because metric system conversions leave me cold. Topping that off are the exchange rate calculations. Throw those in and I doubt that even Albert Einstein knows what the price of Canadian fuel is. I know the cashiers in those Canadian gas stations certainly don't. I asked two or three of them how many gallons I pumped and I got the same look I would have had I had asked them to give me three uses for the Rosetta stone. Suffice to say fuel was expensive and I felt sorry for the poor people who had to pay those inflated prices until yesterday when I saw it for two dollars and fifteen cents right here in central Indiana. If the price keeps going up, my Alaskan trip may turn into an overnighter to Terre Haute, Indiana.

(G2 note: When I wrote this and was considering the Alaskan trip, Diesel fuel was $2.15. Today, it's three dollars and more in some places and the Alaska trip seems even more far fetched.)

On top of all this, I hear the mosquitoes in Alaska are the size of turkey vultures and we'd need the protection of something other than a Camper Shell to avoid the possibility of being eaten alive.

Even if the price of fuel stabilizes, we're still going to have to deal with the weather. When Fionna stays behind, the weather can have much more of a negative effect on camping. We should have given that more thought when we're sleeping in the back of the truck. We experienced several weather extremes on the trip home from Seattle, spending a night in a motel in Montana because the temperature was in the nineties and then the next night, huddling together in the back of our truck in forty degree weather. Added to that was the rain.

In a cold rain, our camper shell gathered moisture from condensation which provided a steady drip every thirty five seconds on our face as we laid in bed staring at the ceiling, some eleven inches from our noses. Were we on our honeymoon, say, it wouldn't matter because, well, just because it wouldn't matter. But we're not on our honeymoon. We're just laying there wondering what in God's name possessed us to come up with this cockamamie idea. No more trips until we solve the condensation problem.

Another consideration for this method of camping is that we will be a year or more older when we're ready to go. We are somehow going to have to remain limber enough to shimmy our way into bed. Maybe that Yoga I keep telling myself I'm going to study will help but I suspect we'll have to sign up for some bullfighting or maybe some break dancing lessons. The agility required for either of those activities is on a par with wriggling over a tailgate into a twenty two inch high enclosure. We are also going to have to find a way to get things out of our storage space under our sleeping quarters. Susie knows that I have slight claustrophobic tendencies but when she wants a pair of shoes out of a little space that most self respecting ferrets wouldn't go into, she still expects me to do it. When I slither under the bed, performing maneuvers best left for prepubescent gymnasts, hyperventilation sets in within a few seconds and I end up sitting on the tailgate with my head in a paper bag.

We had driven seventy three hundred miles over hill and dale and spent thirty five nights uncomfortably holed up in the back of our truck. Now I'm at the end of the allotted space for this story and we still don't know if traveling in less than spartan accommodations is an acceptable way to see Alaska. Maybe if I bought a tent camper and tried ….. tried….. OH. Ouch.

Get Away. sdfkdfj . kjtfdsa' gfdfsdg. %&*/?# Squawk. Squawk.

* * * * *

Testing. Testing. Can anybody hear me? This is Susie, Mrs. G2, talking. I'm in control of the computer now. I had to wrestle the keyboard away from this crazy man who spent all that money on a truck cap and now is thinking about buying a tent camper when we have a perfectly good fifth wheel. Is there no end to this? I'm beginning to believe my mother was right. He is an idiot.

I wish I would have thought of that.

This is the story of a large family; eight children, soon to be nine. And the house was anything but large. Oh sure, the mom and dad considered it a two story home but it was really only a story and a half and not much of a half at that. Outsiders might say the family was too large to be living in such a little house but the family made do. The homespun maxim: "A place for everything and everything in its place" could have originated here.

The house sat on a small quiet side street of the city's near south side. The large front porch that stretched across the front of the house added precious space and was always in use except on the coldest of days. It was a good place to do homework or play when there was time for such things. The one bathroom in the house was kept busy most hours of the day and into the late evening. The kitchen table was long enough to accommodate the ten of them which it did every morning and every evening every day of the year.

The routine of church, work, school, meals and sleep went by on a daily basis without interruption until a particularly warm, spring day in nineteen fifty two. A new television, the first in the family, sat proudly in a place of honor in the living room. The long table in the kitchen was still loaded down with the supper dishes as the family finished eating and immediately gathered around to watch their newest possession. A little girl, second oldest of the eight children and almost ten, sat with her parents, five sisters and two brothers watching the grainy, black and white picture being beamed into their living room from the tall tower on Bluff Road in Indianapolis.

This little girl watched, mesmerized, taking her eyes off the screen only long enough to give her baby sister, whom she was holding, a fresh bottle of milk. The picture on the television showed the waters of a huge lake and a man standing on the bank was calling it the Great Salt Lake. It was an interesting story and perhaps because it was the first thing they'd seen on their new television, the little girl wanted to see it in person. She turned to her mom and dad.

"Do you think we could visit there?" she asked, not knowing she might as well have asked for a trip to the moon.

Her dad looked at her mom and said "Not right now but maybe someday."

"That's okay. When I get big, I'll take you guys." The little girl told them. The show ended and the television was turned off. Baths were taken and lunches made in preparation for school the next day. The Great Salt Lake was forgotten and the years passed. The little girl grew up, met a handsome stranger, married and began to raise a family of her own.

That could have been the end of the story but it wasn't. Fast forward forty odd years. Susie and I are in Salt Lake City preparing to do a little sightseeing.

"I want to see the Great Salt Lake." She said.

"Okay, Susie dear, but first, I plan on seeing the genealogy library." I hated changing my plans and she was well aware of it but that didn't sway her.

"I don't care about any library. I want to see the lake." She was vehement about it.

"Okay." I said. If the truth were to be told, the handsome stranger wanted to see the lake also. We drove west until the great waters loomed before us and found a place to pull over on the edge of the water. Susie got out and rummaged around in the back of the truck.

"What are you looking for?" I asked her.

"Nothing." She replied and walked to the water's edge. She bent over and tasted it. "Yep, it's salt, alright."

I took some pictures while she waded along the shore.

"It sure is big." She said, barely speaking above a whisper. "But not near as big as I imagined."

"What did you say?" I asked, not hearing her since she was so quiet.

"Nothing." She took one last look around and we headed on west.

Seven weeks and a long trip later, we returned to Indiana. We spent a couple of weeks getting the garden back in shape and then one afternoon found ourselves on the south side of Indianapolis.

"How far is it to the cemetery?" Susie said. "I'd like to go see my Mom and Dad."

"Not far." I told her. "We'll do that."

I drove down South Meridian Street to the wrought iron cemetery entrance. We don't get there very often, maybe a couple of times a year and we always have trouble finding her mom and dad's graves. The cemetery is immense and all the graves are marked with flat headstones level with the grass. It makes the place easier to mow, I suppose, but it also makes it devoid of any distinguishable reference points from which to find a grave. Adding to the confusion was the lack of foliage. I knew the general location and could use the landscape to find the graves in the summer but the leaves were all gone and the trees all looked alike.

There was more than a hint of fall in the air as the cool northerly breeze scattered the leaves that had lost their battle to remain on the tree. Those left clinging to the limbs shuddered as the pesky breeze assailed their precarious position.

"Just find me the little red Maple close to the road and I'll take it from there." She told me.

We wound around on the road through the cemetery because there are lots of small red maple trees next to the road and most have lost their leaves. Oddly enough, a particular tree felt like the right one.

"Stop here." Susie told me but I was already putting my foot on the brake. We got out and looked at the seemingly endless rows. The breeze stiffened some and I pulled at my jacket collar as Susie went down one row of headstones. I went down another, looking for the familiar 'Speck' name.

"Here it is." I heard her say, her voice tailing off as she stopped and pointed. I walked over to join her but before I could get there, she knelt down on both knees, oblivious to the grass stains on her jeans and brushed the dust and dead strands of grass off the flat grave marker. First, 'Russell 1908 – 1975' and then 'Agnes 1912 – 2001' appeared as the names and dates were swept clean.

A metal vase that was supposed to fit neatly into a slot on the stone, sat at an angle, filled with artificial flowers. Susie first straightened the vase which had come loose from its mooring and then fluffed out the flowers into a pretty bouquet. From her jacket pocket, she took a small plastic bottle, one of those that healthy people keep their drinking water in, and poured the contents around the perimeter of the marker. She knelt there a minute longer and then got to her feet.

"What was that all about?" I asked her.

"Oh, just something I wanted to do."

"Well, what was it?" I persisted.

She sighed. "I wanted to take my Mom and Dad to see the Great Salt Lake. I promised them I would." She slowly screwed the cap back on the bottle.

"I was just a little kid but that promise meant something to me. I forgot about it for years and oddly enough, only remembered it when Daddy died. It was too late for him but I promised myself that when we had the time, I would at least take my mom."

She stopped and wiped her eyes one at a time, switching the now empty bottle from one hand to another as she did so. Her voice rose a little as she continued.

"Our own kids were little then so I had to wait." The tears began to flow freely so she took a tissue from her pocket and wiped her nose. Her voice cracked with every other word as she continued. "Then mom died just about the time we were free to take her out there." She twisted the empty plastic bottle in her hands until I thought it would snap. "I didn't get to take either one of them to that lake so I did the only thing I could think of to do." She smiled though the tears and held up the empty bottle. "I brought the lake to them. I hope they like it as much as I did."

She stuck the empty bottle back in her pocket and walked towards the car.

PART EIGHT
The Florida Keys

Now that's a new use for a sock.

During the summer of 2004, we submitted our application to volunteer in one or more of Southwest Florida's State Parks for the upcoming winter. We got two offers, both of which were more than we had expected. Long Key State Park in the Florida Keys wanted us for six weeks before Christmas and Koreshan State Park in Estero, south of Fort Myers, had a three month slot available stating in early January. This was perfect and it was a good deal for both us and the state of Florida. They get some unpaid help and we got a place to park Fionna, our fifth wheel.

In late October of 2004, we loaded up Fionna with all the things we need to live our everyday lives and headed south. We arrived at our workplace for the next two months in the little town of Layton on Long Key, some sixty miles from Key West. It's an idyllic, tropical area so everything was green and overgrown and the insects came in two varities; the tiny no-see-ums and the large, economy variety. The mosquitoes, of which there were several, are about the size of canned hams but the rangers told us they would be gone after the first cold spell.

"When's that?" I asked.

"Lemme see." He said, grabbing his jaw with the palm of his hand. "We had one back in '87."

Our campsite was right on the ocean and was quite breezy so that kept the skeeters and the no-see-ums from being more than a nuisance. I could not believe our good luck, parked on oceanfront property not more than ten feet from the water. It was wonderful. I did have a few misgivings when the wind picked up a couple of nights after we got there. My God, had some hurricane gotten in under the radar? The whole island couldn't be more than a couple of feet above sea level and a good storm surge would have carried us halfway to Cuba. I slept fitfully that night but the most beautiful sunrise I had ever seen occurred in the morning over a calm ocean and I quickly dismissed all of my fears about bad weather.

We soon settled into our routine of maintaining the trails in the park and keeping the shoreline clean of debris. The primary topic of conversation amongst the rangers was the festival going on in Key West. Apparently, we had arrived just in time to take part in it.

The people in Key West called their celebration "Fantasy Fest" and it had something to do with Halloween. Susie and I love festivals so we couldn't wait to get there. One of the reasons was food. I love Festival food. I was hoping the Key West Volunteer fire department would be serving those square processed fish sandwiches that are inedible at home but for some reason, are delicious standing in the middle of a firehouse surrounded by firefighting equipment.

All the different church booths would probably be serving chicken and noodles or barbeque sandwiches. The fraternal organizations and the Little League people would probably all have little fundraisers; the basketball shoot, a penny toss, maybe even a 'dunk the Mayor' booth. I couldn't wait.

We arose early and were on Overseas Highway 1 about sun up the day before Halloween so we would be sure to get a good parking spot. There were not a lot of people on the streets when we got there but the city employees were busy setting up barricades for the Grand Finale parade later that night. I looked around for the amusement rides but I didn't see any. I should be able to see the Ferris wheel, at least. What kind of festival would this be without any kiddy rides to keep the little tykes amused.

We wandered onto Duval Street where the festivities were to take place. No church booths. That's strange. Where are the kindly old ladies dishing up chicken and noodles? No dunk stand, no penny toss. What kind of festival was this, anyway? Susie went into a shop and I followed her. When we emerged sometime later, I quickly found out what kind of festival it was. Being fresh from Indiana, I was totally unprepared to see people of the same gender holding hands and being very demonstrative about their feelings for one another.

"My Gosh, Susie." I said. "I think this is a Gay festival."

"Oh no it's not." She said, pointing at a near naked couple, one of each sex, passing by. The female had a painting of a sunset on her bare chest.

"How much film we got?" I asked Susie.

"We have a digital camera, remember?" she told me.

We walked by several artisans that were air brushing practically naked women and men as fast as they could get it done. By early afternoon, the streets were filled with people, many of whom were wearing only enough covering to be 'street legal' and the painted chests were as numerous as the mosquitoes at our campsite. It got to the point where we could barely move and I was going crazy trying not to rub up against somebody who had no clothes on.

It was too much for us so we left the main part of the crowd and went in search of some ice cream. We bought two cones and Susie headed for a sea shell shop across the street. My feet were killing me so I found a picnic table and sat down. A man and woman approached the ice cream stand. The lady had a sea horse painted on her front from head to toe. I judged her to be in her early forties and she was wearing, in addition to the sea horse, only one little patch of cloth that wouldn't hide a quarter but I suppose was keeping her out of jail. She sat down across the picnic table from me and smiled. Her nearly naked husband, wearing only a Pirate hat and one sock that was not on either foot, brought her a cone and walked over to join the line of people who were buying hot dogs.

"Where does he keep his money," I wondered. I stole a glance back at the lady across the table and she smiled again. I tried not to look at her sea horse but it was right in front of me.

"Oh God, Susie, where are you?" I was in a situation that I would have given a hundred dollars to be in when I was fifteen years old but now all I could think of to do was to get back to Indiana.

"Pretty refreshing, isn't it?" she says to me.

"What's that?" I say, panic stricken. My God, was she talking about her sea horse?

She holds up her cone. "Oh, the ice cream." I said, my voice cracking. "Right. The ice cream. Yes, very refreshing."

I stared at my feet and suffered through an uncomfortable silence that seemed to go on for an hour.

"How long did all that painting take?" I asked finally, my eyes going every which way but in her direction.

"Three hours." She told me.

"Three hours??" I said. "Boy, you must have gotten up before breastfast, no, not breastfast, I mean breakfast."

She ignored my Freudian slip. "It also cost three hundred dollars. Are you interested?" she said.

I shook my head in the negative about three hundred times.

"You do have to be comfortable with your own body." She tells me.

That took care of that. Never in a million years. I've not been comfortable with my body ever since my chest went south,. I removed the mirrors in our house about ten years ago and put one up for Susie in the utility room where she can check herself out but not me. I don't need to know what I look like.

Susie returned from shopping and I took my leave from the lady. The parade was still hours away when I got up from the picnic table but we never did make it. By this time, the drinks were flowing freely and I could see the makings of a wild evening ahead. Nope, not for us. About thirty years too late. We walked back to the truck, loaded up our Midwestern values and headed back to reality.

Eight thousand dollars? Sign me up.

Volunteering in state parks does not normally generate a lot of excitement but our stint at Long Key recently got us a little thrill as well as a first hand look at a current American controversy. We were sitting in our camper having breakfast in the State Park on Long Key in the Florida Keys when there was a knock on the camper door.

"Hey Gordon, can you come out here and back me up?" The voice was that of the ranger on patrol in the campground.

"Back me up? I said.

"Yeah." He answered. "I've got some Cuban refugees out here."

Cuban refugees? Back me up? What the heck's he talking about? He had to be kidding but I decided to go along with it. I grabbed my Florida State Park Volunteer hat so I would look official and stepped outside.

Holy Smokes. There he stood with four people. They were casually dressed but you could tell instinctively that they weren't campers. Three young men and one young woman were lined up along the back of the Rangers pickup. The girl wore shorts but the men were in long pants and they were wet up past their knees where they had waded ashore. I looked behind me towards the water and saw this dilapidated boat tied to a post a couple of campsites up the way from us.

I suddenly remembered the ranger's 'back me up' request. My God, who does he think I am, Dirty Harry? I sucked in my stomach, took up my patented John Wayne gait and sauntered over to where they stood, sizing them up as I walked. I knew I could handle the girl if trouble broke out so I leaned over to the ranger and quietly said

"Tell 'em to go ahead and make my day." I tried to sound like Clint at his meanest but my voice cracked and it came out sounding more like Pee Wee Herman.

Susie, joined the group and assessed the situation. Her motherly instincts came out right away at the sight of the young people.

"Are you hungry? She said. The taller of the three shook his head. "No Ingles."

"Eeeee-aaa-ttt?" Susie said slowly, motioning with her hand, putting her finger to her mouth and chewing what I supposed was an imaginary ham sandwich. They brightened up as they understood. Before we could go any further, The ranger, who was on the two way radio, turned to us.

"No contact. The authorities said we're not to talk to them until immigration gets here." This struck Susie the wrong way.

"I don't work for the authorities and I'm a U.S. citizen so if I want to give them something to eat, I will."

I could see tears forming at the plight of these young people and having been around her a while, I knew her hackles were up and I thought I should warn the ranger. I wasn't covering his back on this one.

Susie continued, ever the inquiring reporter and asked the taller of the three men. "How is it over there in Cuba?"

He shook his head, not understanding. But she persisted, drawing her words out slowly.

"What about Castro? Good, bad?" She did the international thumbs up, thumbs down symbol. "Castro?" She said again.

He shook his head, either not caring to voice an opinion on his former leader or else he had decided he wasn't telling anything to this crazy gringo who had just been stuffing her fingers in her mouth.

The ranger interrupted. "We don't know that they're Cubans. They could be terrorists."

That slowed us both down and unlikely as it sounded, it still could be true. Living in the Midwest had us out of our comfort zone here so I asked Susie to stop talking to them. The border patrol van arrived in less than ten minutes. The four refugees were loaded into the van and taken away.

There's a real story here, I thought, having visited the newspaper office enough times now that a little of that printer's ink is flowing through my veins. I ought to report it but I didn't have the slightest idea how to begin.

"How did they find this place?" I said, imagining that flimsy looking boat out in the middle of the ocean.

"Probably the lights." One of the rangers offered. "You can stand in Havana after dark and see the glow of Key West."

Wow. This was good stuff. I thought, assuming a Jimmy Olsen stance and already composing this column in my mind. Another of the volunteers, a retired high school science teacher, had joined the growing crowd and jumped into the conversation.

"Key West Lights." He said slowly, shaking his head. "Not really. With the curvature of the earth, you can see, at best..." he shaded his eyes and looked towards the horizon. "Only about ten miles."

I guess teachers, retired or not, are driven to teach but I liked the Key West lights theory better. I didn't want science and facts. Steering towards the lights on the distant shore was romance and intrigue. That's what this story was about. I was already mentally picturing the female refugee with a greatly enhanced bosom on the cover of a Harlequin Romance. There might even be a movie in this.

I decided to ignore the curvature of the earth story because I'm not winning any Pulitzer prizes talking about Pythagorean theorems.

"So what happens now?" I asked? That's when the controversy I mentioned earlier started.

"They'll be taken to a processing center." The ranger told me. "If they're really Cuban refugees, any relatives in this country will be contacted and each of the four will be given medical care, temporary housing and eight thousand dollars to get themselves established in this country."

"Eight thousand dollars?" I said, incredulously.

"It's more than that this year." A workman, who was in the park working on the new bathhouse, offered. "My trailer was damaged in Hurricane Charley." He said bitterly. "I haven't got any help yet and these people will be set up for life before I get home this weekend."

This was way too serious a subject for a guy whose writing talents are usually directed at making fun of Knozone Action days so I backed away.

So much for romance and a book deal. I have not had a chance to verify the amount of money, if any, the refugees are given but as soon as I do, you might see me, Spanish dictionary in hand, in my kayak out on the Atlantic paddling furiously towards the lights of a brave new world.

Paddle for your life.

Whiling away our days in the Florida Keys in the late fall of the year can get to be monotonous as far as the weather goes. Being a TV weather person down here must be the easiest job in the Western Hemisphere. Oh, there's the occasional hurricane watch to break up any weather related boredom but by and large it's pretty much the same; a beautiful sunrise, a warm, almost cloudless eighty degree day, a walk across the highway to catch the beautiful sunset and then a breezy tropical night. We're almost wishing the Christmas Holidays would get here so we can get back to Indiana for a break from this sameness. There's no excitement to this kind of life but it's our own fault.

We ended up working as volunteers in the Florida State Park system because we wanted to spend some time around the water. We might have gotten more than we bargained for. Our campsite at Long Key State Park was about one hundred and forty miles north east of Cuba. The Key is an island that in places might be a half a mile wide but where we were parked, it's only seventy five yards from one side to the other. The Gulf of Mexico was across the road from our camper and the Atlantic Ocean was right behind us. Our campsite was maybe a foot above sea level and it seemed to be a lot less than that at high tide. It didn't take much for this landlubber to envision the whole place being swallowed up by a storm surge during some unnamed tropical depression.

It's a pretty remote place and because of this, television reception was very poor. I realize that's an odd thing to say in this age of satellites and co-axial cable but we had neither of those. Our little antenna mounted on the top of our camper had to strain to pick up one fuzzy Miami station. This in itself wasn't bad because we don't watch much television but I did try to watch the weather faithfully every evening. You know, that unnamed tropical depression trying to sneak in on us.

Unfortunately, the hard news people at the fuzzy TV station seem to think that the world ends at the Miami city limits so they don't talk much about anything beyond that. As a matter of fact, most of their conversation centers around Shaquille O'Neil who recently rented himself out to play basketball in their town.

Even the weather segment is spent talking about what Miami has accepted to be the second coming in the guise of an overgrown basketball player. Of course, in concentrating on Shaq, the weatherman was neglecting to inform me what the chances of an overnight hurricane are so I went to bed on numerous occasions wondering if there was a category three out there on the horizon. It made for a restless night, especially when the wind was blowing.

To make matters worse, A friend of ours, a very nice lady whom we'll call Judy, loaned us a book called Isaac's Storm. This book documents in very graphic detail the early twentieth century Hurricane that killed six thousand people in Galveston, Texas. It probably should not be read while your feet are dangling in the ocean less than fifteen miles from the memorial to the Nineteen thirty four hurricane that destroyed much of where I sat.

While lying awake at night listening for sounds of excessive wind, I found that I could draw a little comfort by also listening to the traffic out on the Overseas highway, the only route in and out of the Keys. As long as at least some of the traffic is going south towards Key West, I feel certain there is no evacuation order that I missed because Kobe Bryant couldn't get along with Shaquille O'Neill, forcing Shaq to move to Miami.

When we were not watching for hurricanes or doing our camp host duties, I would get my kayak out and put it in the water behind our campsite.

We did this for a week or so and finally Susie insisted I get in the thing. Having been raised where a ten year old kid could throw a rock across the largest body of water in the area, I was still a little suspect about putting a molded piece of plastic with me in it into any bodies of water you can't see across. This is not exactly like floating down Eagle creek or the White river. It's the Atlantic Ocean and even if there were no hurricanes, it still tended to make me a little nervous.

Some of this is because of the Jaws movies. I can't remember where I put the car keys twenty minutes ago but I will never forget the image of that shark terrorizing the quaint little New England town. When I'm paddling around out there, it takes very little imagination on my part to see a monster fish of the Jaws variety come shooting up out of the water to bite off about six feet of my kayak as well as the two legs tucked in where the front of the boat used to be.

It took all my willpower to push that image to the back of my mind as I actually climbed into the thing and pushed off shore. While I was busy double checking my life jacket, I really got in trouble. I noticed that the nose of my kayak seemed to be swinging towards Cuba no matter how hard I paddled in the opposite direction. I whipped the paddles furiously. Push. Pull. But it didn't do any good. My God, I was caught in the Gulf Stream and it was sweeping me out to sea.

I was doomed. I was either going to end up in one of Fidel Castro's jails or at the bottom of the ocean joining my assigned link in the food chain. Either way, I would never see my family again.

"Goodbye kids", I yelled, even though they were a couple of thousand miles away safely ensconced in Indiana, a place I fervently wished I was at the moment. I waved at Susie, standing on the beach, getting smaller by the minute as the tidal forces carried me farther out to sea. I never got the chance to tell her I'll always love her. Seeing my flailing paddle, she jumped in the boiling water, trying to save me.

"Don't do it, Susie. Save yourself." I tried to yell but the gale force winds that had suddenly sprang up out of nowhere pushed the words back into my throat. She paid no attention to my frantic pleas and I watched in horror as she continued wading out to my kayak.

She grabbed the side, leaned over and said, "Hey there, Hiawatha, What do you think you'll be having for lunch?"

Tricky Dick Nixon does it again.

We finished up our assignment in the Florida Keys without any major traumatic damage and went home for Christmas. We returned to Florida in early January to begin a stint as volunteers at Koreshan State park, just south of Fort Myers. Our duties in this park were much different than at Long Key because this park was built around a historical site. The Koreshans were a late nineteenth century group of Midwestern people who banded together to follow their prophet, a man who called himself Koresh, to Southwest Florida. Here they were to live in a commune and while away their days in the pursuit of happiness. Their vision actually lasted for half a century or so before the group all died out. Eventually part of their holdings, including the settlement, was donated to the state of Florida for a park.

The park, among other things, uses volunteers to take care of this settlement and also volunteers serve as Docents, or Guides, to winter time visitors. In exchange for a camping site, Susie and I each did twenty hours of work per week in and around the settlement. We had varied duties to perform, all of which were pleasant and interesting.

Unfortunately, all that almost ended when the park's assistant manager asked me to clean the campground bathrooms, I was going to object because of my hypochondriac tendencies. It seemed to me that public restrooms would be a good place to catch some God-awful airborne disease or worse yet, one lurking about in the Commodes. I had read 'The Andromeda Strain' so I knew the damage those tiny buggers could do.

However, in my golden years, I'm trying to put most of my irrational fears behind me so I agreed to do it. It is a very humbling experience to clean up after your fellow man but it also builds character, at least that's what I told Susie.

"Not a chance, Buster." She told me. "They asked you to help, not me." She went on with her duties in the settlement leaving me to the bathrooms.

My cleaning lessons were provided by the volunteer who had been doing it for the last two months and was now preparing to move on down the road. His name was Bill and he is a retired bio-chemist from Cleveland. He assured me it's perfectly safe.

"With long handled brushes, rubber gloves, high powered hoses and spray bottles, you won't need to touch anything nor will anything need to touch you" he said. I checked him out, looking for signs of pestilence or a pox of some kind or other but he looked as healthy as a ten year old.

Nevertheless, I also decided to be prepared. The day before I was to start my duties, I went to the Hospital emergency room where I borrowed a white hairnet and booties. I was also going for a surgical mask but the nurse on duty drew the line after giving me the first two items. This was a problem because I knew I wasn't going in there without something to cover my face. Luckily, I remembered that I had a Richard Nixon Halloween mask stored under my side of the bed.

Why is that, you ask? Some years ago, in a fit of weakness, Susie told me she was terrified of waking up some morning and finding someone in a Halloween mask lying next to her. This fear was undoubtedly a holdover from watching an old Vincent Price movie as a child or something else just as frightening. I never gave it much thought but I happened to be in one of the big box stores shortly after her revelation and found this mask of old Richard on sale. I bought it thinking it might be fun to have Susie wake up some morning and discover she's in bed with Richard Nixon.

I could not have been more wrong. Richard touched her shoulder and announced "I am not a crook. Boo." and she reacted quite violently. I was conked on the head with the alarm clock that morning. This was in early December of nineteen ninety seven and a knot on my forehead persists today and all because Richard Nixon tapped my wife's arm and said "Wake up, little Susie."

That mask brought back some unhappy memories but I still planned to use it when I was cleaning. I was up early the day I was to start my restroom duty and discovered a slight problem. The mask had holes in it around the various facial orifices to accommodate breathing and vision. I couldn't go in there providing the germs easy access via these openings so I solved this by wearing my snorkel goggles complete with snorkel tube over the mask although Richard Nixon's nose made it a tight fit. I also put on green latex gloves that reached almost to my armpits and then tied a Willie Nelson Bandanna around my forehead to make sure the white hospital hairnet didn't blow off.

I wore knee length socks and put the booties over my tennis shoes. Always thinking ahead, I wrapped rubber bands around the legs of my jeans so no germs could scurry up inside and attack my nether regions. I considered wearing my swim fins over the booties but was afraid people might think me weird.

I decided to do the men's room first because I had not yet worked up the courage to go into the Ladies side. The little dispensers on the walls in there frightened me almost as much as the germs. I put out the 'closed' sign in front of the bathroom door and attached the disinfectant sprayer to the garden hose. The Park service had given me a push broom and I leaned it against the outside wall planning to use it to push the water out of the area after I hosed the place down. Satisfied that I could survive an anthrax attack in this outfit, I walked inside the bathroom dragging the hose. I turned the water on and foamy stuff shot every which way soaking the ceiling and both paper towel holders. I wrestled the hose under control and with my superior mechanical knowledge, it took only a few moments for me to master the disinfecting technique.

'This ain't so bad.' I thought. I could almost see the little germs with their enormous teeth, back pedaling up against the porcelain bowls, their hands in the air in surrender.

I had been at it a few minutes, more than likely having slaughtered millions of the little devils, when a little kid who obviously couldn't read walked into the bathroom. I whirled around with my spray bottle of disinfectant, just missing him with the full force of the spray.

He took one look at me, screamed. "Mommy, Mommy" and ran outside as fast as his little legs would carry him. I shut down the hose and poked my mask covered head out of the door to make sure he was okay and the little kid's mommy whacked me right on my forehead knot with the state issued broom handle. The snorkel tube slowed the handle down some but the errant blow still stunned me.

There was a cosmetic change involved, as well. The alarm clock induced knot on my brow now protrudes from the back of my head.

Epilogue

Slow down and smell the sweet corn.

Being on the road was and is everything we have dreamed about. The freedom to go as we please is an enjoyment whose only requirement is to get old or become independently wealthy or do both. Despite Susie's protestations to the contrary, we're out here because we're in the first category. We're old but we're also blessed with good health and a decent outlook on life so being senior citizens hasn't prevented us from striking out to see the country.

We still spend our summers in Indiana with Fionna parked on our 3 acre hideaway. Here, we both can spend time with family and friends; Susie can tend her flowers and I can grow my vegetable garden.

Staying in one place also gives me a chance to make a little extra money mowing grass. Last summer, that little enterprise presented me with an experience, the story of which seems to be a good way to end this book.

I was in Greenwood, a suburb of Indianapolis, trying to finish mowing a customer's grass before the rain started. I could see it coming from the west and I hurried to finish but the rain arrived before I was half done. It came down so hard I had to put the mowers on my trailer and quit for the day.

Instead of going home, I was supposed to go to my daughter Julie's home where the family was gathering for dinner. When I got there, the sky just to the south of us was black with rain and I decided to go on home, get the mowers out of the weather and put on some dry clothes. I also knew I had left one of Fionna's windows open and I was afraid our bed was getting soaked.

I told the family to eat without me and I headed for the truck as angry clouds, almost a dark green and seemingly within arm's reach, boiled overhead. Thunderstorm warnings were being broadcast on my truck radio and as I went through the little town of West Newton, a mile or so from Julie's, the storm sirens were blaring their warning of impending bad weather. I cursed my forgetfulness in not closing the overhead vent. Good Lord, our bed was going to be soaked.

The rain slackened as I hurried west and by the time I reached the four way stop at the north end of town, the rain was little more than a light drizzle. Things were looking up. Three more miles and I'd be home. It appeared as if it hadn't rained that hard out in the country and perhaps our bed wouldn't be so wet after all. I started down the steep hill where County Line road intersected with Highway 267 that runs north out of Mooresville.

Halfway down the hill, spying the stop sign just ahead, I applied the brakes and nothing happened. The truck didn't stop. The hill, my hurrying, the weight of the two mowers and the trailer, a little loose gravel and the wet pavement all combined to propel the truck into the northbound lane of the highway even as I frantically pumped the brakes in a vain effort to make it stop. I looked south and saw a motorcycle heading northbound not fifty feet from me. In what seemed like slow motion, the rider swerved left to avoid the front end of my truck, went across a ditch and through several of the manicured lawns on the north side of County Line road. I could see it was a young man making his way through the grass and doing a masterful job of keeping the motorcycle upright before wrestling it to a stop.

At the same time, a semi truck in the southbound lane loomed large in my view and by the time it reached where I had been, Smoke was pouring from the truck's brakes and the air horn's blast was scaring the water out of me. The driver's actions and possibly the grace of God avoided an accident. I couldn't do anything. My truck slid across both lanes and out of harm's way. I got the truck stopped on the other side and sat there wondering what had just happened.

The traffic, oblivious to what could have been a tragedy, continued to flow in both directions as I got out of the truck and walked back to where the motorcyclist was working his way back to the road. I apologized profusely. He was very gracious, saying only that I owed him a new set of underwear. I didn't even get his name or where he was from as he moved back onto the highway and continued on his way.

I went home, put the mowers away, got into dry clothes and returned to my daughter's house. I also found the vent window closed; all of that worry and possibly getting killed for nothing. I had a sick feeling in the pit of my stomach that caused me to forego dinner and that night, I couldn't sleep. I couldn't get over how quickly my life could have changed. There wasn't even time to be afraid until I lay there in bed thinking about all that could have happened.

Two seconds one way or the other and I could have killed the young man or that semi could have killed me. Images of my family sitting down to eat without me kept going through my head and I tried to make something mystical out of the episode, thinking maybe God had let me live for some purpose I didn't yet know about.

I quickly dismissed that idea, realizing that it was just luck. I tossed and turned, thinking of all the places I had not been and all the things I had not yet done. I had never been to Rome or the Cayman Islands; I was still terrible at playing golf. I'd never owned a brick house. I'd never plunged down a mountainside covered with snow on a set of four hundred-dollar skis. I'd never caught a Marlin off the coast of Mexico or walked on a glacier in Alaska. I'd never even owned a four wheel drive truck.

I finally drifted off to a fitful unconsciousness thinking that there was still a lot of living to accomplish and I vowed that starting the next day, I was going to do it.

I woke up, groggy from the night's restlessness, to a bright sunny morning and still acutely aware of my mortality. I was also suddenly conscious of how much Susie, my kids and my granddaughter, Riley Marie, meant to me. After breakfast, I drove the four miles to town along Greencastle Road and thought of all the times I had watched the farmers plant these fields lining both sides of the unlined blacktop. All the times I had watched as the plants miraculously rose from the dirt and watched again as the crops were harvested. I marveled at this yearly cycle and wondered if it was as satisfying to the farmer as it suddenly was to me.

I got into Mooresville and made the rounds of people I needed to see. I stopped Rex Nichols, a good golfer and a fair to middling insurance man, on the sidewalk. Every time we talk, I like to pull his chain about insurance men playing golf all the time and this day was no different. I asked him why, he wasn't on the course on such a sunny day.

I said hello to Jack Teagarden at his motorcycle shop. I made a quick stop to see Tom Warthen, a town councilman and the man who services my lawn mowers. He also does radiator repair and had a funny story for me about the traveling radiator salesman.

I stopped at the bank to chat with my friend, Mike Shea and with the bank's tellers, who almost always have a smile on their faces. Even though that might be company policy, those smiles still seemed genuine. I looked around the town and thought what a comforting place Mooresville, Indiana is.

That evening, Susie and I went to church, went to Gray's cafeteria for dinner and later had ice cream with friends at Ritter's custard stand. Somewhere during that day, it dawned on me what a satisfying life that I already have. That frightening slide down the hill had initially made me think that I needed an expensive set of skis or a trip to the Cayman Islands before I go to my final reward but in the end, it made me realize all I need is what I already have. That other stuff isn't me.

Who I am is a guy who loves his family and friends and who makes fun of Governmental edicts like Kno-zone Action days. I'm just a guy who grows more vegetables than we can ever eat and a guy who loves pointing our truck in a direction we've never been. I'm also a guy who is extremely glad to be alive and who, for a few days, at least, would savor every waking moment that God will grant me. This revelation alone was almost worth the scare of that out of control truck.

I know I'll soon be back to my same old ways, scurrying here and there, never stopping to realize how fragile life can be and not slowing down enough to appreciate everyday that we get to spend on the right side of the grass. I doubt that I can maintain this outlook on a daily basis but today, at least, I can say with certainty that life doesn't get any better than this.

Would we do it again?

Well, the time has come to wrap up this book. When we set out on our adventure, a book on our travels was the last thing I had imagined would come out of it. We just wanted to explore this great country and with a few changes in our original idea, we have done just that. The book was an accidental but very rewarding by-product of the trip.

As you know if you've read this far, we have modified our original plan of going wherever and whenever we want. Even before the birth of Riley Marie, we found it's impossible to just drive away into that sunset I mentioned earlier. It was tough enough leaving family and friends and while we were still trying to get used to that idea, Riley Marie was born.

It made for a tough decision about our future.

On the one hand, we've got the lure and the freedom of the open road. There's gloriously wonderful scenery to see and great regional meals to eat. The Rocky Mountains, the desert southwest, the great northwest and the historical east coast are all beckoning to us.

But On the other hand, we've got Riley Marie, a four year old weighing in at a little over thirty pounds. She has filled our lives with joy and when her hand comes up to grasp ours as we walk down the street, we're ready to abandon any plans to leave her behind. But there is still something in us that says 'Go.'

There are a great number of people our age who revel in their grandchildren and would not leave them if a gun was held to their head. Rightfully so; but we have our own lives to live and with e-mail and internet pictures, a visit home at Christmas and a cell phone with a liberal calling plan, we have managed to keep that little darlin' close to us. Oh, there are days when a new picture arrives by E-mail and we both wonder if we've lost our mind. All it takes for reassurance that we did the right thing is grilling shrimp bought fresh off the boat or watching a sunset from an ocean front campsite to bury those thoughts.

We are both sure the day will come when we want to abandon this lifestyle and we have two wishes for that day. The first is that it's not anytime soon and the second is that when the day does come, the hope is that the decision will come from both of us. If not, by the grace of God, we'll just work it out then.

About the Author

Gordon Grindstaff is a retired Information Technology Consultant, but writing has always been his first love. However, the early attempts at storytelling coincided with the discovery that his children were big eaters and writing as a profession provided for only small portions at the dinner table.

His current business card identifies him as a humorist and while his wife Susie might disagree, his writing will back up the title. His humor springs from the experiences of being raised in a post WWII small town in Southern Indiana. Raising 4 children tested his sense of humor and on more than occasion, had it down on the mat for the 3 count. However, that experience, along with 40 plus years of marriage, the world of Corporate silliness and life's everyday situations has sharpened his wit to the point where he is considered one of Monrovia, Indiana's premier humorists.

He and Susie retired in 2001, sold practically everything they owned and set out in their RV to see the country. Their travels led to a self syndicated Newspaper column published weekly in four newspapers in two countries as well as a monthly piece for Senior Life Magazine of Southwest Florida.

His work also appears occasionally in at least 3 other publications but has been largely ignored by a couple of hundred rags whose editors have resisted Mr. Grindstaff's constant whining.

His readership, at last count, now numbers in the dozens and spans the United States from North to South and east to west not to mention the Mediterranean Coast of Spain.

Sometimes hilarious, sometimes sentimental, once in a while nostalgic and always entertaining, his words will touch your heart and your funny bone. They have also been known to cause some of his more uncouth readers to snort loudly through their nostrils.

Made in the USA
Lexington, KY
05 February 2013